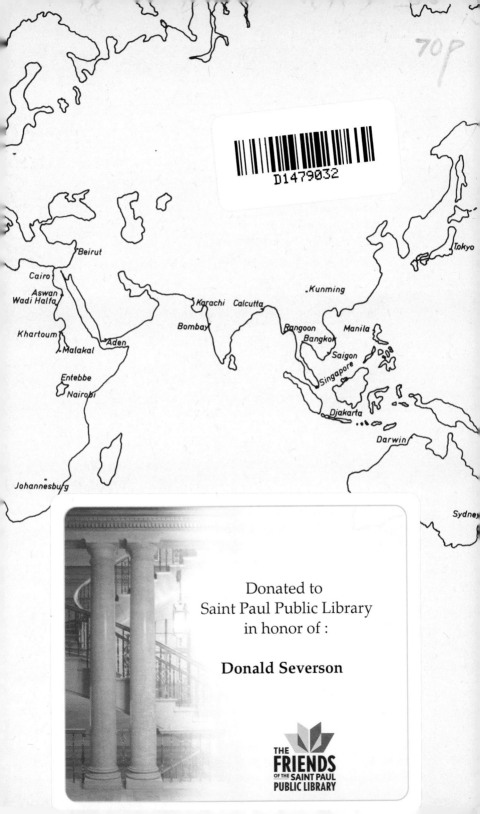

70P

Beirut

Cairo

Aswan
Wadi Halfa

Khartoum

Malakal

Aden

Karachi   Calcutta

Bombay

Kunming

Rangoon
Bangkok

Manila

Saigon

Singapore

Entebbe

Nairobi

Tokyo

Djakarta

Darwin

Johannesburg

Sydney

Off The Beam

RT CHANDLER 1969

t published 1970

ound in Great Britain by
r Ltd, Frome and London

© ROB

Fi

Printed and
Butler & Tan

FOREWORD

THERE are all too few books on British Civil Aviation and its history and, so far as I know, there are none written from the point of view of the Radio Officer. Bob Chandler in this book has, therefore, provided a new outlook on Aviation, the outlook of a Radio Man, as he has experienced it. He is well-known in British Civil Aviation circles since he has been about for a long time, firstly at Croydon before the Nazi War and then again in British South American Airways and in British Instrument and Radio development subsequently. Over the years we have heard much from the pen of the pilot, but not before have we heard from the Radio Officer so naturally and clearly.

This book covers the period from the early 1930s on to the end of the author's active flying career. It is a period of which the British people should be extremely proud. At that time, in spite of all our shortcomings and difficulties, including "the depression", we led the world in almost all aspects of aviation. Imperial Airways was one of the great airline pioneers and showed the world how to raise the standard both technically and in aircraft and operational matters and also in giving high-quality service in every possible way. I myself can recall carrying heads of overseas airlines who had come to study Imperial Airways' methods so as to go back home and develop their own particular lines similarly. Some of these lines today are the greatest in the world.

In those earlier days there was, of course, no such thing as radio telephony for instant and easy communication with the ground and each aircraft relied tremendously on the skill and ability of its "key puncher"—the wireless operator, using the Morse Code only. Bob Chandler was one of those and can, therefore, be placed in the category of those who helped to introduce air safety by radio aid in the air. Every bearing taken in those days was a matter of importance and the Radio Officer took such bearings or obtained them from the ground station by morse code, often in appalling conditions of air turbulence and of interference from "atmospherics". His responsibility was great.

Of my Atfero—the Atlantic Ferry Organisation—Bob Chandler tells many and varied tales. He tells not only of Atlantic crossings, but also of deliveries to many different theatres of war activity. He

v

was one of those who made it possible to bring enormous numbers of aircraft built in the peace and security of America to the active fighting fronts of the world. It is not always realised in the commonplace of today's Atlantic travel that the Atlantic Ferry Organisation was the first to "debunk" that route at a time when it was a highly precarious risk even in summer. The Atlantic Ferry Organisation delivered thousands of aircraft and did so with remarkably few losses.

The author was one of those who made this possible and they are the band of men to whom little credit has ever been given.

After the war I was fortunate to have Bob Chandler join British South American Airways when we started that airline to South America, an area in which British Aviation had never previously operated. He was one of my crew who took off from Heathrow Airport on January 1st, 1946, and thus opened what is now London's number one airport, to fly to South America with a full load of journalists, freight and mail. This was at a time when the facilities on the route were at a minimum and when the functions of every member of the crew were vital. Radio aids were extremely limited and the importance of the wireless operator was thus the greater. They were interesting and exciting days and Bob Chandler took a very active part in them.

In the history of British Civil Aviation the importance of the Radio Man has always been overlooked or understated. This contribution, personal though it may be, has helped to fill the gap in the record. It shows the work of one man in this field. The "radio man" has made a major contribution to the development of British Civil Aviation throughout the world. I welcome this record of one such man and I hope that the public will be more conscious of the wonderful work which Wireless Operators have done for us in the air.

Don Bennett

CHAPTER ONE

My last flight as an operational aircrew member came to an end one glorious sunny morning in 1957 at Hatfield when I climbed down the steps of Comet V.C. 5302, which we had just flown over from Canada. The usual badinage was exchanged with the ground crew as to what we had been doing in Toronto. As I smelt burnt paraffin and hot engines a wave of nostalgia swept over me for I realised that twenty years of flying was finished for ever, all ten thousand two hundred hours and forty minutes of it. I had an un-diagnosed complaint in my left leg and now needed a stick to walk. Aircraft cockpits and walking sticks do not go together. I had to find another job but no job open to me would be like the one which had taken me all over the world in a multitude of aeroplanes flying behind many pilots, always with the responsibility of ensuring that they were kept fully informed of the weather conditions en route as well as ahead and behind us, with the not small task of producing navigational information from the radio equipment. My life as an air radio operator had begun twenty-two years earlier.

As a young man I had not intended to go flying for a career and had started as a radio operator in merchant ships. After eight years in tramp steamers the monotony of the job and the isolation from civilisation brought the realisation that this was a poor way of life. As I came to this conclusion I was posted in 1935 to a collier in the Bristol Channel, she carried dust coal to briquette works in Northern France and then went down to Spain and loaded iron ore for Port Talbot. Life aboard during the loading and discharging was a dirty noisy business. A particularly filthy cargo of coal dust from Barry Docks to Nantes which was loaded and discharged in continuous rain was the final straw. I had heard that there were vacancies in the airlines at Croydon for radio operators and decided to try and get a job in civil aviation as a flight radio operator.

On the train from Cardiff to London, the enormity of what I had done came home to me. I had little money—the only money I had saved was in the form of an allotment and this was withdrawn from the bank for the usual "King for a Day" type of leave to which I was prone—and I had only the vaguest idea of how one set about getting a job as a flying radio operator.

My family were pleased to see me; they were obviously disturbed that I had thrown away eight years' seniority in the radio company, but made no comment. I found that I should have to obtain another radio licence, my marine one having no standing in the flying business and I enrolled in a school at Croydon that ran monthly courses. The last of my allotment money was withdrawn from the bank and with a small loan from a friend it looked as though I should just last one month out; I had to pass first time or not at all.

In those days a necessary qualification for a first officer in Imperial Airways was a flying radio licence and a number of the pupils on the course were first officers in Imperials, some of whom later became famous. The rest of the course were radio people from the three Services. The big problem for them all was reaching the required twenty words per minute to pass the telegraphy tests; in comparison, I was an expert telegraphist and was able to devote the whole month to the technical aspects of the licence. I passed easily. The simple part of my plan was now complete, the not so simple part was to get a flying job.

Croydon airfield in the nineteen thirties was the centre of civil aviation in the United Kingdom and the terminus and starting point of most overseas and internal flights. It was a large grass field with a dip in the middle into which some of the smaller aircraft would vanish from sight when taxiing to a take-off position on the airfield boundary. There were no runways and the east side of the field was bounded by the Purley Way with its string of overhead sodium lights. On the south and west side of the field houses had been built right up to the edge so that their back fences constituted the boundary of the airfield. The Airport Hotel was on the Purley Way and was flanked by a distinctive square control tower. In front of this was a concrete apron on which the aircraft parked to embark and discharge their passengers. A number of hangars and aprons were located round the edge of the airport and these were used for routine aircraft maintenance and parking. The bottom storey of the control tower was used as the main booking hall for the airlines operating in and out of London and it was also used for the Customs clearance. The garden of the Airport Hotel was a fascinating playground during the holidays for the schoolchildren from miles around; it gave them a grandstand view of all the arriving and departing aircraft and they collected aircraft registration letters as other children collect railway engine numbers.

The two main British operators of aircraft were Imperial Airways and British Airways, the pair merged eventually to form BOAC.

Other British operators appeared at Croydon, flew for a few months, sometimes a few years, and then vanished again. Wrightways delivered the daily newspapers to Paris for some years in their smart white and yellow DH.86's. They left Croydon early in the morning and came back about midday. International Air Freight flew daily freight services to Holland and Belgium. Personal Airways operated a charter service with a very smart DH Rapide. Radio Luxemburg had their own bright green Rapide for carrying broadcasting material to and fro. Surrey Flying Services operated sightseeing flights over London with a Fox Moth and a Dragon. The foreign operators were an unending source of interest. Air France with their Wibault and later their Marcel Bloch 220. Lufthansa with their Junkers 52 and later their Condors and KLM with their Fokker stable.

There were many other companies, sometimes with only one aircraft and one pilot. It was difficult to know just who to tackle for a job. I applied to Imperial Airways for a post without getting a reply and I visited every company at Croydon that owned an aeroplane. They were all most friendly but it was now autumn and they did not fly much in the winter . . . they would probably need a man next spring when they were really going to branch out, meanwhile if I would leave my address . . . etc. etc. I could only return home. The only solution to my problem was to go back to the radio company and explain what I had been trying to do; I couldn't expect to go back with the same seniority but at least it would be a job. I considered this off and on without coming to a decision for almost a week and, on the point of deciding to return to sea, the magic letter arrived. A company at Croydon were in a position to offer me a job as a radio operator and they would be pleased if I would call at their Croydon office at my earliest convenience.

I arrived in Croydon and after a long wait I was shown into the office of the owner and chief pilot of the airline. He was a small man, scruffily dressed with a deadpan face and hard eyes. "You know we operate a daily service Croydon–Dublin–Croydon with an '86?"

I nodded.

"Well we reckon we can fill two services a day with passengers next summer and I have my eye on another '86. I know you have no flying experience but I have been studying your application. You're an ex-marine man and have plenty of operating experience, I would like to give you a break. The present radio man can't get along with the pilot on the Dublin service and he can't get along with me, so I am getting rid of him."

3

I didn't know the radio man that was to be sacked, and I didn't care. An '86 was a four-engined biplane and you sat in the cockpit alongside the captain and there were full controls on your side. I would get along with the devil himself for a job like this. The manager went on: "The job is yours if you want it—over to Dublin in the morning, back in the afternoon, six days a week, how about it?"

How about it indeed. "Yes please, I'd love the job, I am not worried over the fact that I have not flown before, I can do the operating and maintain the gear. How much money will I get?"

"Well that's difficult, you have no experience but I am willing to let you gain that experience on our aircraft and next spring, when we start the expanded service, we will give you £5 a week."

The utter impossibility of the offer struck me like a blow. "I haven't any money to keep myself until next spring, can't you pay me eating money for the job?"

The manager jumped to his feet. "That's the offer and a damned good one too for a man in your position, take it or leave it."

I too stood up. "Sorry, I just can't, I haven't money to buy myself a lunch today, how could I possibly live out the winter?"

He opened the door and I stumbled through. "So much for my great flying career due to start on this date," I muttered on the bus to Waddon station. I heard later that he had made the same offer to half a dozen others. So high had been my hopes that I had brought my kit with me and I now retrieved it from the left luggage office and climbed on a train for Victoria. I had a return ticket home and six shillings, I had a marine licence and an air licence but I had no job—something desperate had to be done.

I still wanted to fly and felt sure that something would turn up in the spring. Unfortunately, that was six months away. To go back in tramps meant that I could be away for two years. The only chance was to go to sea in trawlers—they come back to port every twenty-one days at least. I knew nothing about trawlers except that it was a grim life; if I could put up with it, at least I should be in England in the spring.

My former employer's head office was on the Embankment, so, after parking my luggage at Victoria Station, I presented myself to the manager of the Small Craft Department. He examined my sea-going licence and discharge book and raised his eyebrows. "You hold a first-class marine ticket, what the hell do you want to go in trawlers for?"

"Thought I would like a change. I have heard plenty about them, at least the job seems interesting."

4

"Interesting be damned, twenty-one days out, thirty-six hours in port," he replied. "I know the Deep Sea Manager is looking for a bloke for a new cargo boat in Glasgow—forget this trawler nonsense and go and see him."

"Sorry, I don't want to go deep sea again and would appreciate a job in your section, how about it?"

"Got some woman in trouble I suppose and want to keep handy. You ought to get the hell out of it but it's your funeral, when can you start?" he asked.

"Right now," I answered. "I am down to my last few bob."

"I will give you an advance of £3 and a railway ticket to Milford Haven, will you leave tonight?"

"Yes, I'll go and report to your local office in the morning."

He shook hands. "Good luck, laddie, you'll need it. I'll ring Milford and tell 'em you're on your way."

I arrived in Milford Haven at six o'clock on a pouring wet morning. There appeared to be only a dozen milk cans and me for this particular destination and I sat in the cheerless waiting room until about half past eight when, on instructions from the porter, I set off for the docks. The radio company's office did not open before nine.

The marine superintendent had obviously heard from London of my impending arrival and I was soon shown into his office. "There is a tanker out in the haven that has put in to land the radio operator with appendicitis; there's a new man on his way from Cardiff but you can take her if you like," he said, "it could save a few hours."

"Sorry, but I want to go in trawlers," I replied. "I haven't been in one before but I want to keep handy."

"It's a hell of a life, you know, I can't imagine anyone joining a trawler from choice but it's your funeral. You can work with the inspector around the dock for a few days just to get the feel of things," he said.

"Sorry I can't oblige on that tanker and thanks anyway. Know where I can stay in Milford as cheaply as possible?"

"Try the Mission to Deep Sea Fishermen," he answered, "that's not at all bad, at least it's cheap and clean. Get yourself settled there and come and see us in the morning."

I trudged back to the station, picked up my kit and set out for the Mission to Deep Sea Fishermen. As I had been told, it was clean and cheap. I was given a cubicle that was open at the top and bottom and contained a bed and a chair for four shillings a night. Next morning, after a decent breakfast in the communal dining room for one shilling, I set off for the docks. A pleasant surprise awaited me in the company's office, the inspector with whom I was to work turned out to be an extremely pleasant little Welshman with whom I had sailed as a junior some years before.

"I think the first thing is to take you aboard a couple of trawlers that are sailing on the tide just to let you know what you have let yourself in for," he said. "You are going to find this very different from deep sea, the boss tells me you turned down that tanker."

I then told him my story as we trudged round to the dock gates where four trawlers were waiting to sail. "Well that explains your odd determination to sail in trawlers and I can only agree with you and hope you eventually get your air job, your only trouble is going to be the fact that you have never worked ashore. It took me a long time to get used to it but I've got my wife and family settled in a nice little house in Milford and have got used to the bills rolling in, you wait and see how expensive living ashore can be."

We jumped aboard the *Milford Duke* which was waiting at the dock gates and made our way up to the enclosed wheelhouse. The radio operator was on board and showed us his equipment in a tiny hutch at the back of the wheelhouse; he also showed me his bunk which looked more like a coffin, in the main cabin aft. The trawler alongside the *Milford Duke* was a similar type; I was most certainly not going to live in luxury. I pottered around the dock for a week, repairing equipment, changing accumulators and getting used to the smell of fish. Then came the day; I was appointed to the *Milford Queen*, a Strath class trawler that did her fishing off the west coast of Ireland. With an advance from the office, I purchased a straw mattress, blankets and a pillow. I attended the owner's office where the manager briefed me on the code used for reporting and the schedule for contacting the rest of the fleet. Twice a day all the trawlers owned by this company, that were at sea, sent a coded report of their last twenty-four hours' catch to the "control" trawler who then sent them all together to the owners in Milford. By decoding all the messages being sent to the "control" trawler, it was possible to know exactly who was catching the fish.

The radio in the *Queen* was in the skipper's cabin, which was a square box under the wheelhouse and reached via a trapdoor in the wheelhouse floor. The sleeping berth was in the main cabin aft, the walls of which were lined with bunks. They had sliding doors that were closed to keep you in during heavy weather.

The crew consisted of Emil, the skipper and a naturalised Dane;

Fred from Lowestoft, the mate; first, second and third hands and two deckie learners or apprentices; two engineers; two firemen; the ex-Army cook, Taff, and myself. Uniforms were unknown and I caused much amusement by dressing in an ancient plusfour suit and Wellington boots, this was capped by a yellow sou'wester.

The trawler was a lively ship in a sea and the first two days steaming out to the banks I was thoroughly seasick. This soon passed and I settled down to the life—it was rough and hard after deep sea ships but it was made bearable by the innate kindness of those deep sea fishermen. I remember asking Fred, the mate, the second day out about the lavatory. He directed me to the engine room where the chief directed me into the stokehole, I stated my request to the coloured fireman who with a wide grin handed me a shovel. "Use that Mr. Sparks and give it me back to put on the fire, can't waste nuthin' in this old bucket."

Washing facilities were equally crude, hot water from the engine condenser in a bucket was the limit, while shaving during the trip was taboo. Certain words and expressions were said to bring bad luck; pig was known as Irish lamb and whistling was strictly forbidden because it encouraged the wind. There was always food on the table in the cabin aft and there was always tea brewing on the galley stove. I found I was spending most of my working hours in the wheelhouse which was handy to the captain's cabin where I kept the radio schedules. This was an unpleasant business, for the Danish skipper was an old man who spent as much time as possible resting on his bunk. He suffered from a stomach ailment and fed himself only on condensed milk. All portholes were tightly closed and the stench was horrible; one didn't hang about after a radio schedule, I even did the decoding up in the wheelhouse.

After three weeks the fishholds were full and we steamed back to Milford, an extremely smelly and whiskery band. My own growth of beard after three weeks was the subject of much comment—the colour was right but the growth was very patchy. Circumstances made me shave this off before we actually arrived in Milford. I was sitting in the galley eating a slice of bread and treacle when Fred the mate came in, he caught the slice of bread and treacle a flick with the back of his hand which neatly plastered the whole thing into my growing beard. Whiskers and treacle are very difficult to shave off with a safety razor.

After thirty-six hours in port we were off again. The pay was poor—£3 a week and five shillings for every £100 of catch sold. This averaged about fifteen shillings for a three week trip—some

7

£3 5s. a week and a rough and difficult life, but one accepted it and after five trips I had quite settled down. Then came the great day, the offer of a job as a radio engineer/operator with a company at Croydon that equipped and maintained aircraft radio. Twelve hours later I was on a train from Milford to London in a vastly different frame of mind from that in which I had made the reverse journey some six months before. My aviation career was about to begin.

CHAPTER TWO

THE radio company had an office in the main hall at Croydon and a workshop at the back of one of the hangars. The pay was £12 a month and five shillings for each test flight. The company had maintenance contracts with most of the firms owning aircraft fitted with radio in this country. There were two shifts in the workshop —7.0 a.m. to 3.0 p.m. and 3.0 p.m. to 11.0 p.m.—which were loosely supervised by a popular character known as "The Colonel". I started as junior on the afternoon shift. The leader of the shift was an elderly gentleman by the name of Dymwoodie; he was naturally called "Dim". He had made one trip to sea as a radio operator and had then spent years in radio shops before joining the radio company. He was interested only in routine maintenance and disliked the flying side of the job, but he still wanted the five shillings for the test flights. When I knew him better, I used to do his flights and let him claim the money.

The radio equipment carried in aircraft in 1935 was at about the same stage of development as had been reached in marine equipment. The aircraft transmitter had a large single valve for an oscillator with smaller valves for amplifiers. The filaments were all bright emitters, rather like the filaments of electric light bulbs. They would light up the whole aircraft at night but had the virtue that it was easy to distinguish which of them had stopped working. Each frequency had to be set up manually as it was required. Communication was by telegraphy in the medium frequency band with the morse key screwed in any accessible spot. The receivers had much smaller valves of the same type and the approved method of finding which of them was faulty was by finding which one was cold. Most aircraft had two aerials, a fixed aerial strung between the wing-tips and the tail and a trailing aerial of some 200 feet of wire with a lead weight at the end. This was on a reel which was wound in and out by hand. Power was supplied by a wind-driven generator which turned at a constant speed regardless of the speed of the aircraft. This was done by means of a slipping clutch or feathering blades on the shaft.

I found the operation and maintenance of this equipment reasonably simple and after a few weeks I was competent to cure any

9

ordinary fault that was likely to occur. I was alone in the work-shop one evening when the phone rang; it was British Airways reporting that one of their Lockheed Electras on its way back from Malmo had broadcast a message to say that the flight was proceeding normally but that the radio receiver was not working. It was due on the tarmac in twenty minutes. With some trepidation I set out for the arrival area in front of the control tower with my bag of tools. Right on time the Electra appeared from the east, made a perfect landing and rolled up to the control tower. I hung back until all the passengers had gone into the terminal building and then walked towards the steps into the aircraft. I was met by the captain at the cabin doorway, a large, smiling man who said, "Hey, you the radio man?" I gulped and nodded. "Well for Christ's sake go and put that lad out of his misery, it's his first trip alone and he has worried himself sick all the way from Malmo about that receiver packing up. I told him it didn't matter a damn, we could see the English coast 50 miles out."

The hangar foreman had followed me. "Let me know if you can't fix it because this aircraft is on an early morning departure for Paris."

This I agreed to do, first trip radio operator and first time engineer. This looked far from healthy, I thought, as I climbed forward to the radio compartment directly behind the cockpit. Here I found a harassed man of about my own age dressed in a blue flying overall.

"I am sorry old man, but it's all most odd, I can hear nothing on the receiver yet the tubes are all right and the tuning eye works, the transmitter keys and radiates but I can't hear any side-tone."

I tried to put on the calm, confident air that is reputed to help at times like these. "You've got a stinker here but we will soon sort it out, give me your telephones and we will do some checking."

He pulled the headset off his head and as he handed it to me he found the plug was pushed into the top pocket of his flying overall. A look of horror came over his face, "Christ, I haven't had the phones plugged in," he cried, "a couple of the passengers came up before take-off to look at the cockpit and I stowed that damn plug in my pocket when I got out of my seat to let them through."

I felt a great wave of relief. I had cleared my first snag but the radio operator was not finished yet.

"This is my first trip and if I'm lucky enough not to get the sack, I shall never live this one down. Can't you cook up a real snag for me?"

10

I thought this out. Yes, a respectable fault would not hurt my professional reputation either, and I replied, "Yes, I'll cook it if you will insist on a test flight afterwards."

"Sure, that's worth money to you isn't it?" he agreed. "The skipper's a good egg and will fly it for us. I'll catch him before he goes home," and he rushed off down the aeroplane.

I fiddled around with the telephone leads, broke a lead in the receiver plug and resoldered it. The hangar foreman poked his head into the compartment. "So you've fixed it Sparks, and now you want to fiddle a test flight?"

I started to explain that although everything was now fine on ground test, I thought that for safety's sake . . . the foreman laughed, "You're all the same—after the five bobs—using anything you can find wrong. I know you."

He was interrupted by the captain. "Let the lad be, Red, he has fixed it and I can beat up the missus at Redhill and she can fetch me in her car—it'll save me train fares." He turned to the radio operator who had followed him up the cabin. "You come along too, Junior, and check out the gear. The radio genius can sit in the copilot's seat."

I was so excited that I could not adjust the lap strap. The pilot leant across and fixed it and then spoke out of the side of his mouth, "First time, son?"

I nodded, too full to speak.

"You'll enjoy it. Gotta start some time; the real problem in this business is knowing when to quit."

The foreman stood on the tarmac in full view of the skipper and the port engine burst into life with a roar, shortly followed by the starboard engine. The pilot turned. "All clear your side?"

I raised my thumb in the approved fashion and we started bumping across the grassy field to the fence by the scent factory where the pilot swung the Electra into the wind.

After carefully scrutinising the sky, he turned to me and shouted above the increasing roar of the motors, "Keep your seat and your head laddie, we're on our way."

With a lurch the Electra started rolling, the hangars on the other side of the field seemed to rush towards us and then suddenly vanish. I was airborne on my first flight. The pilot busied himself lifting the wheels and the flaps and pulling back the throttles, then set the aircraft in a gentle turn.

"We'll go and see if the missus has got rid of the lodger," called the pilot.

I laughed dutifully and turned to the side window. A thousand feet below spread the sprawling suburbs of South London and on the horizon I could see the hills of Kent and Sussex. It was a beautiful, clear, still evening; perfect weather for my baptism to flying. Within a few minutes the pilot pulled back the throttles and pushed forward the wheel and the Electra started a long dive towards a white-painted house standing alone in a field. As we drew closer, he called, "Look out for a woman with a tablecloth."

I glued my eyes to the side window and as we swept low over the house, I saw a woman dash out of a side door waving a white cloth. As we climbed up again, I shouted my information across the cockpit, he nodded and grinned, "That's settled then, radio all right now?"

I felt a wave of guilt, I had forgotten completely the reason of the flight and turned to the radio operator. He smiled and raised his thumb.

"It's okay now, Sir, let's go home."

The pilot nodded and a few minutes later we were lining up on the scent factory for our landing. The factory vanished and the green sward of Croydon airfield came up at a terrific rate. Suddenly the field vanished under the nose and with a gentle thump the main landing wheels and the tail wheel touched together. I had made my first flight. The radio operator and I became good friends and our paths crossed several times before he was killed some years later in a flying-boat accident.

A few days after my first flight, while engaged on routine maintenance on Air Dispatch's big fleet of DH Dragons, I was called upon by a young gentleman with a title. He owned a DH Rapide, of which he was inordinately proud, and it had recently been equipped with radio. This was in the cabin and he controlled it with a set of Bowden controls on the cockpit wall. His complaint was that sometimes when he was using the radio, he would receive an electric shock in his bottom. On the last occasion this had happened, the shock had made him jump up so violently that he had almost put his head through the cockpit roof. He showed me a large bruise to prove his case. I was at a complete loss as to what could be wrong but agreed to have a look at the Rapide installation. I sat in the cockpit and the radio operated normally and then I asked him to sit in the cockpit and to try and recreate the snag.

"I have tried that a dozen times without any luck. Come up in the air and you will see what I mean," said his Lordship. Sitting in the front passenger's seat was not going to be as exciting as in the cockpit of an Electra, but five shillings was not to be turned down and I eagerly accepted his offer.

After a remarkably short run, the Rapide lifted quietly in the air. I flew a lot on this particular type later and it was a pleasant aircraft in all aspects, its only known vice was a weakness to stand up on its nose if it was braked too violently on landing. It was a beautiful summer day and I was fascinated by the panorama of the streets of London spread below me, when a roar from the cockpit brought me back to the job in hand.

"Got me right in the bloody arse that time," howled his Lordship. "Now say there's nothing wrong with it."

I leant forward and pressed the key that was fixed to a cross member on the cockpit wall. The reaction was instantaneous—his Lordship tried to leap to his feet, banged his head on the cockpit roof and roared out a string of profanity. My luck, however, was in, I had seen what was happening. The lead in from the aerial came through the cockpit roof just behind his head, where there was a rubber-covered joint which connected to the aircraft transmitter. The rubber covering had been torn and if he leant back and used his radio at the same time, he simply earthed the transmitter through the metal seat. I persuaded his Lordship to lean forward while I padded the insulating rubber cover with tape; the next problem was to get him to try again.

"You get in the seat and burn your own bloody arse," raged his Lordship and started to climb out of the cockpit. I firmly pressed him back, explaining that I couldn't fly and this was only my second time in the air. The Rapide meandered gently round the sky as the argument went on.

"Look," I said. "I'll hold a cushion seat over your head so that if I haven't cleared the snag, at least you won't bump your nut again."

"To hell with you and your bloody cushion, why should I burn my arse to prove your rotten radio?" he shouted.

At last we compromised, I wore the headphones and he worked the key while I held the cushion—no shock. His Lordship's manner changed when he found that we had cleared the fault on his beloved Rapide.

"Good show, that's settled. It's a lovely day, anywhere you would like to go?" I asked for a trip along the South Coast where I was born. It wasn't the dramatic beat-up of the Electra, but it was interesting to see a well-known countryside from a new viewpoint. I landed back at Croydon, five shillings better off and two more hours' flying time for my log book.

My next job was a Railway Air Services Rapide in which the pilot complained of a strong smell of burning every time he used his radio. I found a badly charred aerial plug which I showed him and then replaced. The pilot was a first officer in Imperials whom I had met on the radio course. I explained about the five shillings and that I was trying to build up flying time.

"I can't give you more than twenty minutes, the fault is too simple to stand any more flying time but you are welcome to that."

I agreed and off we went for half an hour on yet another sunny afternoon; I was slowly building up time.

The years at sea had left one indelible mark. I could not break the habit of spending any money I had in my pocket and £12 a month was just not enough. There was plenty of freelance flying to be picked up around Croydon but my contract with the radio company specifically forbade flying unless directly instructed to do so. The company's rate for our services was much too high for the smaller companies so I decided to make my own arrangements. I approached Air Dispatch and the manager offered me all the flying I could handle at ten shillings an hour by day and fifteen shillings an hour by night and agreed to keep his mouth shut about it. I explained that my hours were from 3.0 p.m. to 11.0 p.m. and he at once offered me a flight to Paris with a load of papers, leaving at five the next morning and getting back about midday. The aircraft was a DH Dragon and the flying time about five hours. I jumped at it, two pounds ten, almost as much as the company paid me for a week's work.

I finished my shift at 11.0 p.m., my mind full of the coming trip, and tried to get a few hours' sleep in my digs, but I was too worked up and at 3.0 a.m. I got dressed and set out on the mile walk to the airport. It was a damp, foggy night and I found the Dragon standing forlornly outside the hangar. She was not locked and I climbed forward and sat in the radio seat just behind the cockpit bulkhead. It was 3.30 a.m., an hour and a half to wait.

It was getting light by four-thirty when a ground engineer arrived on his bicycle. "You're pretty early," he said. "New to the job, aren't you?" I agreed. He said that the paper van would soon be along and perhaps I would help load up. A few minutes later the van arrived and backed carefully against the door of the Dragon and the engineer and I manhandled the bundles of papers into the cabin, stacking them to leave a narrow central gangway. As the van drove away, the pilot climbed into the cabin; he was a famous local freelance known as Scruffy Thomas. He was dressed in the Croydon uniform—sports coat with leather-patched elbows, flannel trousers, both items carrying the odd oil stain. As a concession to the early morning chill, Scruffy had on a tattered raincoat and an equally decrepit trilby hat. I remember thinking that he was really living up to his name. He was a pleasant enough soul, though, and I had been told that he was a most reliable pilot.

"I hear you haven't made this trip before," he said. "Piece of cake. The only thing I want you to do is to watch the weather at Lympne, Le Touquet, Beauvais and Le Bourget. Last night there was a fair chance of fog the whole way. The old box is heavily loaded and I want to know about the weather so that we can lob in if it really starts closing in."

I said I would do all I could.

"Just one more thing. I know that you laddies think that the yard-stick of a good radioman is the number of QDMs you can shove at the pilot in a minute—if I want 'em, feed 'em in to me nice and slow, we only have a magnetic compass."

A QDM was a course for the pilot to fly to reach the airport and was calculated by a radio bearing of the aircraft at the ground station and passed to the aircraft by telegraphy.

"Let's hop off then. This may not be a hayride."

Scruffy and I settled in our seats while the ground mechanic pulled over each engine by hand. He then held up his thumb and swung the port propeller. There was a cough and a bang and the Gipsy Major settled down to a healthy roar. The same procedure was repeated with the starboard engine. Scruffy gave them both a short burst and waved the mechanic to pull away the chocks and we started bumping across the grass to the take-off point.

It was ten minutes past five and the fog had lifted enough to see the hangars on the other side of the field. I peered ahead and hoped that there would be clear weather at Le Bourget. Scruffy checked the magnetos on each engine and then waved a hand through the door.

"You all set?"

I stuck up my thumb. "All set, Skipper."

With one last look around the sky, he brought both motors to take-off revs and we started to trundle across the field. The speed picked up slowly, too slowly, even to my uninitiated mind. At last Scruffy pushed the wheel forward, the tail rose heavily and the airspeed dropped back. He banged shut the throttles and the Dragon went bumping round in a wide circle. "What you got back there, bricks?" he yelled over his shoulder. "There's no wind and

I am going to take the longest run I can, if those Majors can take another belting like that."

Again the engines roared at full throttle and after what seemed an age, the bumping of the wheels over the rough grass smoothed out. We were flying at last. Slowly Scruffy eased back the throttles and turned the aircraft towards the south in a gentle climb. Within seconds she plunged into a wall of fog and I turned my attention to the radio. I was the only aircraft about and my departure message was acknowledged at once by Croydon and Le Bourget. The latter immediately passed me his present and forecast weather—thick fog at the moment, hoped to clear in about two hours. Le Touquet then chipped in with his weather, then Beauvais, and they were both the same as Le Bourget. Scruffy studied my outstretched logbook. "A bit worse than I thought but Le Bourget should be clear enough for us, we'll keep on."

I settled down again getting bearings from Croydon and Lympne every fifteen minutes and passing them to Scruffy. He plotted them roughly on his map.

"Good work," Scruffy called. "We are coming along fine, try and get two bearings as we cross the coast in about ten minutes, we shall never see anything in this."

I waited until the time was up, obtained the bearings and then pushed the logbook in front of him. Again he plotted and then turned.

"Tell Croydon and Paris we have just crossed the coast."

I nodded and said, "Seems as though the fog is getting lighter."

"That's just the sun getting up, I am going to climb," replied Scruffy.

At 8,000 feet we suddenly burst out of our grey world into brilliant sunshine. The change was so violent that it was like a physical blow, the clouds below were a sea of cotton wool shot with black shadows, it looked beautiful and safe and solid. For twenty minutes I sat and watched this incredible picture and then suddenly everything was changed. The port engine gave a great cough and stopped, the prop jarring to a stop in a manner that shook the whole aeroplane.

I leant into the cockpit.

"Lost the port engine, that'll never run again. She can't maintain height on one with this load, dump all the papers, dump everything you can," shouted Scruffy.

I rushed back to the door and forced it open. The sun shining on the sea of cotton wool was still there but it didn't look beautiful any more—it looked damned sinister. The papers were in bundles which I now rolled to the door which the slipstream kept closed. I sat on the floor and heaved away at the bundle with my feet, it took me twenty-five minutes of frenzied work to get them out and I was only vaguely aware that we had gone back into cloud again. A glance over Scruffy's shoulder showed that the Dragon was down to 2,000 feet.

"I have been circling over the sea and now I want you to guide me to Lympne. She is barely holding height even now, but we should make it okay. Feed me about three QDMs a minute."

Lympne replied to my first call with the pressure setting for the altimeter and said he had quarter-mile visibility in fog and asked me to transmit for a bearing. I now stood in the cockpit door and wrote each course in large figures in the log as they came through. Scruffy would read them and then adjust his compass to the new heading. For twenty minutes we gradually lost height, we were now down to 1,000 feet and flying in fog that was sometimes dense enough to block out the wingtips. The last QDM was accompanied by the signal "MS".

"Motors South," I yelled and Scruffy put the aircraft into a slow turn.

"MW," said Lympne.

"Motors West," I cried to Scruffy.

He nodded. Then "MN" and "ME" were signalled, and at last "MS" again. Scruffy broke off the turn and headed south.

"Start the QDMs again. I've got the field position set, but not too fast."

For a while we flew south and then he turned again and adjusted to a QDM which would take him due north to the field. The routine commenced again but now we were also steadily letting down—900 feet, 800 feet, 700 feet.

"Shout if you see anything," said Scruffy.

500 feet, 400 feet, 300 feet, and then with my eyes starting from my head with concentration, I saw a shadow flash under the nose. Lympne radioed that she could hear our motors to the south again.

Scruffy nodded, "Keep watching." Suddenly a large black area seemed to leap out of the murk under the nose. "A wood," yelled Scruffy.

One more course and he suddenly jerked the throttle shut and pulled back on the wheel; the boundary fence flashed underneath and we thumped down firmly in the middle of Lympne Airport. Scruffy turned round in his seat, his face was white and strained under his dilapidated old hat. "Thanks. I don't want that bloody lot again. You were a great help." He turned back and gazed morosely at the port motor. "Those two take-offs were too much for the old girl, cracked an oil pipe and frozen up solid now I expect." He taxied over to the buildings and switched off the remaining motor.

We were met at the aircraft door by one of the night shift radio operators.

"That was as near as you want to go," he said chattily. "We couldn't see you until you were on the ground."

"Near enough," agreed Scruffy. "I'm going to leave her here and go back to Croydon by train."

The night man agreed and said he would get the petrol truck to run us to the station. There was a train to town at 7.45 a.m. I looked at my watch—7.15. The whole thing had only taken two hours but plenty had gone on. It also dawned on me that there was more to flying than had at first been apparent.

We arrived back at Croydon about midday and after lunch at my digs I went on the afternoon shift at three o'clock, bursting with a story that I couldn't tell. A day or so later I received a registered letter from Air Dispatch containing £1—two hours' flying at ten shillings an hour.

CHAPTER THREE

SOME weeks later an engineer told us in the workshop that there was an aircraft in trouble overhead. It was a fine sunny day and we set off for the tarmac to see what was to be seen. A large crowd was watching a DH.86 which was droning steadily round the airport; the turns were very flat and sloppy, and the flying seemed to be most erratic and the control tower had no contact on the radio. The aircraft had been returning from Paris after delivering the morning papers, and about twenty miles south of Croydon his radio had gone off the air. It had arrived overhead at 1,000 feet but was now down to 500 feet through losing height in turns and poor flying generally. Then suddenly the aircraft seemed to come to life; it made a wide turn to the south and throttled back to make a perfect landing. Later on, the story of what had happened leaked out. The captain and radio operator had flown together for over a year and the captain had taught the radioman enough flying to keep straight and level while he had a rest. On this unhappy day he had handed over to the radioman some miles south of Croydon while he went aft to the lavatory. No sooner had he got inside than the door slammed to behind him and the lock fell out on the cabin side. The pilot was firmly locked in. He immediately started banging and shouting to attract attention, but a tense situation was also building up in the cockpit. The radioman was extremely short-sighted and the pilot had taught him to fly on instruments. He now realised that his ETA for Croydon was up and the captain hadn't come back; he darted a frightened look down—yes, they were over Croydon all right, and he now concentrated his strictly limited flying ability on staying there. This he did by flying by instruments with the odd glance outside to confirm his position. He claimed afterwards that the aircraft was completely bewitched—every time he took his eyes off the instruments, it tried to climb, dive or roll over on its back. In the lavatory the pilot now sat on the floor, put his feet against the door and his back against the after wall and heaved mightily. The after wall gave way and he was deposited in the tail of the aircraft on top of the control cables. Gingerly he climbed back, after an initial pitch up which the radioman seemed to have controlled. He now began methodically to smash the door with his shoe; at last he could get his arm through only to find that the lock had dropped out. He continued his destruction until he could climb through the top half of the door. He dashed forward, jumped into the cockpit and grabbed the controls from a very relieved radio operator. When either the pilot or the radioman were in the airport bar, an infallible way to start trouble was to sing the ditty about the three old ladies locked in the lavatory.

Just before eleven o'clock one evening, a company that was engaged mostly on joy flights rang up to say that they had three hours' Army co-operation flying to do. The freelance radioman had failed to turn up and they would like to hire one of our people. I was alone in the workshop and said I would do the job for fifteen shillings an hour if they would keep quiet about it; they agreed instantly but said I must come over right away. This I did and found the aircraft, a gaily painted Dragon with the glamorous title of "Blue Mist", with its engines running, the pilot in his seat. He slowed the port motor while a mechanic helped me pull open the door and struggle in. I hurried up to the cabin, tapped the pilot on the shoulder and within minutes we were climbing into the night sky. They had told me on the phone that the aircraft was to fly up and down over Reading for two hours at 6,000 feet for the Army to train their predictors on. This was my first night flight and I remained for the first half hour completely fascinated by the wonderful fairyland made by the lights of London. I made a couple of attempts to talk to the pilot but he was wearing a leather flying helmet and didn't appear to hear me. I felt that he didn't want to hear me because he shook his head irritably each time I tried to talk to him. For an hour we trudged up and down over Reading. I heard several planes that were on Army co-op return to Croydon and then we seemed to be the only one still at it. I checked with Croydon and he asked me how much longer we would be. I replied about one and a half hours. He then asked me to wait. His next message was to the effect that they were expecting fog in the early morning; it was just starting to form and they advised an early return from the exercise. I poked my head into the cockpit and tried to shout the information to the pilot but he didn't seem to understand. I then turned on the light on the cockpit wall and held the log book under it. Suddenly the pilot snatched off his helmet, releasing a mop of shoulder-length fair hair—the pilot was a woman.

"Why can't you keep quiet," she stormed. "I can't stand people nattering at me when I am flying."

I considered that I had been badly put upon by the joy-riding company. "Nattering be damned," I shouted. "Croydon are expecting fog and want us to return."

"The Army pay only for time over the area and we have only been here about an hour," she answered. "We can always land somewhere else if Croydon shuts in."

This wide blue-up-yonder attitude irritated and frightened me. "Where the hell do you go to at two o'clock in the morning? If we stay to the end, how much fuel will we have?"

She waved at me. "Go and sit down and get on with your radioing; I'll make the decisions."

I slumped back in my seat. I had a feeling that there was going to be a sticky time ahead, and told Croydon bluntly that the skipper refused to return until the operation was complete. I finished my signal with two long exclamation marks. Croydon answered in similar fashion and then said wait while he talked to the aircraft owners. Within minutes Croydon keyed out in plain language "Return immediately", and signed the message with the owner's name. That settled it, and with bad grace the pilot turned the aircraft towards home. Croydon gave a steady series of QDMs which I dutifully showed to the pilot, but she treated them with disdain— she was quite capable of finding her way back without my help. She was too; visibility was getting poor by the time we got back, but she found the field and with a vicious side-slip landed just over the boundary. We were met at the parking area by the owner and mechanic; they both greeted me warmly, they were pleased to see their aeroplane back, but the pilot treated me with complete indifference. I heard later that this lady was quite a character; she resented deeply having anyone on board who was capable of assisting her with the operation of the aircraft. Looking back, it was perhaps that she was unsure of herself and any offer to help she considered was made only to show up her incapabilities. I never flew with her again.

There was an aeroplane at Croydon which all the freelance pilots and operators treated with great respect, it was a Monospar fitted with two Gipsy Major engines. It had originally been fitted with two Pobjoy engines, when it had been a joy to fly; the installation of the heavier and more powerful engines had made it into a real handful. I was still in a state of acute financial distress and was picking up any freelance work that came my way. I was getting bolder about it now, my attitude was that if the radio company didn't like it they could fire me.

I contracted for three hours' Army co-operation flying in the Monospar with a pilot known as Slim. He was one of the characters for whom Croydon was famous in those days, his particular foible being the wearing of a white helmet when he was flying. I found the Monospar outside the Rollason hangar and as I settled down alongside, Slim told me that we weren't going far, the beat was Sutton to Cheam—about seven miles in all and about ten miles from the field.

"The Met. people say we may get some fog later, so if we lose the Croydon lights, home we go."

I agreed, this looked like being a reasonably easy flight. It was a clear, still evening; we took off easily and were soon established on the beat. It was about three minutes long and we settled down to a system of flying two headings with me acting as timekeeper. During the next two hours, Slim flew steadily while the long summer twilight dwindled into darkness and then he began to fidget.

"That last pint wants to get out," he shouted. "I shan't last until we get down."

I gazed around the tiny cockpit. "Not a damn thing to use unless you use your helmet," I shouted back.

Slim took my joke quite seriously and immediately pulled off his white flying helmet. "Now I will turn on to the next heading, level her out and then I want you to hold her straight and level while I use this helmet. When I've done, I'll hand it to you and you can empty it out of the window—use the chin strap for a handle."

Slim waved "She's all yours," and started to fill his helmet. I glued my eyes to the airspeed and the straight and level instruments and started concentrating desperately on keeping right side up. The Monospar was extraordinarily sensitive; my slightest movements seemed to cause wild gyrations which Slim smoothed out with his free hand until she really showed how jinxed she was. The starboard engine stopped dead, she dropped the starboard wing and within a second was trying to turn on her back. Slim dropped everything and fought her back on to an even keel, but unfortunately when he dropped his helmet we were on our side and it landed in my lap. By the time we had things straightened out the horrible truth began to dawn on me. Slim had his hands full getting the Monospar back to Croydon but he found time to howl with laughter. He made a perfect single-engined landing and rolled it to the hangar. I climbed out of that aeroplane damp and smelling strongly and a proportion of my earnings had to go to the drycleaners. Slim later offered to pay the bill but I refused with what dignity I could muster. The joke was all over the aerodrome in a couple of days and it inevitably got to the ears of the "Colonel" but he chose to ignore it.

By November things had become very quiet with only the regular companies operating their aeroplanes; freelance flying had fallen off to next to nothing and the company decided that this would be a good time for my holidays. An excellent idea, but as usual I was broke. Slim, of Monospar fame, then came to the fore. He was now flying for a firm that operated Curtis Condors between Croydon, Amsterdam and Brussels and his radioman had been flying continuously for eighteen months. Slim suggested that I took his place and his wages for two weeks. His radio operator agreed at once and the Condor people had no objection. I took my holiday to start on Saturday morning and I met Slim outside the aeroplane at eleven o'clock. The Condor was, I believe, originally built as a night sleeper in the United States but she made an ideal freighter, with a big roomy fuselage, biplane wings and retractable under-carriage. Slim showed me round the "office"; the pilot and radio operator sat side by side in a wide cockpit. It was luxury com-pared to most other aircraft. We had a mixed freight which was stowed under nets down the cabin walls and we were soon bump-ing across the field to the take-off point. I remember thinking that this trip would surely go better than my last attempt to fly out of England. Slim tested the magnetos and turned the big craft into the wind. I had a wide view from the big windows, the radio was easily accessible behind the pilot's seat—I was going to enjoy my fortnight's holiday. The din from the big radial engines was tremendous when they built up to take-off revs, but she was soon off the ground and settling down for a long climb into the east. From my vantage point, I could see the whole of the London dock system and I remember feeling that I had really improved my lot; I might have been joining one of those elderly tramps for a two-year voyage instead of sailing over them at 2,000 feet on the way to Rotterdam.

I busied myself with the weather reports and a couple of QDMs that Slim didn't want and then he pointed out the Dutch coast through the haze; we were nearly there. Lunch in Rotterdam and then on to Brussels where the last of our cargo was discharged and we were loaded up for the return journey. As we climbed into the cabin, our ears were assailed by a twittering noise that seemed to fill the whole aircraft—we had a cargo of day-old chicks. I don't know if the chicks stopped while we were flying but they were certainly full of song when we left the aircraft in Croydon after an uneventful trip from Brussels. For two weeks we flew this route steadily and I came to recognise the land contours and take an interest in the navigation. Slim showed me what little he knew but admitted that the best thing was to fly a course for a time and then look around for something you recognised.

It was on my last day on the route that Slim took the day off and his place was taken by a gentleman against whom I had been warned many times. A tall, thin character, complete with a wealthy accent and toothbrush moustache; he had recently taken up civil aviation on leaving the Royal Air Force. My casual greeting the next morning was frozen in its tracks; I was curtly informed to get aboard the aircraft and until we landed back in Croydon I should always address him as "Sir". This was a far cry from the easy relationship in which I had done my flying so far but I consoled myself with the thought it was for today only. As we climbed into the cloud, I went through the usual routine of collecting the destination and alternate weather, but this was firmly stopped. I would do nothing until I was specifically given orders to do so. At both Rotterdam and Brussels I ducked out of sight until we were ready to go—at the latter I did not see him around so I climbed into my seat to wait. He joined the aircraft a few minutes later followed by two men and a horse; the latter was to be our return freight. The loaders suspended the horse in a sling with its feet just touching the floor and its head in the cockpit. Meanwhile I was receiving a stern lecture about aircrew behaviour.

"I am generally thoroughly displeased with your conduct on this trip," said the pilot, fixing me with his slightly protuberant eyes. "I have been very tolerant, but your daring to scuttle aboard and take your seat before I am aboard, I will not stand for. I shall report you when we get back to . . .'

My temper flared. "Listen, you stupid sod. I am only relieving the regular man on this route and this is my last flight. I hope he can put up with you because I wouldn't."

Mr. G. stared at me in amazement and anger. I was about to start again when he turned away and started his cockpit drill. We took off for London in a noisy but icy atmosphere. The horse was enjoying the ride and repeatedly nibbled my shoulder with his soft lips. I fed him the remains of my lunch and two oranges that I had filched from the cargo a couple of days before. Mr. G. watched in icy silence. When I looked again he was staring fixedly out of the

24

port window, so I leaned forward and taking his lightweight uniform cap from the scuttle, offered it to the horse. He nuzzled it for a bit and then taking a grip of the soft top, he started to chew. The pilot's head swivelled round but his nerves were good, his two hands remained on the control yoke and he never said a word. I don't know if his lack of reaction put the horse off his meal but after chewing away for a few more seconds, he dropped the badly mauled cap to the floor where it remained throughout the trip. As I climbed under the horse's neck, I backheeled the remains into the cockpit but the pilot had the last laugh. When I received the cheque for the two weeks' work, it was less the price of a new uniform cap.

My return to the radio company was something of an anti-climax; it had become general knowledge throughout the company about my freelance activities and I was told by the "Colonel" that they would have to stop. I agreed with him; freelancing was pretty well finished until next spring—why get the sack now?

CHAPTER FOUR

THE winter and spring of 1936 and 1937 were very quiet at Croydon and the only flying that I could get were official test flights—after an overhaul we checked the radio and were then expected to go on the test flight to ensure that it was working properly. For the first of these flights I hung around for weeks; it was on one of the two famous Short landplanes operated by Imperial Airways on the Paris and Cologne runs. They were the monsters of their day, biplane wings with four Jupiter engines in a row between them and a fuselage attached to the lower plane that was somehow reminiscent of a flying-boat hull. They had two enormous main landing wheels and a tail wheel. They were called "Scylla" and "Syrinx" but were more generally known as "JJ" and "JK" from the last two letters of their registration. I remember one of these monsters landing in bad weather and running into the public enclosure which was fortunately empty at the time and the only damage sustained was to the iron railings of the enclosure. The two big wheels just rolled them flat.

At last came the great day—"JK" was to make her certification of airworthiness flight at 10 a.m. I was in the Imperial hangar at nine o'clock and was later told that I spent most of the time standing on one leg. True or false, at 9.30 "JK" was towed out of the hangar for the engine runs, when these were completed an Imps crew climbed aboard with me firmly attached to their tail. The cockpit was wide and square and the radio station was a desk, no less, attached to the starboard cockpit wall behind the first officer. The Imps radioman settled down in the cabin with his newspaper and left me in the huge cockpit with the two pilots. Unless one has flown in "JJ" or "JK" it is impossible to understand the differences in the atmosphere of the take-off between them and the types with which I had become familiar. The hammering of the engines at full revs, the juddering of the fuselage with all the instruments jigging around before your eyes, this I had grown used to; I was unprepared for the smooth sweep across the grass—you couldn't tell when you were airborne—and the gentle climb into the sky. Everything seemed to happen so smoothly, I decided then that this was the easy way to earn a living flying. The pilots carried out their series of tests while I tested the radio on both fixed and trailing aerials and confirmed that the wind-driven generator was working. Aircraft in those days took all their electrical power from the batteries which were continuously charged when in flight from a wind-driven generator. I returned to the cabin and told the Imps man that all was well. He signed my form and returned to his newspaper. "It's all yours, do you good to get some practice." I agreed and returned to the front "office". Watching the pilots going through their drill I was again impressed by the stately way in which "JK" carried out the manœuvre, the only discordant note I could see was the airspeed—she seemed to fly at about 80 mph and dropped below this even in a gentle turn. I checked the weather and told the pilot; he said that we would land at twelve o'clock. I can only describe the approach and landing as a progression back to earth. I watched through a porthole beside the table, the big starboard landing wheel turning gently; there was a gentle thump and it started to turn rapidly, we had landed.

For some weeks we had been plagued with an intermittent radio fault on a Handley Page 42, I think it was "Hanno". We couldn't reproduce the fault when we tested it on the ground and the log entry against the fault of "Ground tested and found okay" was beginning to cause some hostile feelings between the engineers and the Imps radiomen. Both sides claimed that the other side was not doing their job efficiently and the Imperial superintendent decreed that an engineer would accompany the radio officer on "Hanno's" next trip to Paris. The "Colonel" picked me for the job; the night before the flight I took all the radio equipment into the workshop and gave it a thorough going over; I tightened everything that could be tightened, I resoldered joints that just looked slightly tired, I cleaned switches, changed relays and valves and then reinstalled it all again in "Hanno"; I then signed my name to the unpopular entry in the log "Ground tested and found okay".

I joined the crew on the tarmac the next morning and explained to the captain who I was. The captain, E. R. B. White, known as "Erby", was one of the real old timers—a calm, efficient man to whom flying was strictly a way of earning a living.

"Glad to have you along," he said. "This fault has let us down on the last three trips in "Hanno", each time the weather hasn't been too bad but it could really catch us out on a bad day."

I agreed that it was all obscure but I had hopes of pinpointing the problem.

"There's no seat for you unfortunately, but I'll get the steward to put a stool for you alongside the radio."

I thanked him and we climbed aboard. The cockpit was not so wide as "JK"; the pilots sat up on a pedestal while the radio operator sat down in a well behind the captain's seat and beside the cockpit door. I sat on my stool beside him in the gangway. A radio officer once told me that he was very busy going into Le Bourget when a sudden roaring told him that something was amiss. He turned and found himself looking down on the roofs of Paris from no great height—the door had opened as the aircraft turned to port. Nothing like this happened today, however, the aircraft drummed along for about two hours while the radio worked like a charm. The captain said that they would be landing in about ten minutes. The flight was short because of a strong tail wind but it had been rather boring. I was still in the state when flying fascinated me and all I had seen this trip was the strip of sky between the two pilots. During lunch, Erby turned to me, "It looks as though you have frightened that snag away for the time being."

I explained what I had done the night before and the whole table laughed. 'That's what I call using a trip hammer to crack a peanut. Who pays for that lot?" asked the first officer.

"Don't worry, the maintenance is on a flat rate. The company will be the loser," I replied.

"Sure you stuck to radio?" smiled Erby. "The port outer's a bit rough, sure you didn't change that?"

I denied this and then he suggested I sit back and take things easy on the way back—they would call me if I was wanted.

The weather had deteriorated considerably on the journey back and Croydon reported gale force northerly wind with poor visibility in heavy rain. The aircraft was almost empty and I sat in the front seat of the cabin and watched the '42 wallow through almost continuous cloud. I sometimes had a quick view of some soaked fields in Northern France; once I saw a town which should have been Beauvais and later a quick glance of a sea that was white with spray—it was blowing all right. Meanwhile the steward served afternoon tea.

"As far as I am concerned you're a passenger, but I can't give any to the blokes up front—not allowed you know."

I nodded, there had been a battle going on for weeks about whether or not the crew were entitled to meals in the cockpit; the company said they were not. This attitude was changed some time later when a very senior captain was found to be carrying his lunch in a red pocket handkerchief attached to a stick over his shoulder!

After some three and a half hours, the engines were throttled back and we started to lose height. We should have been at Croydon by now, but it seemed doubtful. At about 600 feet we broke clear, still in rain, and in a few moments I recognised East Grinstead. We were about twenty miles from Croydon and the captain was now obviously following the road home. "Hanno" rolled and tossed below the clouds; it reminded me of the *Milford Queen*. Gazing fixedly at the road, I saw that we were slowly being over-hauled by a yellow van which passed beneath us and was soon lost in the rain ahead. Those twenty miles took us another thirty minutes. Erby White made his usual immaculate job of landing and taxied the wildly lurching aeroplane into the lee of the hangars. The wind was gusting to forty knots and he was well aware that the huge biplane wings under these conditions could well turn "Hanno" on her back. As he passed into the cabin to disembark, he patted my shoulder. "Fixed that just in time. Trip hammer or not, we needed that radio today and badly, thank you."

I left "Hanno" walking eight feet tall.

This trip brought home to me the fact that I knew nothing about navigation. I thought, quite incorrectly, that local progress in the R/O business was to become a navigator as well. I enrolled on a postal course and one year later became the proud owner of a Second "N".

The next job that came my way, and this time, undoubtedly for my sins, concerned a venerable Wessex. This had been fitted up to display at night over large cities the illuminated word OXO. The Wessex was a high-wing monoplane with three Genet engines and she had been equipped with two wind-driven generators, one for the radio and one for the illuminations. The radio occupied one side of the cockpit after bulkhead, and the controls for the illuminations, fuses, rheostats, etc. occupied the other. The frame-work carrying the OXO letters took the form of a lower main plane with the letters some four feet long. I examined the aero-plane in the back of the hanger in the twilight of a November day. The radio had been fitted by the company and was quite normal, but the illuminations appeared to have been put in by some firm of heavy electrical engineers. No one seemed to know anything about it; the hangar foreman positively sneered when I asked him, "Just selling it hangar space?"

The pilot turned up later, his attitude was he was a freelance pilot with a contract to fly a Wessex over London for one hour between 8.0 and 9.0 p.m. that evening displaying the word OXO. He was an irascible little man and snapped at every question but I did get him to say that he had never flown this particular contraption before. The "Colonel" was equally non-commital; when queried he just shrugged his shoulders.

"Just an hour's flying on a Wessex; I always thought you liked flying and would jump at the job."

I met the little pilot at about twenty minutes to eight and I found that with the assistance of the hangar foreman he had rolled out the Wessex and run up the engines; he was ready to go. I started to explain that I had found no way to illuminate OXO on the ground, we would just have to fly it and pray. He immediately bristled up, "I can't stand funny men, let's go."

Within a few minutes we were making a climbing turn around the field before setting course for London at 2,000 feet. The radio was all right and then with some trepidation I tackled the illuminations; there were no cabin lights that I could find and I had to hold my torch in one hand. Each letter seemed to have a rheostat, a switch and a fuse. I checked that the wind-driven genny was giving out, put each rheostat to maximum and then switched on each letter. Through my window a ghostly circle of light appeared. I shot across the cabin and found an equivalent circle on the other side; it was working but only dimly. I now inched back each rheostat and soon we were sailing over the heart of London with a brightly illuminated sign. Very pleased with myself, I leant into the cockpit.

"What a job, she flies like a handcart with all that garbage trailing along and now your sign has completely obliterated my panel lights," snarled the pilot. "Try and damp it down."

I returned to the panel to turn up the rheostats when there was a flash and a bang; X had blown his fuse. The fuse was red hot and I needed pliers to get it out. I blew on it and waved it around until I could insert some more fuse wire. As I went to fit it back, there was another bang—Port O had gone out—another fuse. Again I struggled and at last had OXO at full strength. Seconds later we flew through a flurry of rain and I lost both Os; before I could get them back X packed up. I now found that the whole panel was overheating. I received a nasty shock trying to find what was wrong with X and then burnt my fingers trying to change yet another fuse. X suddenly returned to life, glowed briefly for about a minute, and then starboard O blew up. I saw a puff of smoke through the window. Sweating from shock and burnt fingers, I shoved my head into the cockpit.

"Let's go home, the whole caboodle will go on fire if I switch it on again."

There was no argument and in a few minutes we were back at Croydon. I heard later a discussion in the bar of the Airport Hotel about a new form of skywriting that had been tried out over London the previous night. The aircraft had apparently tried to spell out the sign in lights but no one could make sense out of what he was trying to spell; the odd letters that could be seen went off and on in a most erratic manner! I believe the whole thing was scrapped soon afterwards.

Radio direction finders in their earliest forms had been appearing on aircraft for some time. Their use was limited as it entailed turning the aircraft until the radio signal was zero; this meant that you were pointing directly towards the station that was giving the bearing. You went on from there to plot your bearing line; the operation was cumbersome and little used. Most aircraft obtained their bearings on request from the ground stations. The company had a request from a firm in Cambridge that an aircraft radio was u/s (unserviceable) and would they send an engineer. The clerk who accepted the request neither asked what was wrong, what type of equipment nor what aeroplane; the job was passed to him with the instruction that someone must get to Cambridge and fix it as soon as possible. I was selected to go and caught a train from Liverpool Street the next morning and settled down to read my way to Cambridge. I was not particularly concerned; I knew that the company in Cambridge had several aircraft fitted with our equipment. A chauffeur met me at the ticket barrier and whisked me out to the field. He led me to the office of the owner of the company; I remonstrated that I would rather go to the hangar, fix the fault and visit the head man on my way out, but this was not to be and I was soon ushered into the office. The head man was a tall, pleasant character but what he had to tell me was far from pleasant. He had a Stinson Reliant that had arrived in this country with a device called a radio compass. It didn't seem to work and would I fix it before 3 p.m. (it was now midday) as he wanted to demonstrate it to a customer.

I was escorted out to the field and the Stinson was standing on the tarmac, complete with a ground accumulator and a mechanic. Great things were obviously expected of me and the only thing

I needed was a miracle! The mechanic gave me a large manual that had arrived with the aircraft and I settled down in the cockpit to find out just what I was looking for. I first read up how to operate it and with the assistance of the mechanic switched it on. A wave of relief washed over me as I put on the headset—the receiver was working. Sticking close to the book, I now made a series of tests and found the radio compass was operating extremely well. I found the receiver under the back passenger seat and for good measure I fumbled around the plugs to ensure that they were tight. It was an important young man that marched back to the owner's office and claimed that the fault had been "fixed".

"That's good. Neither I nor the man to whom I am trying to sell the aeroplane really know how this thing works. Come along on the demo. and show both of us," he replied.

This was not exactly my plan. I had hoped to get him to accept it on the ground and get back to Croydon before it went unserviceable again. I was given an excellent lunch and we then climbed into the Stinson. It was the best appointed aeroplane I had seen; the interior was sound-proofed in an attractive shade of grey, carpets on the floor, ashtrays and deep comfortable seats. I sat in the co-pilot's seat and the prospective buyer sat behind on a bench type seat. The radial engine fired at once and the Stinson seemed to leap into the air after a remarkably short run; within minutes we were at 5,000 feet over the flat fields of Cambridgeshire. Visibility forward and downward from my seat was wonderful and I was settling down to some practice in mental map reading when the prospective owner asked me about the radio compass. Just to make sure I tuned in the most powerful transmitter I knew—the BBC programme on 200 metres—and demonstrated how the radio compass worked, finishing up with a homing flight towards Droitwich. After a three-hour flight we landed back at Cambridge, all very satisfied. I am sure that there was nothing wrong from the start but no one had been quite sure of just what it was supposed to do.

The next flight that came my way was a delivery flight to Nairobi on a DH.86B; this was a real thrill—if the pilot was willing, I could try out some of my new found knowledge of navigation. The radio company had appointed me to do the flight so it was no longer necessary for me to skulk round the aircraft after dark. I met the pilot and was at once impressed; he was a tall, dark man—a freelance with plenty of experience and, incidentally, plenty of money. I explained my aspirations in the navigation field and the state of learning that I had then reached. He was quite pleasant and suggested that I do the flight plans and try to navigate the flights while he would supervise what I did. The aeroplane was ready for collection at Hatfield, the route had been laid down and there were only a few outstanding matters to be settled and we could get on our way.

Some days later the pilot and I climbed into a brand new 86B. The radio was in the cabin behind the pilot's seat; there were only the two of us—it looked like being a trip to remember. We climbed away from Hatfield through 6,000 feet of solid cloud and then settled down between layers at 8,000 feet; four hours to go to Lyon. I went through the radio checks and then set about the navigation. For the next three hours I must have been an absolute pest to the ground stations. I asked for bearing after bearing which I plotted; I kept an air plot which further confused the issue by proving that the actual and forecast winds were diametrically opposed to each other. After three hours I was in a state of mental collapse and the only certain information I had was that the aircraft was over France. The pilot then waved me up to the cockpit and into the copilot's seat.

"I have been watching you at that navigation and you have one fault—you're working so bloody hard you are not thinking straight," he laughed. "Now look, we are three hours on our way, you know our estimated ground speed—see where that puts us."

I darted back into the cabin, worked out that simple sum and plotted it, then clambered back into the copilot's seat. "DR (dead reckoning) puts us over Avallon, but my DR plot and the met. wind . . ."

He waved me to silence and said, "Look over your side and you'll find Avallon just passing under the starboard wing." He was right. "Don't try and do too much; try and fit your navigation to the conditions. It's been gin clear since Paris and you have worked yourself into a lather—you didn't even find time to look over the side," he said. "Now just sit there and map read while you get your second wind; let's have a position, say, every fifteen minutes."

We flew on in beautiful weather and then let down on to the aerodrome at Lyon, where the pilot made what I came to recognise as his characteristic landing. He always rolled on the main wheels and then gently dropped the tail wheel; he once explained that he liked to feel the surface with his main wheels first—at some places you never knew what you would find.

We stayed in a small hotel close to the aerodrome that night and the pilot insisted on paying for the dinner; he knew my limited funds and throughout the trip was unobtrusively helping me financially. Without being pedantic, he pointed out the relative importance of each operation in navigation and stressed the importance of completing each operation without haste.

"If you've lost yourself and taken three hours to make a good job of it, you can spare three minutes to find yourself again," he laughed.

The next morning, the pilot checked over my flight plan to Rome. "Yes, let's call it four hours dead. Now today don't try and run an airplot—get a position every thirty minutes and use all we've got—pinpoints, radio or DR and we'll try and put a degree of confidence against each one."

We left Lyon in sunny weather and set course for Rome at 8,000 feet when the pilot called me up into the cockpit. He pointed ahead and there in brilliant sunshine were the Alps. The jumble of snow-clad peaks against the deep blue made a truly wonderful sight. When I commented, the pilot laughed. "Fair enough on a day like this but in bad weather those peaks stuff themselves into clouds and produce some bloody awful turbulence." I was going to scramble out of my seat for my first position when he restrained me. "There's a road, a railway and a river in a valley crossing our track at right-angles soon, get your fix from that." I consulted the topographical map; yes, it was undoubtedly the best position available.

For the next thirty minutes I sat mesmerised with the beauty of the Alps and then the Italian coast came up out of the haze ahead. Rome reported no ceiling and a visibility of ten miles in haze as we flew out to sea, while the Italian coast unfolded on the port side. I had the position of the aircraft accurately now and I asked the pilot several times our distance away from visible landmarks. His judgement of distance was almost uncanny. We crossed the Italian coast again and I had a good view of Elba, and then, with about twenty miles to go, he commenced a gentle let-down to the aerodrome. The pilot knew Rome well and we were soon settled in an inn at a village about five miles from the field. In the morning we flew to Brindisi, had lunch, and in the late afternoon landed at Athens. The last part of this flight was most interesting when we flew low over the Corinth canal for the pilot to take some photographs. The next morning we were up bright and early for the longest oversea flight of the trip—Athens to Alexandria—it worked out at five hours. Our fuel reserve including the internal tanks gave us approximately six hours twenty minutes—we should do the job comfortably.

The first two hours of the flight passed pleasantly; we were flying over the Greek islands and our position was never in doubt as each pinpoint appeared out of the haze and passed beneath. Then away to starboard a line of rugged coast appeared—the island of Crete—and then dead ahead was Cape Sidheras, giving a first-class point of departure for our three hours of sea crossing to Alexandria.

I now started navigating furiously and in twenty minutes again found myself in a muddle; the pilot was most patient. "Rub it out and start quietly from the Cape," he said. "That's the last thing we know with any degree of certainty; don't bother with an air plot for at least an hour."

I carried out his instructions and the '86 droned on in a bowl of haze; she seemed to be quite stationary in the sky. At last I could raise Alexandria who gave me a third-class bearing. I plotted it and it put us east of track; ten minutes later another second class bearing put us west of track. I plotted away and it seemed that the aircraft was definitely west of track. As we drew closer, the bearings were upgraded to first class. If my sums were right, we were west of track by about fifty miles. When I told the skipper he laughed. "Excellent. We will carry on as we are and then when we see the coast we shall know which way to turn to find Alex." My faith in my ability as a navigator was not very strong and I started to worry that if we turned east, would it be right? I called for yet another bearing but by now Alexandria was used to me; he replied with the bearing and, as though he had sensed my worry, added, "You're a bit west of the usual Athens–Alex route bearing." I could have jumped with relief. I now established where I thought we should cross the coast and when I showed it to the pilot he handed me his topographical map. "Okay, we'll see when the coast comes up."

I glanced at my watch and gazed fixedly ahead into the haze. It was ten minutes to the coast and they were the longest ten minutes ever. When the time was up, there was no sign of anything; my hands began to get sticky and my mouth to dry out. I had made a mess of a simple flight again. I gazed ahead and then looked down and there it was—the coast was directly beneath us. I had not appreciated that forward visibility was almost nil, although you could see directly downwards. The pilot throttled back and started descending, keeping the coast in plain view. Soon the desert gave way to the green of the Nile Delta and there was the airfield at Alexandria beneath us. Over a beer in the rest house, the pilot again stressed the virtue of not worrying if things didn't immediately fall into place. I was feeling better about my efforts but not much; it had become painfully obvious that the simple navigational problems worked out much better on the landlady's kitchen table than they did in an aeroplane.

The next four sectors of the flight were literally following the valley of the Nile, with the temperature steadily building up. Alexandria to Aswan—we were tempted to try and make Wadi Halfa but were warned of the possibility of sandstorms south of Aswan, so we spent the night in the rest house there. Next day, a long flight to Khartoum which started by following the Nile for about fifty miles, then 250 miles of Nubian Desert and then in the haze ahead appeared the Nile again—a strip of green in the sand. We fixed our position crossing the river and set out across the desert for Khartoum. About 200 miles farther on the Nile came angling in again from the port side; we then followed the river for the last seventy-five miles to the aerodrome at Khartoum. We landed in a swirl of sand and in intense heat in the middle of the afternoon. I had encountered heat in the Persian Gulf but this seemed much worse; it turned the comparatively cool aeroplane into an oven in seconds. After a hot and restless night, we were glad to get away for Malakal—a comparatively short trip of about 400 miles. This trip we had the White Nile in sight the whole time, first on one side and then the other. I was getting a lot of map reading practice but still had to use mental dead reckoning to identify some of the places we passed over. Malakal was even hotter than Khartoum and we spent another restless night. We set off for Kampala in the morning, another 250 miles of desert and we picked up the White Nile coming in from the starboard side; we fixed ourselves over Juba and then flew on to Kampala over scenery that gradually changed from desert to the deep green of the tropical rain forests. Kampala was civilisation after our last three nightstops but the pilot was in a hurry to deliver the aircraft to Nairobi and early the next morning we set off on the last leg of the flight. For the first time since Northern France we ran into cloud; it was a rough and rainy trip but fifty miles from Nairobi the clouds broke up and we landed at Nairobi in clear, sunny weather. Under the watchful eye of the captain, my navigation stood the strain of some three hours of blind flying; my position agreed with the actual position when we broke out of the clouds.

The owners of the '86 wanted the pilot to stay on for three months to check out their own pilots on the aeroplane, but I was to be sent home by sea. After an hilarious farewell dinner, I caught the morning train to Mombasa, then a Union Castle boat to Southampton. With deep regret I heard some time later that the pilot had been killed when the roof blew off a Hillson Praga aeroplane that he was testing for someone.

CHAPTER FIVE

WHEN I returned to Croydon, Army co-operation flying was in full swing and with an acute shortage of both pilots and radiomen. By flying on every possible occasion I was able to keep the wolf from the door, and although I did not grow any wealthier, I added a lot of flying hours on Rapides, Dragons and '86s to my logbook. On one flight in a Rapide, I made the mistake that was always waiting at the end of a flight; I had contacted to do three hours' Army co-op at Grantham and we left Croydon about 5.0 p.m. to position the aircraft at Grantham for the night's work. We completed the flight and left Grantham for Croydon about 1 a.m. At Croydon the visibility was varying quite rapidly between half a mile and nothing at all in moving fog. The ground below was obscured and we flew steadily towards Croydon on a series of bearings until they told us they could hear us overhead.

To operate medium frequency radio in an aircraft at maximum ranges, it was necessary to trail out 200 feet of wire for an aerial. To keep this aerial in position, it had attached to its free end a string of lead beads called the bead weight; in some countries a single lead weight was used. The procedure was to use the trailing aerial until close to the aerodrome and then switch over to a fixed aerial—the great thing was then to remember to reel in the trailing aerial. Croydon aerodrome had houses on the airfield boundary on three sides and 200 feet of wire with a lead weight at the end flailing behind a landing aircraft could cause damage.

Now it was my turn. The visibility at Croydon had gone up to half a mile, but we still required a series of bearings to make a safe approach. I was using the fixed aerial and then over the last row of houses on the west side of the field there was a sharp crack and a few feet of copper wire flew back out of the fairlead—I had lost 200 feet of wire and the lead weights somewhere in the Waddon Road. I didn't tell the pilot—there was a chance that it had hung up in a tree and had done no damage. I was on duty at 7 a.m. the next morning and until eleven o'clock all was routine; then, as I was discussing a problem with the "Colonel", there was a heavy knock on the workshop door and in marched a large and ponderous policeman complete with 200 feet of copper wire and a lead bead weight slung over his shoulder. "Clean through the back window, smashed both top and bottom. Tidy little bill for one of your blokes to pay."

Before the "Colonel" could remonstrate, the constable plunged on. " 'Bout four o'clock this morning the people said; only aircraft landing about that time was B——'s Rapide, according to the Control Tower. B——'s Rapide had been to Grantham and was on its way back. They say they had one of your blokes on the radio."

The "Colonel" swung round and one look at my face was enough —"Private enterprise again I see. I hope they paid you enough to square up for that window."

After concluding an agreement with the owner of the house, the profit from the flight was about six shillings.

During this period Imps began to take delivery of their DH Albatross aircraft. They were low-wing wooden monoplanes with four Gipsy-Twelve aircooled engines streamlined into the wing; they carried twenty-two passengers. Unfortunately they had a tall electric undercarriage with single leg each side which soon led to trouble. Returning from a Paris trip one afternoon, an Albatross was taxi-ing on the grass—a high cross wind causing her to slide sideways— when the tyres ran against the concrete in front of the control tower. This instantly stopped the sliding and the aircraft collapsed on its belly. Only the undercarriage and propellers were damaged and within an hour she had been towed away to the hangar. Some time later an Albatross arrived over Croydon with one wheel down and one wheel firmly locked up. A DH engineer was hung head first out of the bay and with a spanner tied to his wrist he winched the offending undercarriage down by hand. It took a long time but eventually she made a safe landing, the only casualty being Captain Oliver's voice which had turned into a harsh croak. Yet another morning the door of number one hangar was firmly closed when we reported at 7 a.m. Entrance was gained through a side door and it was discovered that an Albatross had been jacked up during the night. Excessive weight had been put in the nose and she had promptly put her nose on the hangar floor and her tail in the roof. Again the only serious damage was vocal—the nightshift foreman was reputed to have completely lost his power of speech.

I made several test flights in these aircraft and they were a joy to fly in; the cockpits were soundproofed and the crew accommodation was spacious and comfortable.

British Airways were now receiving their Lockheed 14; there seemed to be some stalling problems in the early days and two senior captains were killed near Bristol, but they soon had this particular problem cleaned up. The military version of the '14 was to become known during the war as the Hudson.

At about this time, also, Imps started accepting their Armstrong Whitworth Ensigns. They had been much delayed by the R.A.F. re-armament programme and were even now not ready for airline service. They were a high wing metal aircraft fitted with four Armstrong Siddeley Tiger engines. When delivered these engines gave 880 bhp, which was not enough for this heavy, thick-winged aircraft, and they were uprated to 925 bhp. Even this was not enough and in 1940 they were re-engined with Wright Cyclones of 1,100 bhp. During this period I was involved in test flights when the aircraft was in its middle stage—925 bhp. The cockpit had not the comfort of the Albatross—the pilot and copilot sat on a high pedestal; behind the pilot sat the radioman in a well with his seat in the middle of the gangway facing outboard with the motor-driven auxiliary power unit behind him. I remember on one flight the captain calling down to me, "Radio, go and look at the two engines on the port side; something to tell your grandchildren about." It most surely was, the two engines had literally blown up, two cylinders had been blown off one engine and the two pistons were stuck up in the airstream, the other engine had lost one cylinder. As I slipped back into my seat, the captain shouted, "Tell Croydon what's happened and tell them to make it an emergency." Croydon acknowledged the message and then I just had to sit tight and wait in my dark hole. After a period of intense concentration by the two pilots, I saw the control column move back, followed by the thump of the landing wheels. At this time I had not developed the technique of going "with equanimity" through an emergency in an aircraft without being able to see or hear what was going on.

A great effort was made by Imperials in 1938 to carry all overseas Christmas mail by air and the Ensigns, although still not carrying passengers, were conscripted to assist in this operation. The results were catastrophic; one Ensign got as far as Cairo before being stopped by engine trouble, the rest just fell out along the way with the same complaint. Out of their failure came my next long flight. Imperials chartered anything that would fly to move this stranded mail onwards and I was hired for a Rapide to carry mail from Paris to Cairo. The pilot was a pleasant character and was happy to let me try out my small navigational ability. He was one of those placid characters that seemed to doze away the hours in the cockpit; then fifteen minutes before arriving at his destination he would pick up his map, fix his position exactly and go on to land. He would let me work away to my heart's content and would accept all the information I passed up to him but I don't think he made any use of it. The first leg of our journey was from Croydon to Paris where we loaded up the mail bags. The flight onwards was uneventful—Dijon, Marseilles, Nice, Genoa, Rome, Brindisi, and there we ran right out of luck—we had an engine failure. It happened as the pilot was running up the engines before switching off, and spare parts from England were needed. It was decided to ship me home, and the next day an '86 on its way back to England after delivering a load of mail to Cairo gave me a lift home. I was given the copilot's seat but my offer to assist in the navigation was politely refused. The crew had been together for a long time and they didn't need any help although the pilot did let me do a few spells of straight and level flying.

I found Croydon very quiet for the first few months of the new year and then I was posted to Weston-super-Mare as radio engineer/operator for Weston Airways. I have a feeling that the radio company wanted me moved from Croydon because my free-lance flying activities were not setting a good example to the junior engineers.

I found Weston Airways suffering from severe growing pains, short of pilots, radio operators and office space; I set up shop in a tea chest in a corner of the hangar. They had a large, but very mixed fleet of aircraft—Dragons, Rapides, Percival Q6s, Dragonflies, Short Scion Juniors—and besides several established routes, they flew a lot of Army co-op. The previous engineer had just not been able to stand the pace; Weston Airways needed radio operators more than radio maintenance and he hated flying. When they found I was keen to fly, I was made most welcome and fly I did, every day and all day and carried out maintenance in the evenings if there was no Army co-op work. The half dozen radio operators were a mixed bag and one in particular was an everlasting source of trouble. He was on the Manchester run in a Q6 and he was persistently sick; after one particularly disastrous trip to Manchester and back the pilot refused point blank to carry him in the afternoon and I was asked to take his place. This particular run then became my "beat" for the summer. It was two return trips a day—Weston, Whitchurch (Bristol), Elmdon (Birmingham) and Ringway (Manchester); the aircraft used on this route were two Percival Q6s, one with a retracting undercarriage and one with fixed. It was about this time that I was inadvertently passed two invoices from the radio company for my services to Weston Airways. The difference between what I was paid and what Weston Airways were being charged was so incredible that I took them direct to the manager and offered to do the job for six pounds a week. He agreed at once; I had to give six months' notice and he said he would insist on my staying at Weston until the expiry of my notice. So began what was to be the most intensive flying of my career.

When not on the Manchester run, I went on some of the other routes, Weston/Cardiff/Swansea, where we landed on the sand at Mumbles. Weston to Lands End—the aircraft circled Barnstaple while the traffic officer cycled around like a shepherd's dog and cleared the sheep off the aerodrome. There was the incredible Weston/Cardiff ferry; this took fifteen minutes and cost a fraction of the train fare, the train taking four and a half hours. In the height of the summer aircraft just skittled to and fro and the holidaymakers loved it; there was a bus service to the City passing its gate. It was nothing to see a party of children with labels attached come across in the morning and go home at night after a day by the seaside. I only know of two accidents on this route; an empty Dragon on a positioning flight to Cardiff crashed on take-off and killed the pilot and, before I went to Weston, a Dragon crashed on the mud on its approach to Cardiff with three intoxicated passengers. It appeared from the positions of the bodies that an attempt had been made to pull the pilot out of the cockpit.

The summer went by and my flying hours piled up by sometimes ten hours a day, but only one flight really stays in my mind. Weston Airways had several coloured pilots and on a very hot, still Sunday afternoon one of these pilots and myself were scheduled for two hours' Army co-op flying over Wellington in a Dragonfly. We stuck the tail in the fence and held on to the brakes as long as they would hold at full revs and then started the take-off—the Dragonfly was not exactly famous for its take-off. Slowly we built up to flying speed and then, too soon, the pilot pulled back on the control column, the Dragonfly gave a little hop and settled back firmly on the grass; three times he pulled the control column back too soon and then we were faced with a five-foot high hedge. Somebody shouted, it was probably me, and then the pilot hauled the column right back into his stomach. The Dragonfly hopped neatly over the fence and landed again very firmly in the next field without any assistance from the crew. I looked at the pilot, his chocolate brown face was grey white and the aeroplane was filled with that smell so impossible to describe—the smell of fear. The next day the ground crew brought the Dragonfly back to the aerodrome—via the gate.

Then one Sunday morning we found we were at war. All civil flying stopped and we were made up into two-man crews and incorporated into National Air Communications. NAC was formed of civil aircraft and civil crews to ferry equipment and personnel for the three services. Our first job was to report to Abingdon to ferry plasma to France. We reported to Abingdon and were stuck there for three days. Everything was in chaos, nobody knew where the plasma was and even if we had found it, the chances of finding anyone who knew where it was supposed to go were remote. After pestering the RAF Movements Control for about a week, we were told to go back to Weston until we were called for. The Rapide to which I had been assigned was eventually sent to Worthy Down and we delivered all kinds of supplies to France. All the civil aircraft were involved—HP.42s carrying beer with an immaculately uniformed crew and my old pal "Scruffy" with a decrepit Dragon and a radioman in a fisherman's jersey carrying blood plasma; everyone did their bit. I had several pilots during this period and had dropped any aspirations I may have had of becoming a navigator.

One flight I shall long remember; we had delivered a load to Rheims and were told that the aircraft was to be returned to Weston to allow some modifications to be made. That night we fell into bad company and it was two very tired and depressed men that climbed into the Rapide the next morning. The weather was thick and hazy with considerable turbulence and the pilot decided that we would stop at Rouen to have something to settle our stomachs. This we did with a fair degree of success and some three hours later took off into the haze for Weston. I saw the French coast pass beneath us and thought I recognised the mouth of the Seine but immediately dismissed it and settled down to wait for the Isle of Wight to come up. I was aroused out of a deep sleep by the pilot. "I just saw land beneath us, for Christ's sake, where are we?" I checked my watch—just under an hour since we had crossed the coast and still in thick haze—where were we indeed? The pilot was letting down and soon we could see the fields below. "Looks like France to me, certainly not the Wight," called the pilot. I wasn't prepared to agree, when we passed over a field of corn that had just been cleared with a man and a horse working in it.

"I'm going to land and ask that chap where we are," said the pilot, and without more ado he landed and I jumped out. The man walked across, blue dungarees, a beret and not a word of English. Schoolboy French did not help and in desperation I handed him a map. I can see his gnarled brown finger even now questing over the map until he found the town of Vauville on the Cherbourg Peninsula. He pointed to the place and then stretched out his arm and said something about kilometres. Thanking him profusely, I shook him warmly by the hand and climbed up to the cockpit. The pilot and I stared at each other with amazement.

"How the hell did we get there?" asked the pilot.

"What was your course for Weston from Rouen?" I replied, and then a gleam came into the pilot's somewhat bloodshot eye.

"Same as Amiens to Rouen—I forgot to change it."

I felt a wave of relief—no complex navigational problem this—just a first-class blunder.

As the war swung against us and the troops began to fall back, we were sent to a forward airfield to evacuate a special party of RAF people. We found the field but the party had already left; in fact, everyone had left except for a corporal and a few men doing demolition work. We offered them a lift but they refused; they had some trucks waiting for them. "Things are pretty confused," the corporal told us. "I don't know how long to stay but there's no point in your hanging around." We agreed and he then suggested we load up with champagne from the officers' mess and presented me with a Vickers G.O. gun and a pan of ammunition.

We were in the '86 and I put the gun in the front passenger seat. We had the sky completely to ourselves until the English coast when we had to share it with a few seagulls.

"Let's have that gun up here," said the pilot, "see if I can shoot a few of the beggars down; you fly her straight and level."

He inched down his side window and I handed him the gun. The next second all hell broke loose, the cockpit seemed full of red hot cartridge cases, one fell in the open top of the pilot's flying boot and one landed in my open shirt; the corporal had forgotten to attach the collector bag to the gun before handing it over. That was my last flight with NAC—we were shortly disbanded and sent back to Weston.

CHAPTER SIX

FLYING back to Weston at the end of NAC, I wondered what I would do next. Civil flying was finished until the end of the war and the RAF were not taking aircrew with glasses. I found, however, that Weston Airways had taken on a contract with the Government to set up an Air Observers' Navigation School, AONS, and that I was to be its chief radio operator and direction finding instructor. These schools, set up soon after the outbreak of war, were to train observers, later to be called navigators. Twelve Avro Ansons were sent to the school, they were just shells and we started to equip them with radio.

I was now to find that pre-war RAF development in the field of aircraft radio was not as advanced as in the civil aircraft industry. The receivers were powered by two volt wet batteries and the high tension voltage was supplied by dry batteries one or the other of which in spite of repeated checking and routine replacements was always failing in flight. The receiver and the transmitter both had large boxes of coils which had to be plugged in to cover certain frequencies and as only one frequency was used in the school, a large number of these boxes were soon scattered all over the hangars. Part of the communication receiver could be used as a radio direction finder. It was decidedly on the crude side but some of the more skilled operators became able to use it quite accurately. It would perhaps only be fair to say that radio in the pre-war RAF had not the importance that it had in civil airlines as most Service flying was over comparatively short distances with the ground always in sight.

I was extremely fortunate in getting half a dozen ex-marine radio operators who had been instructing at the RAF School at Yatesbury and were familiar with the RAF equipment. This was before the selective employment laws were passed and these men were only too keen to get away from teaching morse; they had no flying experience but they took to it like a duck takes to water. The rest of the staff were an odd mixture—I was forced to employ anyone who could send and receive the morse code. They were good, bad and indifferent, but as they only had one station to work and only one message to send every half hour, they got by. The radio station was

45

our own, equipped with the same type of equipment as were the aircraft.

One elderly radioman, who claimed to have been in the Navy, was the only one that really caused me any grief. He disliked flying in bumpy weather and always had a good reason for ducking out of a flight; we were so shorthanded that it meant having to go myself or taking over the ground station to release the duty radioman to take his place. One morning he went on strike; I had a lecture in the school and I said he would just have to fly and that, I hoped, was the end of the matter. After the Anson landed, he vanished from the field. I sent round to his house after a week to be told that he had become mentally deranged and his wife was taking me to court over it. I was next called for by the secretary of Weston Airways and given a letter which proved conclusively that Captain Bligh was a cooing dove compared with me. I had driven this man into the air and while flying, he had fallen and injured himself on the aircraft direction finder. On checking up I found that the aircraft in which he had been flying was not fitted with a direction finder and that was the end of the matter.

The flying was confined to the west of England, the longest flight was to Land's End and back and the only complaint I heard against the Anson was that she was cold and draughty. The school was eventually moved to Outschoorn in South Africa and all the civilian aircrew and instructors were either put into uniform or discharged. Because I wore glasses, I was unsuitable for the former and Weston Airways gave me a job as radio/electrician in their hangar. Before this happened, however, I was to have a flight in an Anson which I shall never forget.

The last course was finished and four of the students had been posted to Jurby in the Isle of Man. It was decided to fly them to Jurby and at the instigation of my landlady, I put myself on the flight. She claimed that Manx kippers were out of this world and strongly recommended that I go and collect some. The flight to Jurby was uneventful but then came a problem—the pilot found some old friends on the field and decided to stay the night. I went to Douglas by bus after we had agreed to meet at the aeroplane the next morning. I arrived at nine o'clock, complete with a box of kippers but there was no pilot; he turned up at about 10 a.m., looking decidedly the worse for wear, muttering vaguely about delaying twenty-four hours. His friends had other views and poured him into the Anson and started up the engines for him. I gingerly took the copilot's seat at his request "to help with the bloody undercarriage" as he put it. With intense concentration he started his run directly from the parking area and more by luck than good judgement we eventually found ourselves in the air on a southerly heading.

The pilot turned and fixed me with a glassy eye. "I'm done," he mumbled. "You fly her for a bit." We changed seats and then he went back over the front spar and curled up with his head on my Mae West and passed out cold. I was frightened; ahead of me was a huge bank of cloud over the Welsh Mountains; I had to go through and I wasn't even competent to do a gentle turn. The undercarriage was still down and there was climb power on the engines. I shouted until I was hoarse, I even tried flying with one hand and reaching back over the spar with the other to wake him up; it was useless, I had got to fly that Anson whatever happened. Gradually we approached that wall of cloud, climbing slowly up to 8,000 feet, and as we drew near I could see that it wasn't solid but a collection of towering cumulo nimbus clouds with wide paths between them. I altered course slightly for the nearest gap and then my troubles really began. The towering walls of cloud same closer and closer and then a chasm opened up to the left. I turned the Anson and then saw my airspeed going up fast—I was diving. I jerked back the controls, up came the nose and the Anson plunged into the cloud on the right hand side. Seconds later she burst out into a wide corridor and after a frantic look at the instruments, I started to get things straight and level again. Then the corridor pinched out and we plunged into cloud; things had been reasonably well under control when we went in and I tried to keep them that way by jamming my elbows into my thighs and my heels into the floor. Again we burst clear and I spared a hurried glance out of the window—I was staring along a long passage in the cloud with a patch of brown rock at the end of it. We were almost vertical. Another frenzied grab—how that dear old Anson worked to save her own life, as well as mine—and she was nearly level again. It seemed to go on for ever, for hours I struggled to keep the right way up, my hands and feet were icy cold, yet the perspiration was trickling down my chest and legs. Then a corridor I was wallowing down turned to sunshine at the end and suddenly, all the clouds were behind me. I spent the first five minutes in complete relaxation; the Anson seemed to say "Leave this bit to me," and I did. The next thing was to find out where I was; the heading had been southerly when I entered the cloud, it still was, but just where I had been between those times was a complete guess. Through my

47

window I could see a little white steamer crossing a fairly wide river, it was going across at right angles, it must be a ferryboat and then, in a flash, the whole picture fell into place—it was the Aust Ferry and I had only to follow the south bank of the river to Weston-super-Mare and home.

Flying in clear air was a lot easier and I wobbled round about 90 degrees and set off for the airfield. Clear of Bristol, I started to ease the throttles and slowly reduce height. I arrived at a height varying between 1,500 and 1,000 feet and commenced a series of flat skidding turns around the field. I also started to try and wake up the pilot. Greatly daring, I even slipped out of the seat and gave him a kick, but this nearly caused disaster, for the Anson immediately stuck her nose down; at last the horrible truth dawned—I should have to get it down somehow on my own. In those days the long powered approach was considered not the thing, but I made one—from Clevedon to Weston—that broke all the rules. I throttled back and started my long drag in, aiming at the airfield. I kept the speed just above stalling but the lower I sank, the faster things started to flash past. This was cumulative—in spite of the airspeed indicator telling me that my speed was constant—and then I was over the last two fields, the road along the edge of the airfield was coming up at a fantastic rate—I panicked, slammed the throttles shut, and dashed for the tail with the thought that the tail of an aeroplane always survived a crash. The Anson had suffered enough at my hands and now took charge; as I scrambled down the cabin, it made a heavy, but perfectly safe, three point landing. It only remained for me to switch off the engines and wake up the pilot. My claims to have landed the aeroplane were firmly refuted by some airmen on the aerodrome boundary who had seen me scuttle back to the tail.

Shortly after this the school left for South Africa and I took up a job in the hangar. Weston Airways were now operating a civilian repair organisation on Fairey Battles and Ansons. The radio and electrical overhaul and repair work on these aircraft was pretty fundamental and I soon became bored with it. In the spring of 1942 the Air Ministry was looking for skilled radio operators for the civilian side of the RAF—Ferry Command, based in Montreal. Weston Airways were willing to let me go and I was called to White Waltham for an interview with Air Transport Auxiliary— a collection of civilians, both men and women, who were delivering aircraft from factory to squadrons within the British Isles. I was frankly staggered by my reception; the interviewing panel was composed of two ATA pilots and a woman pilot who popped in and out—their knowledge of aircraft was less than my own. I produced my air and marine licences and my Second "N" but they remained unimpressed. They asked me how much flying I had and when I produced my logbook with a certified 5,700 hours, they almost added up the hours to check that my sums were right. The woman pilot then popped in and stated firmly that she didn't "approve" of either navigators or radio operators—they were totally unnecessary! The stupid behaviour of the two men followed by the fatuous rubbish from the female sparked off my always uncertain temper. "I have been sent here to be judged as to my ability as a radio operator. You have seen my licences and apparently checked my hours; I don't give a damn about what you think of the necessity for navigators and radio operators."

The female promptly popped out again and the two men started to cross-question me about what I had been doing. After a few minutes, back came the female. "Did you ever fly with Miss —— at Croydon?" I confessed that I had once been guilty but was never likely to be caught again in an aeroplane with that suicidal old bag. This brought the interview to an abrupt end; I was positively whistled through the Accounts Department and delivered back to Maidenhead station.

As I sat in the train back to Weston, I decided there was no hope of joining Ferry Command. They must have put a fair-sized spoke in my wheel because I was not called for until nine months later when they were scraping the bottom of the barrel. Then came the fateful letter—an appointment in RAF Ferry Command—and a single railway voucher from Weston to Liverpool, en route for Canada. At last I was moving again.

At Lime Street station the RTO directed me to the RAF Embarkation Office in the docks; they passed me on to the *Louis Pasteur*, a converted French liner operated, I believe, by the Cunard Company. I eventually located the cabin to which I had been assigned and found that I was one of eight—six Poles going to join BOAC, D——, another radioman, and myself. D—— and I were old friends and had been together in Weston during the AONS days. The nine-day trip to New York was made without incident; the food was especially appreciated after rationed England. Arriving in New York, the RTO gave us some dollars, tickets for the night train from New York to Montreal and a letter informing us that accommodation had been booked for us in the Mount Royal Hotel. The next afternoon found D—— and myself ensconced in the most elegant double room in the Mount Royal; with eight dollars a day living expenses, we could afford to sleep here only—there would be little left over for food. The next day we reported to Dorval, the airfield outside Montreal where Ferry Command had set up its headquarters. I found several old friends from the Croydon days and we settled down to a six weeks' course to familiarise us with Ferry Command operations. We also found a room and board which we shared, the price of which was much more in keeping with our allowances than was the Mount Royal.

There were about thirty people on the course and they were the oddest collection. One extremely handsome young man was the son of an English canon; while waiting in Montreal to join his first ship as a radio operator, he had joined an extremely hectic party at which he made a bet that he would marry the first woman who would accept him. In the East End of Montreal a French Canadian prostitute obliged and he collected his bet. All sorts of strings were pulled; he had been returned to England, divested of his Canadian wife and had then returned to Canada in Ferry Command. He failed the course and was again returned to England. Another was a character who had worked for me at Weston; he was an odd bird but knew his job. In Canada he really made a name for himself—he terrorised some female refugees he met in a café into believing that he was a secret agent and unless they agreed to sleep with him, he would have their relatives persecuted in Germany. It worked, and thinking he was on to a good thing, he asked another radioman if he would like to come in on it; this was too much for the refugees, they told the police and the Mounties scooped up our two heroes and deported them to England in very short order. Another strange character was a man who claimed to be a salesman who had joined the Merchant Navy as a radio operator to avoid the Army. After one voyage he had somehow got into Ferry Command. I sat beside him on the course and was rapidly convinced that he knew absolutely nothing about the business. I told the instructor my suspicions and we set a trap. One afternoon a test was called, I answered the questions with the most stupid rubbish and left my answers displayed so that my neighbour could copy them. This he did most accurately—he even repeated my spelling mistakes! He was sent home but I have often wondered if he passed the same examination board as I had at White Waltham. In the final exam D—— and I turned out to be the star pupils—99 per cent each.

The next part of our training was aircraft familiarisation during training flights for pilots. Practical training on the airborne equipment was carried out on the actual American and Canadian radio which was to be in all the aircraft that were delivered to the United Kingdom from North America and it was far in advance of any equipment that I had encountered in my flying career so far. It had been developed for use by pilots and the operation had been made as foolproof as possible. Each frequency was crystal controlled and was selected by a switch which automatically tuned the equipment. As it was to be used for radio-telephone the transmitted power had been made as high as was practicable. Because of the problems of long ranges over which the aircraft had to fly and wartime security problems, we were now to use this high-powered equipment on telegraphy. After the wet batteries and the low power of the Anson equipment, I considered that radio operating in Ferry Command was going to be a comparatively simple job and this it turned out to be. Local flying on pilot-training was an extremely good method for finding your way around the different types of aircraft that were being delivered.

The pilots were far too busy to bother what you did and I spent my first two flights trying to understand the rapid fire instructions given from Dorval control to the pilots on voice radio. Then came the great day, I was to go on a Hudson delivery to England, the captain was an Englishman, the copilot a South African, the navigator a RAF sergeant fresh out of an Empire Training School. We all met at the briefing meeting on the afternoon before departure; it looked all right from a weather point of view, take-off was 7.30 the next morning. A collection of buses toured Montreal City in the early morning collecting aircrew from fixed points, I joined mine at Sherbrook Street. At Dorval the weather was confirmed, I collected the codes, route books, etc. and we all climbed into a brand new Hudson, first stop Gander. The captain was one of the free-lance fraternity from Croydon but we had not met before; the copilot was a South African mining engineer who had worked for a company where flying the firm's Rapide had been part of his job. They were both in their late thirties. The navigator was barely twenty and had been working in a tailor's shop when he had been called up. The trip to Gander along the Canadian Airways system was uneventful and called for little effort on the part of myself or the navigator. I did notice though that he had my complaint—he worked furiously away in the nose the whole time and arrived in a state of physical and mental collapse. The country over which we passed was very different from anything that I had seen before;

for a time we followed the St. Lawrence, passing over airways stations with strange names that were soon to become part of our vocabulary—Three Rivers, Quebec, Rimouski. We crossed the Gulf of St. Lawrence to Newfoundland, with airways stations at St. Andrews and Stephenville; the country below looked really rugged —forests and lakes by the score and no apparent signs of civilisation. Definitely not the country to force land in to ask the way!

Gander was a big field hacked out of the muskeg and they gave us a welcome in the form of an excellent late lunch and then allocated us a bunk in the wooden huts standing behind the hangar. The young navigator collapsed in his bunk and passed out cold; we had great trouble in waking him for the met. briefing in the early evening. Some thirty of us collected in a barnlike room at the back of the hangar where we were addressed by the chief met. officer—a man later to become famous for his Atlantic weather forecasting. Tonight he was quite uncompromising—"Tonight it's not on chaps, not any of the routes—Bluie West is out, Iceland's out, Prestwick's all right, but I can only promise you a 50 knot headwind the whole way; tomorrow won't be so bad." He then went on to say that they had a film of the approach to Bluie West One and he recommended those who hadn't been there before to watch it; a showing would be made after the briefing. We stayed and watched it—it had been shot in clear weather but it gave a very clear indication that BW.1 was not the place to be in bad weather.

We spent the twenty-four hours until the next briefing sitting around and reading, the navigator was now completely recovered and raring to go. This time the weather was right and, although both the copilot and navigator were all for going into BW.1, the pilot decreed a direct flight to Reykjavik—1,570 miles and over water all the way. We took off in the dark of the early evening, climbed through cloud to 9,000 feet and set course for Iceland. For an hour I was able to hear Twillingate and Gander and gave the navigator cross bearings and then he was on his own. Within a few minutes of getting to altitude, we were in contact with Reykjavik, Prestwick and Gander and the first confirmed that the weather for our time of arrival was unchanged from the forecast. The navigator now really got busy; he clambered from the nose to the cabin to take star shots, he clambered back to work them out, he asked me for high frequency bearings from as far away as Bermuda—all of which he plotted religiously; he even took a time of sun-up for the longitude and worked that back. For hours we roared on over the cloud; we ate our box lunches, we drank coffee,

52

all except the navigator—he was too busy. At last there was only an hour left and I realised that the navigator had been quiet for some minutes. I peered between the copilot's legs and found that he was sprawled over his chart fast asleep. I told the pilot—he laughed "He got us within an hour of home; set up the direction finder and I will home it the rest of the way." This he did and ten minutes before ETA he nosed down into the cloud. At 5,000 feet we broke clear and ahead of us was Iceland. "Wake up young Vasco da Gama and tell him the last ETA he gave us before he passed out was accurate to the minute," said the captain to the copilot.

My few weeks in Canada had made my memories of the shortages in England rather distant but the RAF staging post at Reykjavik brought us to our senses with a bang. We were assigned beds in a dirty Nissen hut, coarse sheets and three squares of heavy grey felt that went by the name of army blankets. We were served a meal of stew and mashed potatoes, rhubarb and custard and a mug of tea. The bar would open at six o'clock. I had made my first Atlantic crossing in an aeroplane but I didn't seem to have impressed anyone, except myself. At six o'clock the captain started drinking, by eight he was becoming a nuisance and by ten o'clock he was poison. The copilot, who had resented not being captain in the first case, took this opportunity of going to the RAF CO and asking if he could take over command as the captain was incapable. Fortunately, the CO was a tactful man and said he would delay his decision until he had seen the captain in the morning. This he did and after a stiff lecture about behaviour he set us on our way; unfortunately, to stress his point, he told the captain that his crew led by the copilot had refused to fly with him. This was rather unfair on the navigator and myself who had been fast asleep when the unpleasantness started. The trip from Reykjavik to Prestwick was made in clear weather but the atmosphere in the Hudson could hardly be called clear, the only one unaffected by the cockpit hate was the navigator who immersed himself in one of his marathon navigational exercises.

As we were circling to land, a Hudson ahead of us crashed on landing and burst into flames and we were instructed to go and land at Heathfield. We were met there by a bus from Prestwick and relieved to hear that the crew had all jumped clear. Prestwick airfield was run by Scottish Aviation and a first-class job they made of it. The hutted accommodation was clean and dry, the restaurant meals were as good as local conditions would allow and their staff became most adept at handling the streams of transient aircrew that passed through Prestwick in their hundreds.

Movement Control had our marching orders ready; the navigator was sent on leave prior to joining a bomber OTU, the captain was sent on leave while the copilot and I were on the departure list for the return ferry to Montreal the next evening. The return ferry was run by BOAC with Liberator bombers converted to carrying passengers with the minimum of comfort. They operated between Montreal and Prestwick—winter and summer—sometimes in truly appalling weather, and continued to do so until the end of the war. The crews were a mixture of Dutchmen from KLM, Englishmen from Imperials and British Airways and Polish wartime airmen. Their operation was extremely efficient, but one of the few losses was E. R. B. White of the HP.42 "Hanno" who crashed on the Isle of Arran. Passenger accommodation was the best possible under the circumstances but it was pretty crude. Eiderdowns were laid on the bomb-bay and aircraft floor and the passengers in full flying kit, including Mae Wests and parachute harness, then lay down across the aircraft. To economise on space, you laid alternately head to feet and you were then covered with eiderdowns. On my first return ferry the captain decided to make Montreal in one hop and for 16½ hours, at temperatures well below freezing, we lay under those eiderdowns. A trip to the Elsan in the tail meant extricating oneself from two other people's feet and then stumbling across the rest of the prone bodies. The temperature in the Elsan compartment was so low that it made you forget the object of the whole exercise. I slept for the first six hours and for the next ten alternately read and gazed at the roof; reading was made difficult by the fact that it was dangerous to expose the hands at these temperatures and one had to wear gloves. At long last we were released from the belly of the Liberator in Montreal. In command was a famous Dutch pilot, Captain Moll, who, when one of the ferry pilots complained of the cold and the altitude at which the flight had been made, replied, "You always fly high with Moll, but you never get your feet wet." He survived the war but was killed in a Constellation at Prestwick in the late 1940s. I had now flown the Atlantic both ways.

CHAPTER SEVEN

I NOW had some two weeks to spend in Montreal before my next trip, and Montreal during the war years was a wonderful place to spend a holiday. There were about a dozen Canadians in my lodgings and they supplied me with unlimited advice on where to eat and where to go afterwards; I found the $8 a day allowance quite adequate for a thoroughly good time.

Then one morning the phone rang and it was the crewing people from Dorval; my second trip was to be in a B.25 or a Mitchell as the RAF called them, briefing the next day at 2.0 p.m. The Mitchell was a twin-engined midwing aircraft with a bombardier in the transparent nose, and pilot and copilot, and then behind them the navigator. Next came the bomb-bay which extended almost to the roof of the aircraft and in an isolated compartment behind it was the radio operator. The only physical communication between the radio operator and the cockpit was a narrow tunnel on the top of the bomb-bay which terminated over the navigator's desk. In the event of an intercommunication failure, the navigator and the radio operator could communicate with each other by means of an endless cord, attached to which was a metal clip to carry the message. The cord ran through the tunnel and was anchored to the roof of the aircraft above the navigator's table. On the few occasions I had to use this device, I found it almost impossible to make the navigator look up and, if the message was urgent, it meant wriggling along the tunnel. This was extremely difficult as the sides of the tunnel were used to position all the special equipment added after the Mitchell was completed. One radio operator made an enemy over that tunnel. His B.25 was en route from BW.1 to Prestwick one night when, just before the point of no return, he received a message to return to Greenland—head winds over the rest of the route and poor landing conditions at Prestwick made the flight inadvisable. Both the pilot and the navigator had discarded their head sets for the more comfortable baseball caps not realising that the intercom call light system had gone out of action. For about ten minutes the radio operator jiggled the message in its clip above the navigator's head but, completely immersed in his sums, he did not look up. Realising that the further they flew the longer they would take to return to BW.1, he decided to try and wriggle along the tunnel. He was a big man, made even more bulky by his heavy flying kit, and the inevitable happened—he stuck. His chin was just at the end of the tunnel and for some time he shouted and whistled but the navigator was in the middle of a star fix. In desperation he spat squarely into the navigator's chart. Telling the story later he said he had never seen such rage on a man's face as on that navigator's. Even when they had returned to BW.1 and the situation had been explained, the navigator still maintained it was a poor way to treat the first three star fix he had taken in earnest.

At Dorval the next afternoon I met the rest of the crew; a Canadian flight lieutenant who had just finished a spell as an instructor at Trenton, he was now on his way to the UK to join a bomber squadron. He introduced himself as Jack and Jack he was for the rest of the trip. The navigator was an Englishman, a sergeant who had completed his training and was returning to the UK. They were both keen on calling at as many places as they could on the trip and they even hatched a plot to land at Meeks Field, the American base in Iceland, in mistake for Reykjavik. We found that the aircraft was at Houlton in Maine and that we were to leave Montreal by train that evening. This pleased Jack and the navigator—another place for them to visit. We were met at Houlton station the next morning by the RCAF Liaison Officer who drove us out to the base and settled us down for lunch in the officers' mess. In the afternoon he drove us down to the hangar and showed us over the Mitchell. We each checked out the equipment that was our special responsibility and departure was set for 10.0 a.m. the next day for Goose Bay, Labrador.

The Met. forecast the next morning promised clear weather all the way and soon after 10.0 a.m. the Mitchell lifted off the runway on the first leg to England. We sped across the greens and browns of New Brunswick and then the mouth of the St. Lawrence River, with Anticosti Island in the middle of it, loomed ahead. Then we crossed the North bank of the river and we were flying over Labrador. This is a wild and desolate land with hundreds of miles of stunted fir trees and numberless small and large lakes of every conceivable shape. As I peered through the side windows, I gave a shiver—"No place for a forced landing," I muttered, "the most rugged place I have ever flown over." Later I found far worse places than Labrador, at least the locals weren't against you—there weren't any!

Jack called over the intercom system, "I am talking to Goose, climb up forward and then you can see what it's all about."

I squeezed carefully through the tunnel and assisted by the navigator got across his chart table and into the copilot's seat. "Look right ahead," said Jack, "it's hazy but try and follow that line on the horizon, it's Hamilton Inlet and that's Goose Bay just on my side."

Slowly the details of the RCAF base at Goose Bay grew out of the haze. It had been a gigantic task; bringing in heavy machinery by sea during the summer, when Hamilton Inlet was not frozen, a huge aerodrome had been hacked out of the wilderness. It was kept supplied by air from Montreal with fresh food—an operation known as the "milkrun" that used a few Hudsons and Dakotas. This service was flown winter and summer and was much sought after by the Canadian crews because it meant almost every night in Montreal.

We made a good landing and taxied up to the ramp. We were met by a truck which took us to the control tower to report, then on to the debriefing office and along to the transient mess for a late lunch. Most of the big transient messes were open nearly all of the twenty-four hours to cater for the heavy traffic—they served breakfast for seven hours, lunch for seven hours and supper for seven hours and even if you arrived during the hour they were changing over they would always produce something. The American base were showing their film of the approach to Bluie West One each evening for crews making their first flight into the place. The three of us attended and Jack and the navigator came out of the show full of enthusiasm to "get the hell into that fjord and see what them Yanks have built themselves". I was less enthusiastic —I would have preferred to make my first trip with someone who had been there before.

Seeing an urgent need to ferry aircraft with a limited range to Europe, the United States had built a string of airfields across the North Atlantic. Some of them were of limited value but Bluie West One, on the coast of Greenland, was on the direct route for the shorter range aircraft and had become an extremely busy staging post. After a careful survey, the only place that had enough level ground for an airfield was found some fifty miles up one of the fjords. Ice had gouged out a valley down to the shore of the fjord and then retreated leaving a wide valley between snowcapped mountains. There the United States had built a long double runway which extended from the shore of the fjord inland towards

57

the face of the retreating glacier. Except for narrow pieces of coastline, the whole of Greenland is covered with a huge cap of ice some 10,000 feet high; being largely unsurveyed, the safe height to fly over it was 12,000 feet. The icecap was a weather breeder whose behaviour was very difficult to forecast and herein lay the real danger of the airfield. Mist or cloud would roll off the cap and sink to water level; in the fjord that had to be used to get to the field, this would happen without warning.

Another problem was ensuring that the aircraft located the right fjord—the entrances all looked so much alike. If the first fjord to the north was taken in error and this was discovered in time, there was a saddleback over which you could fly into the correct fjord. Any of the others were deathtraps on a bad day with cloud on the mountains, unless the mistake was discovered when there was still room to turn round and fly out. To ensure that the correct fjord was found, a radio range station was located on Simiutak Island, or Bluie West Four as it was called, at the mouth of the right one. The drill was to fly the beam down to Bluie West Four, and then a compass course into the correct fjord.

In clear weather some pilots would fly over Bluie West One at 10,000 feet and then let down directly to the field. I never flew with a pilot who tackled the problem this way, all I flew with wanted the maximum local knowledge that could be gathered and each flight was made as though in bad weather.

With the intention of thoroughly exploring this strange place, we set off the next morning from Goose Bay. We had a first-class weather report and flew low along Hamilton Inlet and then set course for Bluie West Four. The sea was covered with small icebergs from the Davis Strait; they couldn't have been much of a danger to shipping for about half-way across we passed a big trawler that was pushing north through them.

I confirmed that clear weather was still expected at Bluie West Four and Bluie West One and when I reported this to Jack he suggested I scramble up front and "get myself a grandstand seat". This I did and strapped myself firmly into the copilot's seat. Across the horizon ahead of us was a black line of broken cliffs backed by an amorphous white mass that seemed to fade imperceptibly into the brilliantblue sky—it was the icecap. I tuned in the Bluie West Four range station and loud and clear in our ears was the steady note signifying that we were right on track. The black cliffs were drawing closer and Jack dropped the Mitchell down close to the sea. He laughed over the intercom, "If we lose that beam for one

58

second I am getting out of this place fast, it's like flying into a cliff face." Standing between us the navigator for once was deadly serious.

"Christ, yes, there must be a hundred fjords all looking alike, without that beam we would never find the right entrance."

The strength of the radio beam was building up strongly indicating that we were getting close to BW.4 but ahead it was difficult to distinguish between islands and coastline. Then, suddenly, we were over the off-shore islands; the beam signal faded indicating that we were right overhead. "We're there," I shouted, and peering downwards saw the masts of the radio station flash past below us. The navigator gave Jack a course to steer and in no time at all we were roaring into the mouth of a fjord.

The walls towered above us on either side streaked with snow, the green water below was flecked with small icebergs, the deep blue sky was now obscured by a shining haze that rested on the tops of the mountains; we appeared to be flying along a tunnel. I found no means of establishing that we were in the correct "slot" as the Americans called it; I kept the picture of the saddleback in my mind but nothing remotely resembling it showed up on my side. During the construction of the base, one of the cargo boats had run on a rocky ledge and sank to deck level. This had happened on the last bend before the runway and was now used as a warning to prepare for landing. We swept round another bend and there away on the port side was the partly submerged steamer; Jack dropped the wheels and flaps and reduced his speed, a turn to starboard round another cliff and there in front of us was a long double runway. A jeep displaying a large "FOLLOW ME" sign picked us up when we had stopped rolling and guided us to the parking area and a waiting crew car. Again we went through the arrival procedure which terminated in an excellent lunch. The transit camp was a clean and comfortable place, serving extremely good meals, so much so that the pilot and the navigator decided to stay for twenty-four hours and explore the place. They spent the whole day climbing the moraine to the end of the dead glacier and thoroughly enjoyed themselves.

The next morning was clear and Jack decided to climb to 12,000 feet over the field and then fly across the icecap to Iceland. This we did but we saw very little; the whole cap was covered with a light mist through which the sun was shining and it was impossible to decide if you were looking at the cap or at the mist. Soon the rocks and icebergs of the Denmark Strait came up and we crossed the coast. I was later to fly over the icecap several times and always had a feeling of being lost in that shining haze; there was no horizon and nothing visible beneath you, it was somehow quite different from ordinary cloud flying. Crossing the Denmark Strait I passed the navigator a few long range bearings and checked the Reykjavik weather—it was low cloud and rain.

We held a three-cornered discussion over the intercom about landing at Meeks Field. I adopted the view that the weather there would be no better than at Reykjavik so we would not be able to see much, also it would need a lot of explaining away. I won the day and Jack let down gently through some 6,000 feet of cloud and broke through over Faxa Bay. Soon we had landed and were ensconced in the transient mess. The lunch was spam, fried bread and tea and when the navigator and I pointed out that spam was a luxury, Jack's face fell. "You mean there is worse than this to come?" he asked. "Nothing could be worse than this fried-up-bread stuff." Jack's introduction to Nissen huts and felt blankets was even more of a shock, his last remark before going to sleep was, "Is it right to fight a war to preserve this lot?"

We found that the English summer had set in all the way to Prestwick, when we visited the Met. Office next morning—low cloud and high winds—although Prestwick itself was forecasting five miles visibility with 1,000 feet cloud base. We decided to carry on because Jack swore that after a breakfast of powdered egg, he just couldn't face another meal at Reykjavik. It was a long trip and the air was full of turbulence; we were all decidedly worn by the time we landed at Prestwick. That evening I said goodbye to two extremely pleasant people and it was with real regret that I heard some months later that Jack had been killed on his first operational trip to Germany.

I had another ride back to Canada in a return ferry Liberator but this time the aircraft stopped at Gander to refuel; this broke up the flight into two parts which made it much more bearable. I spent a pleasant ten days in Montreal and then came the call for briefing again. It was another Hudson for Prestwick with the English pilot with whom I had made my first trip; the navigator and copilot were two sergeants from the Empire Training School. It was a completely uneventful trip—Gander, Reykjavik, Prestwick—but news awaited the pilot and me at Prestwick, we were to collect a Hampden at St. Athan and deliver it to Patricia Bay in Vancouver. We found in St. Athan that the aircraft was not ready for delivery; the extra fuel tanks had not been fitted, and the chief technical officer promised us the aeroplane in one week. He suggested that we go on leave for a week and he would send us each a telegram when the Hampden had been completed and satisfactorily test flown. I spent nearly two weeks at home before the CTO's telegram arrived and then it was the long journey back to South Wales.

At St. Athan we found that the CTO had done his best for us; he had fitted new Pegasus engines and thoroughly overhauled the aeroplane. The Hampden was a prewar twin-engined bomber with a short, deep but narrow fuselage with a single boom, twin fins and rudders. It had a crew of four—the navigator in the nose, the pilot in the top of the fuselage with his feet level with the navigator's head and then two radio gunners in the after part. We had a crew of three—a pilot, a navigator and myself. The pilot and I test flew the aircraft for two hours and didn't like it. Perhaps our standards were too high but it was slow, noisy and leaked like a basket, the radio was cumbersome to handle and of low power. In fact, only the navigator who joined us the next day had a good word to say for the Hampden, he had just completed a tour of operations in one. He was a flying officer on a posting to Dorval and boasted that he was completely immune to the hardships of Hampden flying. The range of the aircraft had been much increased by the extra tanks but the pilot was quite adamant that he wasn't undertaking any flights of long duration—it was to be short hops all the way. The first hop was St. Athan to Prestwick and I had a foretaste of what my radio problems were going to be like; I didn't raise Prestwick until we were nearly there.

At Prestwick, Scottish Aviation looked the aircraft over and said it was fit to fly and I knew nothing could be done about the radio —that was just the nature of the beast. The next hop was to Stornoway and apart from the port engine cutting out and then starting up again, it was reasonably uneventful. We spent the night in Stornoway and then off early next morning for Reykjavik—some 700 miles of open sea. The forecast was one mile in rain with complete cloud cover at 2,000 feet and it was recommended that we stay underneath. This meant an extremely rough ride and also that we had no radio communication with either Reykjavik or Prestwick—no bearings and no weather reports. About half way across the water, a north-bound Liberator picked up my weak signals and relayed them to Reykjavik, he also gave me the latest weather situation. This was about as forecast so we pressed on. Then at long last, after straining my ears for what seemed like hours, I was able to pick up the range stations at Vik and later Reykjavik. We were roughly on track and were soon circling the airport at Reykjavik and asking for landing instructions. Only when directly over the control tower could our signals be heard and the pilot soon grew tired and hoarse and went in and landed.

It was a tired and harassed radioman that was hauled before the local signals officer to account for the failure to report the aircraft's position and incorrect use of the landing radio telephone procedures. The meeting was unfortunate from the start; the signals officer was a grounded pilot with no knowledge of my problems, his technical sergeant was having a day off and the meeting broke up in some disorder. During the evening another officer, whose job I never discovered, took me aside in the mess and asked me to explain my row with the signals officer. I told him of the problem of operating low-powered radio equipment at low altitude in areas where everyone else used high-powered American equipment and the pilot's R/T equipment suffered from the same complaint. He said he understood the limitations imposed on our operation and would ensure that a special watch was set up for us on a special frequency for the rest of the flight—an excellent scheme about which nothing more was heard.

The next morning in dull, rainy weather, we set off on the next sector—from Reykjavik to Bluie East 8 or Angmagssalik in Greenland. After a time the radio station at Reykjavik could no longer hear us and I could not hear BE.8—a situation to which we became quite resigned. Fortunately the weather cleared up and the navigator was able to add a few sun shots to his DR navigation.

We were churning along eating half frozen cheese sandwiches and drinking the cold tea which had been supplied for our lunch when the port engine cut dead. The pilot opened up the starboard engine and although it gave out a mighty clatter, the Hampden could not hold height. We could just see the coast of Greenland on the horizon. I sent out blind distress calls, the pilot struggled to start the engine while the navigator stared down at the famous Denmark Strait which was steadily getting closer. At 1,000 feet, I realised that the situation was becoming desperate—how long could we last in water as cold as this? Suddenly the port engine burst into life and relief flooded over me like a river as we slowly regained height. The flow of language from the cockpit was picturesque—the pilot had apparently been too busy to be as frightened as I was.

Slowly the Hampden climbed to 6,000 feet and then very faintly I could hear the BE.8 beacon. I took a series of bearings, averaged them out for the navigator and, in conjunction with a sun shot, he found a position which put us in about the right place. Visibility was extremely limited but at long last I heard with considerable relief the navigator tell the pilot he could see the runway. Then followed the usual pantomime with the pilot's radio telephone equipment which ended with the pilot going in and landing without a clearance. We were soon surrounded by the Army personnel who manned this lonely base; we were new faces to them and they gave us a great welcome. The field was alongside a big fjord and again backed by the towering icecap; it was open to sea traffic for a short period in mid-summer and for the rest of the year aeroplanes were their only visitors. They were amazed at our venerable Hampden and refused to consider that the RCAF would seriously use it for a torpedo trainer—it was probably for a museum! However, two engineers volunteered to work on the port engine and the stores officer insisted on supplying us with American flying jackets, trousers and overboots. "Call yourself Brown, Jones and Smith and by the time the stores bashers sort it out the war will be over," he said. Camp beds were put up for us in the communal hut but it was late before we used them—there was so much talking to do.

The engineers reported the next morning that they could find nothing obviously wrong with the port engine except that it should have been on the scrap pile. Rigged out in our new finery and loaded down with the best of flight rations, we climbed aboard the Hampden for the worst sector of all—from BE.8 to BW.1. The pilot had wisely decided that we would make the flight by following the coast of Greenland, south to Cape Farewell and then north again to BW.1—a flight of some 900 miles. It was one of those incredibly clear days that are sometimes experienced in this part of the world; our friends in BE.8 had produced a most comprehensive met. briefing which forecast these conditions for the whole of the flight. Our only worry was the port engine.

We flew at about 3,000 feet some five miles off the coast and what a coast! For long stretches the icecap tumbled right down to the sea and it was impossible to distinguish the icebergs from the shoreline. Then a gravelly spit would push out between some bergs, then a whole series of rocky cliffs with the icecap appearing to spill over their edges. The sea was covered with floating bergs of all shapes and sizes. In the brilliant sunshine, the picture was one of incredible grandeur but it was completely spoiled for me through intensive listening for that port motor to stop working. When we turned Cape Farewell the coastline changed; there was a considerable belt of green country but we now moved out to sea and set course to intercept the beam from BW.4 which would guide us into the BW.1 fjord. As I was the only member of the crew that had been here before, my advice was taken and we aimed to intercept the beam thirty miles from the coast and then fly down it with plenty of time to get settled down for the rush up the fjord. At long last the signal from BW.4 built up and then we crossed the beam, the pilot swung round and after a few corrections from me, settled down for the run into the coast. Neither of the crew liked receiving guidance from another crew member whose only visibility was sideways, and as that forbidding coastline loomed closer, the intercom system was loaded with comments about what would happen to me if we didn't make it! We did make it, the navigator got a sight of the radio masts on BW.4 and gave the pilot a new course and then for the second time in my career we were flying up the fjord. Soon the famous signpost—the sunken ship—showed up and we landed on the long double runway. We were met by a crowd of interested servicemen and the usual comments were passed about the Hampden, the pilot told the ramp engineer about our port engine and he was enthusiastic about pulling it down. He had had experience of Pegasus when he was in England and seemed convinced he could find what ailed it. The pilot agreed that we should lay over the three days it would take.

We spent an interesting three days at BW.1; it was high summer and with only two hours of darkness. An almost continuous stream of aircraft passed through on their way to Europe. One incident that reminded us all that a war was being fought was the arrival of a delivery Mitchell with an engine fault. When the ground crew removed the cowling they found stowed between the two bottom cylinders a can of explosive; according to rumour it was a type that exploded after it had been maintained at a certain temperature for three hours; three hours put the aircraft well out to sea on its way to Prestwick! On the third day the engineers reported that the Hampden was ready again. They could find no real fault with the engine that would cause the random dead cuts; we could only lumber on and hope for the best and next morning we set off for Goose Bay. The weather was fair and the flight without incident. The Goose Bay residents—both Canadian and American—turned out to see the Hampden; I heard her described as a "Limey flying machine" and we were all congratulated on our courage.

We now flew down the Canadian airways system to Montreal; as the only radio was in the rear of the aircraft, the navigator found

himself unemployed and left us. After a short rest we set out again
—North Bay, Winnipeg—and then over Lethbridge in Alberta the
trip came to an abrupt end. The port engine stopped again with an
expensive grinding sound which made the whole aircraft shudder,
this was followed by a fierce jerk and I saw a piece of metal fly past
my window. "That's it," came the pilot's voice over the intercom.
"The port engine is jammed solid and now the cowling has fallen
off; I'm going to land at Lethbridge." This we did and in a phone
message to Pats Bay it was suggested we catch the train back to
Montreal and they would send someone down the next day to see
what could be done with the aircraft. This was agreed and we left
the old Hampden looking decidedly shopsoiled on Lethbridge airport. I think three of these aircraft were delivered but at last
disaster struck and one of them ditched in the Denmark Strait. The
three-man crew got away in their dinghy and then set up house on
an iceberg. They were eventually rescued by the US Coastguard
cutter *Bear*, homeward bound from her last trip of the season to
BE.8; the only casualty was the navigator who had frozen feet.

CHAPTER EIGHT

RAF FERRY COMMAND came into being in July, 1941. It took over the Canadian Pacific Air Service (ATFERO) which had been brought into being by the Ministry of Aircraft Production during the summer of 1940. The purpose was to fly aircraft purchased in the United States, directly across the Atlantic, thereby saving precious shipping space and even more precious time. Operational "know-how" was provided by former Imperial Airways flying staff seconded from BOAC. The Canadian-Pacific Railway Company was brought in to do the administration. There was a desperate shortage of trained aircrew and the ranks of Ferry Command were filled by aircrew regardless of nationality, colour or physical standards. A high percentage of them were Americans and, as they were neutrals at that time, their pay was extremely high in comparison with the rest of us. Later, when the Empire Training Schools began turning out aircrew, Ferry Command was further strengthened by members of the Commonwealth military services and the governments in exile. The original crews wore a dark blue uniform very like the Royal Australian Air Force but with metal wings and cap insignia. Eventually the crews became incredibly mixed with a wide variety of uniforms—some worn by the Americans were of their own design. Everyone on a delivery was given officer status until he returned to Montreal where he reverted to a civilian.

The object of Ferry Command was the delivery of aircraft and this remained its main objective even after it became part of the Royal Air Force Transport Command. It was disbanded at the end of 1945. In spite of the mixture of people and allegiances, relationships remained amiable right to the end. Some of the Air Force personnel with a couple of tours behind them resented the free and easy relations that existed between aircrews but they were very much in the minority. Again there was sometimes friction between RAF staff permanently posted to staging posts and transit aircrews, but it was comparatively rare. One crew of which I was a member consisted of an ex-Air France captain, an American civilian copilot, a Canadian/Chinese flight engineer, a RAAF navigator and myself—we worked together quite well.

After my Hampden flight from St. Athan towards Vancouver, I was put on local flying, most of this was circuits and bumps around Dorval with occasional flights to North Bay in a Hudson. It was on one of these North Bay flights that I received a fright which I will never forget. The crew was an American instructor and two RCAF pilot officers as pupils, and myself. The flight to North Bay, where we landed and had lunch, was without incident. Half-way back to Montreal the two pupils were sitting in the cockpit, the instructor was standing in the doorway between them and I was sitting in the radio compartment. The instructor told the pupils to change seats and stepped back to allow one of them to back out while the other one jumped into his seat. For some strange reason, the two pupils tried to both back into the radio compartment at the same time. During this mix up, one of them knocked off the magneto switch of the starboard engine—probably with his foot—the engine stopped dead, the aircraft flicked over on to its back and went into a spin. The two pupils were flung into the radio compartment on top of the instructor and at the bottom of the pile was myself. How the instructor extricated himself from that tangle of arms and legs, I don't know, but he did and dragged himself into the cockpit. The Hudson was now dangerously close to the ground and he just pulled as hard as he could to get her out of that dive. I felt that I was being firmly pushed through the cabin floor; I stopped struggling to free myself from the other two bodies and, quite slowly, a black curtain fell in front of my eyes. My last conscious thought was that I could still see parts of the aircraft structure through that curtain and then I blacked out. When I came to, the aircraft was flying straight and level and one of the pupils was dabbing my face with iced water from a thermos we had on board. The instructor was flying the aircraft and he explained that she was vibrating badly; he said he would stay at 1,000 feet and try and get her back to Dorval. He was given permission to land direct and this he did, landing the Hudson like a feather on the first few feet of the runway, then letting the tail wheel down as though it was touching down on eggs. He stopped her gently in front of the hangar and we all piled out of what was found to be a badly battered aircraft. The skin on the wings was badly wrinkled, so was the fuselage! Oil dripped dismally out on one wheel well and from head-on it looked as though the wings had started to droop. We were whisked away to the MO who checked the rest out as fit and well and said that I had suffered some internal bleeding which would clear up in a day or two.

67

It was during this period that there was an unusual accident on a Ventura on the "milkrun". It was a new aircraft and was taking supplies and four Service personnel to Goose Bay. It was cold in the cabin and they turned on the cabin heater; the cabin was immediately filled with dense choking fumes. They grabbed their parachutes and dived through the door; all the chutes opened and apparently they all made a safe landing in the middle of Labrador, but from then on no trace of them could be found. Months later, two walked out—an ex-Mounted policeman and a radio engineer who had landed close to him. The former's knowledge of living off the bush had been invaluable but the rest were never heard of again.

It was now winter and the weather conditions in Montreal considerably reduced local flying so I was put back on deliveries. The next delivery aircraft was a Dakota, my friend of the Hampden flight had returned to England and I was crewed up with another Englishman. The flight was Montreal–Gander–Prestwick and uneventful except that the pilot was a most odd type. In the air I was aware of his gaze fixed on me from the cockpit and on the ground at Gander and Prestwick he spent most of his time staring into the middle distance. He was never out of my sight for long—we had adjacent rooms in Prestwick and were side by side in the return Ferry Liberator. His conversation was confined to monosyllables; I would chatter away but he wouldn't answer, yet it seemed that he must have company. I was glad to get back to Montreal where I promptly informed the chief radio operator that I didn't want to be crewed again with that pilot; he laughed, "You're about the tenth man that's told me that." Eventually this pilot was returned to England and years later I heard that he had risen to command in civil airlines but his brain had eventually given way. He was under pressure on the one flight I did with him and it is surprising that he lasted as long as he did.

I was next put on the permanent crew of an ex-Air France pilot, he was in his late fifties and had been flying for many years; he was the most polite person I had ever met. He was engaged almost exclusively in delivering Liberators from Montreal to Prestwick during the period that I flew with him, but he really did not need a crew at all. We left on my first trip with a full Service crew, except for Captain Henri, his Canadian flight engineer and myself. Even when flying along the airways to Gander, Captain Henri demonstrated his one man band. He did all his own navigation, collected his own weather but was perfectly polite to all of us. The navigator was making his first trip and was working like a fury; Captain

Henri accepted all his changes of heading, changes of ETA, etc., with profuse thanks. My long-range weather reports from Gander he received with the greatest courtesy and filed them away in his brief-case, but he never read them. By the time we arrived, the navigator was nearly in tears—"Lookit son," said the flight engineer, "I have been flying with old Henri for a year now and he is like this with every crew he has—he just doesn't like to bother people. We will be taking off for Prestwick in a couple of hours and we shall fly the whole trip on 093 degrees magnetic. When we get close to Prestwick, he will tune in the radio range there and will tow into the airfield on that."

The flight engineer's words came true. Over lunch Captain Henri apologised that we could not spend the usual night in bed but the weather was suitable and he would like to take off for Prestwick that evening. He appreciated that some of the crew might be tired but he didn't mind them sleeping on the way across. The keen young navigator made out a most comprehensive flight plan and one felt that he was going to show Henri that he could possibly do without the rest of us but not without him! Henri's flying was somehow an extension of himself; he taxied gently to the end of the runway, meticulously checked all his flying controls and each of the motors and then opened up for the take-off. He stayed on the runway until she really wanted to fly and then he quietly eased her off the ground into a gentle climb—flaps, revs, wheels—he handled everything himself. He disconnected his headset, replaced his cap and settled down for the night on a heading of 093 degrees magnetic. For the next nine hours the navigator worked away at his star shots and long-range bearings; he produced chits asking Henri to alter course a dozen times and Henri accepted each chit with profuse thanks, filing them carefully on a bulldog clip he had hung on the cockpit wall beside him—but we stayed on 093 degrees magnetic. I helped the navigator with his bearings, passed our hourly position to Prestwick and copies of the relevant weather reports and waited for Henri to ask for them—I waited in vain. Half an hour before our estimated time of arrival at Prestwick, Henri donned his headset, tuned in the range station there, and then made a small alteration of course. He contacted the control tower himself and received permission to let down through a thick layer of cloud; he broke out to the North of the field, dropped his own wheels and flaps and went in to make a smooth landing. Over a belated breakfast, the crew discussed Henri who had gone to sit at another table with some friends. The Service copilot was disgusted and asked the table bitterly why he had been included in the crew; the navigator reckoned he had worked like a dog only to produce the same answer as Henri who had obviously done nothing at all. The engineer tried to pour oil on troubled waters. "I keep telling you—forget it, he's always the same, no matter who he has along with him. He flew the Air France/African routes for donkey's years with only a radioman for company and he just developed into a one man band."

Unmollified, the Service boys departed for their various destinations while the engineer and I went to control to find out about a ride back to Montreal. We were told we were on the next night's return ferry and retired to our rooms to catch up on sleep. We returned to Montreal the next night, another 16 dreary hours on the floor of a Liberator. The flight engineer's parting shot was, "See you next week on another Lib—and with Henri." He was right. Within a few days I received a call from the radio office to come in and a letter from Henri in flawless English was handed to me; he had enjoyed having me on his crew during his last delivery flight and had asked the office if it could be arranged for me to fly with him permanently. I pointed out to the chief radio operator that Henri really didn't want a crew and that I would much rather crew up with a pilot that at least used the information I provided, but he was adamant and with Henri I went.

I rode with Henri on three Liberator deliveries in succession and each was a complete copy of the other; we always went through Gander, we never stopped for the night and we always made the crossing on 093 magnetic.

This rather boring routine was stopped when Henri was laid up with a damaged ankle caused through slipping in the snow. I think he must have passed on my name around the Air France pilots for my next trip was with another Free Frenchman on a Liberator delivery to China. His permanent radioman was also from Air France, I forget now why he couldn't make the trip, and the rest of the crew had been together for almost a year. They were the usual mixed bunch—an American civilian copilot, a Canadian civilian flight engineer and a Royal Australian Air Force flying officer navigator. It was a long and tiring trip—Montreal, Gander, Prestwick, Rabat Sale, Cairo, Karachi, Calcutta and then over the Hump to Kunming. Perhaps the only thing of real note on that long trip out was our arrival at Kunming. The Americans had just moved in and were busy building a straw shed around their coke machine; it was just a strip in the middle of nowhere but they were quite certain they had not got mixed in their building priorities. Within an hour of our arrival a battered Dakota appeared, he had been diverted on his way back to Calcutta to pick us up. Perched on the cargo of crates we had a first-class view of the famous Hump over which the Americans were airfreighting supplies to China. We went through it, or rather over it, at 12,000 feet and, in spite of many dire warnings, did not see any of the Japanese Zeros that were reputed to lie in wait for unwary freight aircraft. Calcutta was its usual hot and sticky self but we were on our way within minutes. An American DC-4 freighter was taking off for Karachi, and the US Army hustled us aboard right away. We each made some sort of bed among the freight and went to sleep, tired of box lunches, tepid coffee and of aeroplanes in general. At Karachi our headlong flight came to a stop, there was nothing leaving for either the US or for the UK for a couple of days and we were put in a huge transit camp under canvas. Although we had made a night stop whenever practicable, the whole crew were tired out. My recollections of that American transit camp are hazy—I know I ate a lot and slept a lot and, with the rest of the crew, went to the open air cinema on both evenings.

On the third morning we were told that a Curtis Commando was leaving for Miami at midday and we were scheduled as passengers. The Curtis Commando was a big twin-engined freighter/passenger aircraft with a slightly sinister name for its climb performance on one engine; this worried us not at all, the six American Servicemen who made up the rest of the passengers were going home on leave and the Liberator crew just wanted to get back to Montreal. Among the passengers was the once famous child film star, Jackie Coogan.

Now started what became an endurance marathon—Karachi, Aden, Khartoum, Fort Lamy, Takoradi, Ascension Island, Natal, Belem, Trinidad, Borinquen and Miami. The crew changed, the freight changed but we seemed to be destined to go on for ever; we were fed at most of the stops, we washed and shaved when we could and we slept on the metal floor of the aircraft or tried to doze on the fore and aft metal seats. At Miami International we thought our luck must change but it was not to be, a South Atlantic Ferry Command Liberator was on its way back to Montreal and it had delayed departure to pick us up. It took me a week back in Montreal to recover from that effort.

My next delivery was a Canadian Lancaster with Packard Merlin engines and I found it most uncomfortable compared with

American aircraft. There is no doubt that in British military aircraft, no attempt was made to make the crew comfortable. There is perhaps some wisdom in producing an environment that makes a man tired, irritable and uncomfortable, at least he won't fall off to sleep. However, I appreciated comfort on long flights; I personally worked better that way.

The crew of the Lanc was a full Service crew that had been put together in Montreal for a one-way delivery. At the last moment the radio operator had dropped out and I was brought in to fill his place. The flight was straightforward—Dorval, Gander, Prestwick, but it sticks in my mind because of a long battle I had with the squadron leader pilot. He and the copilot insisted on flying in their shirt-sleeves, it was bitterly cold and the only method of keeping them warm was to run the aircraft heating at full blast. The heating of a Lanc was from exhaust muffs which came into a duct alongside the radio operator's seat. To keep the pilots warm, I had to fry. We had a bitter row in the air between Dorval and Gander, they refused even to put on their flying kit and repeatedly reached over my lap to turn on the heat after I had turned it down. They agreed on the ground in Gander that a winter crossing of the Atlantic in shirt-sleeves was not on. Accepting this, we flew straight to Prestwick but on the climb they took off their jackets and loudly called for heat over the intercommunication system. I stripped down to my underpants and jammed a blanket to stop the duct from burning my leg and so we flew across the Atlantic. I don't know why they behaved so stupidly but they were both very young—perhaps they wanted to prove how tough they were.

A period of persistent westerly gales had almost stopped the return Ferry Liberators and a considerable number of us had to be sent back by sea. We hung around Prestwick for two days and then some fifty of us were put on buses and taken to Glasgow. We were checked through the immigration and then loaded aboard a tender and off we steamed to the tail of the Bank to join the US troopship *General John Pope*. She was a huge, single funnel, grey painted trooper and as the tender came alongside her gangway, I realised that she had no portholes. We were accommodated in huge dormitories with three tiers of let-down cots. The ship was spotless and the food of a high order. It took twelve days to get to Norfolk, Virginia, for the westerly winds that had held up the Liberators had produced some heavy seas in the North Atlantic. The coloured stewards in the saloon knew that the UK was under strict rationing and assumed that the British members of the company at least were on the edge of starvation. They produced gargantuan portions of every course for us and became quite concerned when we couldn't dispose of it all. My table steward said sorrowfully when I had been able to eat only half of a huge mound of asparagus, "You should try and eat that man, your stomach sure must have shrunk some on the starvation diet you bin livin' on." In Norfolk, we were loaded into a train and returned to Montreal.

When I reported to the radio office in Dorval, I was asked if I would like to go on a navigation course. I jumped at the chance and produced my almost forgotten Second "N" as a proof of my keenness. My name was accepted and as the six weeks' course was not to start for two weeks, it was suggested that I make another delivery. This turned out to be another Dakota; the pilot was an ex-bush pilot with the copilot and navigator one trip only Service personnel. The bush pilot and the copilot got along very well and when we set off on the first leg to Goose Bay the pilot took us for a joyride round every lake and strip that he had landed on in Labrador. It was a formidable list and it took hours, we wandered all over the place, we made low runs over this cabin and that lake until the navigator threw up his hands in disgust and retired. Every half hour Goose Bay would ask me when we were due to arrive because we were over an hour behind our ETA. I felt like answering, "God knows, at the moment we are over central Labrador at zero feet looking for a French Canadian trapper called Gasparde. We have found his cabin and we are now looking along his trap line to see if he is all right." I didn't do this but gently reminded the pilot that we were due at Goose a long time ago and they were asking if we were lost. "We're not lost son," he replied. "Tell 'em we're fine and we'll be along soon."

"Soon" was an exaggeration but we did eventually arrive at Goose. I believe we broke the record for the slowest time from Dorval to Goose Bay. We spent the night there and over supper the copilot expressed a wish to see BW.1; no sooner said than done, the pilot had practically opened up the place with a Dak a couple of years ago and that was agreed as our next scheduled stop.

The next morning we found the cloud was down in the fjord and snow was expected at BW.1. I was relieved to hear the operations people say that BW.1 wasn't accepting aircraft, not even a Dak flown by our expert who seemed very well known to them. It was decided therefore that we would wait until the evening, making a flight down to Cape Farewell and then a great circle track to Prestwick. We made the flight in bright moonlight down to Cape Farewell; this was not as impressive as it might have been for the whole of Greenland was covered with cloud. Here we ran into cloud but picked up a fine westerly wind which persisted almost to Prestwick. The navigator was unhappy at being unable to use some of his new-found knowledge of astro navigation for we made that crossing without one sight of the heavens, but I kept him supplied with plenty of bearings. Prestwick was as usual clear, and I could not help comparing this flight with the last one in a Lancaster. The pilot and I found that we were scheduled out on the next night's return ferry but that brave west wind that had helped us across so well would need to change direction drastically if we were to get back directly to Gander.

We found the next night that the flight was routed via the Azores, then Gander and Montreal. The take-off was delayed until the early morning so that the arrival at the new airfield at Lagens on Terceira Island could be made in daylight. The Portuguese owned the Azores and had given permission for this staging post to be built by the Americans. It was also used as a Coastal Command base by the RAF. We landed at Lagens about midday; it was a fine, wide airfield, completely equipped with all the then known radio aids and with accommodation to handle plenty of transient crews. The single runway was laid with PSP (Pierced Steel Plate) and the aircraft were parked along taxiways parallel with this. The captain of the return ferry now decided to delay his departure until the evening and several of us decided to do the tiny town of Angra. We loaded up on a jolting bullock cart and set off. The town had a small square and a few shops but you could sense we were far from welcome. The whole island was desperately poor and seemed numbed from the catastrophic impact of this big base being dumped in their midst. The shops were almost bare of stocks, only the liquor stores seemed to have adequate supplies and that had been brewed on the island. I bought four large bottles of this local brew and stowed it away in my luggage. Later that evening we left for Gander, the flight progressed so well that the Captain decided to fly direct to Montreal and there we landed some fourteen hours later.

Back in my lodgings in Montreal, I decided to try the Azores brew on my Canadian friends that evening when they returned from their offices. We experimented and found it seemed to go best with a drink called "7 up" and they then settled down in my room to build up an appetite for supper which was at seven o'clock.

The results were little short of disastrous, even when diluted with fruit juice it made a first-class paint remover. Surveying the residents at breakfast the next morning, I decided that the sink was the only place for what remained of the Azores "brew".

CHAPTER NINE

I WAS now ready to start my navigation training and joined a class of about twenty radiomen and settled down to try and absorb as much as possible in the time. The instructor's approach was absolutely sound. "I can't make ace navigators of you in six weeks; all I can do is to teach you what to do and how to do it but not why," he told us on the first morning. My previous groundwork on the landlady's kitchen table now stood me in good stead and I found the course very interesting. The Service instructors were more than willing to go out of their way to make sure that we became as competent as possible in the time. Part way through the last week of the course, the briefing officer and the senior instructor went into a huddle in the corner of our classroom; several times they glanced at me and I had an uncomfortable feeling that I was under discussion. At last the briefing officer turned to the class. "Sorry chaps, but we want three radio/navigators for the morning. I know you haven't completed your course, but we shall just have to pick out the best we can." He turned to me. "With that licence you are a natural, so come across to the briefing room and I'll introduce you to the skipper, we'll pick the other two later." As I followed him across the road my stomach turned over with each step I took. Navigating a DH.86 on a summer's day from a topographical map was a different proposition to navigating during winter across the North Atlantic in a high speed bomber. My skipper was waiting in the briefing room, a large, fair-haired Texan.

"Here you are Clyde," said the briefing officer, "the pick of the pack; hasn't finished his course yet and by the look on his face is full of misgivings about the whole deal."

I introduced myself and started to tell him about my total lack of experience. Clyde was a large, calm man, he always called me "Lad" although I was his elder by six months. "I've only delivered one Mosquito myself Lad, but we will make out, you just tell me where to aim it and we'll see what turns up." The rest of the day went in a daze—drawing kit, maps and a sextant which I examined with grave misgivings.

That evening in my lodgings, time seemed to stand still; I had screwed up my courage now and I wanted to get on with the job before it all oozed away, and pick-up time was not until six o'clock in the morning. At last the long night ended and I was standing at the kerb waiting for the early bus. It was full of the usual glum collection of aircrew on their way to the field. Clyde made room for me alongside him and we started discussing the flight. He said that if the weather was right, he wanted to go to Gander today, spend twenty-four hours there and set off for Prestwick tomorrow night. He said he would fly the airways system to Gander, this would make few demands on my navigational ability and in the first light of a winter's dawn we arrived at Dorval.

The Mosquito was parked outside the departure building and I was soon immersed in the pre-flight duties of collecting the paperwork for the flight and making out a flight plan. Clyde unobtrusively helped all the time and at last we got out to the Mozzy with all our equipment—maps, charts, tables, Skyoe cards and the sextant. The Mosquito had a hatch under the nose and while Clyde did his external checks, a ground crewman handed me up the equipment which I proceeded to stow around the cockpit. As soon as I had found a temporary home for everything, I took my seat and then Clyde climbed up the short ladder and settled himself into the cockpit. I checked out the radio, the ground crewman removed the ladder and the hatch was secured. One after the other the Merlins coughed, and then broke into a healthy roar; the tower controller gave us a taxi clearance and then we were bumping along the taxiway to the end of the duty runway. I looked around me at a dreary sight—the edges of the runway were banked with dirty, frozen snow, the sky was grey in the dawn light and appeared to be loaded down with snow—I was glad to be getting away from it all.

At last we were lined up, the controller gave us clear for take-off, Clyde grinned at me across the tiny cockpit and started angling open the throttles. The Mozzy started to lurch along but as the snow banks hurtled past and the speed built up, the bumps smoothed out and then we were flying, the undershoot lights flashed below and suddenly we were in black cloud. Clyde eased back to climb power. "Met. said we could top this lot at 8,000 feet so we'll establish on top in the sunshine, what's the first course?"

I had set out on my first trip as a navigator. The Quebec radio range was loud and clear in my earphones when I first tuned it in and then, as I cut the volume right back, I was able to identify that we were slightly off the beam. "Nothing to worry about yet." Clyde's voice came over the intercom, "Bit south, we will leave it." I next copied Gander weather broadcast and then went back to Quebec radio range, suddenly the signal faded right away and

77

then returned again; we had passed through the cone of silence over Quebec. Consulting the flight plan, I now told the Quebec range radio operator the flight particulars and the ETA at Millinocket, the next range station on the airways system. Slowly the time passed —Megantic, Seven Islands, St. Andrews Field range stations. At each we found the cone of silence. The forecast winds were reasonably accurate and the weather at Gander remained wide open. At last we passed Stephenville and then we could hear the range station at Gander. It was now a clear, sunny day and I peered through the windscreen trying to pick up the field. Clyde watched me peering first at my watch and then ahead. "It won't have moved, Lad, just be patient for another five minutes, your ETAs have been spot on all morning, this one will be all right." It was all right; there ahead were the huge runways of Gander and in my telephones the unemotional voice of the tower operator telling us that there was no local traffic and that we were clear for our final approach. Clyde went through his approach and landing drill and bounced us lightly on to the main runway between the snow banks. As I completed my navigation log by filling in the "finished with engines" time, I noticed that it agreed exactly with the flight plan. I was not to be as accurate as that again for a long time.

In the ops room Clyde stated his intention of a twenty-four-hour layover but it was suggested that we attend the met. briefing that evening to see what we might expect for the next night. The met. briefing room was packed as there was quite a pile up of aircraft at Gander waiting to get across to England. Clyde and I settled down at the end of the back row and then the met. officer exploded his bombshell. "Tonight's the night lads, if you don't get away within the next few hours, you may be stuck here for a week. There's heavy snow along the Maritimes and it's sweeping this way, it will arive tomorrow afternoon, and it's going to shut this field down tight for several days. The winds for the crossing aren't good, you'll get approximately a twenty-knot headwind component on the direct route, but Prestwick will be wide open and so are the alternates."

Clyde turned to me. "It's up to you, Lad, if you think you've had enough for today, we'll just sit it out in Gander."

I thought for a minute. "Got to go sooner or later, let's go tonight."

Clyde nodded. "Yep, we'll figure out the flight plan between us and make our final decision then."

On a direct flight to Prestwick, we made a flight plan of twelve hours twenty minutes. It seemed a long time but it was well within our endurance and we decided to go. Bundled up in our flying kit we stowed ourselves away in the tiny cockpit; it was a bitterly cold, but clear, night and the thought of a long flight over the North Atlantic above complex weather formations with the navigation dependent on my ability to use a sextant through a trembling perspex dome above my head had quite literally scared me stiff. I remember thinking of the navigational dreams I had at Croydon before the war but I had never visualised myself doing anything quite like this. Then the Packard Merlins grunted into life and we moved along to the end of the runway, our landing lights shining on the piled banks of snow. We lined up and Clyde checked out each motor. "You're cleared for take-off," said the tower operator and then a few minutes later, "I have you off the ground at '43 and clear you to climb on course, have a good trip." The game was well and truly started. We climbed away on our first course and I was once again swamped with the thoughts of the dozens of things I had to do in the next twelve hours which must culminate in a landing at Prestwick over 2,000 miles away.

At 25,000 feet Clyde levelled off and leaned off the engines to long range cruise and I settled down to tackle my job in some sort of order. After an hour I decided that I would get a position. I collected HF/DF bearings from Gander, Bermuda and Iceland and plotted them. I drew out an air plot and applied the met. wind to it and was amazed to find that they agreed to within twenty-five miles. All this took nearly thirty minutes and it was time to report my position to Gander which both Iceland and Prestwick acknowledged. Clyde had jiggled with the heating controls and we were comfortably warm. I gazed around the heavens and picked two stars which would give me a reasonable fix. I felt down behind the pilot's seat for the sextant, Clyde's voice came over the intercom, "You left it on the tarmac at Dorval. I didn't see it until we had started up and were taxiing away. You looked worried enough as it was so I didn't bother you any more." I felt relieved; I was much more competent with radio navigation than I was with astro navigation anyway. My only concern now was getting to Prestwick and I could figure out some excuse for losing the sextant by the time I got back to Dorval. The next HF/DF radio fix put us forty miles south of track and about ten minutes behind. Clyde took the alteration of course without comment, he probably thought it was a bit early for course alterations but he refrained from comment. The next fix showed us about on track but twenty-five minutes late—the headwind component must be greater than we had allowed for.

Soon Gander was to pass me a message confirming that the head-wind component was greater and this led to a wild flurry of activity in which the remainder of the flight plan was re-worked with the fresh information. This put us fifty minutes late. Clyde shrugged his shoulders. "It's not serious yet, we'll press on."

Another radio fix about confirmed the new winds, we remained at 25,000 feet in reasonable comfort until we reached our point of no return. Clyde laughed, "Another worry gone, we can't go back now however much you slip the ETA back."

Another two radio fixes plotted us drifting south of track and still losing time. The next fix didn't look right at all. I re-worked the sums and then collected another set of bearings from Gander, Prestwick and Reykjavik to try and find out what had gone wrong. This time Reykjavik labelled his bearing "doubtful". The plotted fix gave me new heart—nothing drastic had happened, Reykjavik had been the faulty one. So we roared on through the night and, as Clyde had said, "We got it aimed right." The horizon ahead was beginning to lighten and before the long range stations faded out, I collected one last set of bearings. We were now an hour behind time but still close to track. Clyde listened to my report and then grunted, "We'll keep this until you can pick up the range at Prest-wick, we can then turn and establish ourselves on that."

As the cockpit slowly lightened, I strained my ears for the Prest-wick range and then at last I had it, "PK", "PK" at just about the same strength; we weren't far off track. Soon we could hear it distinctly, we were a bit south of the beam, so altered course some ten degrees and as the dawn came we were tight on track with two hours to go to Prestwick according to my calculations. Prestwick reported three-tenths cloud cover at 5,000 feet and we decided to stay at 25,000 feet until we got a bit closer. With the rising sun we could see through large gaps in the cloud and Clyde shouted, "I can see an island over here."

I pointed hopefully to Rathlin, "That it?"

"That's it," he said. "How much further?"

"'Bout 90 miles," I answered. We started to descend and at last broke through the scattered overcast with Kintyre broad on my beam and Arran on the bow. We had arrived.

The arrival at Prestwick was a distinct anticlimax. The debriefing people daily met transatlantic navigators with dozens of crossings to their credit and in a short time we hustled through and into the restaurant for a late breakfast.

Clyde and I were returned to Montreal a couple of nights later on the return ferry Liberator. We met in Montreal and Clyde visited Dorval with me to help explain away the abandoned sextant which the ground crew had returned to the navigation stores. He also arranged with the briefing staff that he and I would make a permanent delivery crew. The navigation instructor went over my logs and decided that I would probably get by without further training and I became a fully fledged radio navigator. Clyde unfortunately now went on a short leave and during his absence the briefing people called me in to do a Mosquito delivery at short notice.

The new skipper was a prewar RAF officer with two tours of operations to his credit. He proved to be an impossible character to get along with; when introduced to him by the briefing officer, I called him "Skipper" but I was at once informed that, as captain of the aircraft, he was to be addressed as "Sir" at all times—on the ground and in the air. He had protruding blue eyes which seemed to bulge permanently with indignation and each sentence was punctuated by alternate sweeps at a large, fair moustache. I gazed at him in amazement. "I have selected you for this trip because I understand you are English; I can't stand Canadians or Americans —no sense of discipline," he said.

The Canadian briefing officer turned as I pushed through the crowd to him. "Sorry, I know what you are going to say, but you'll have to go with him, clown that he is. Three of your blokes have refused point blank even at the threat of the sack. Got to get the bastard away somehow, we'll put you back with Clyde when he gets back from leave."

I returned to the squadron leader. "I am the fourth that has refused to fly with you. I don't like your manners, you may not like mine; I agree to keep out of your way while we deliver this Mosquito to Prestwick, perhaps you will return the compliment."

"This bloody shower wants straightening out," he huffed, "and if I had them . . ."

I interrupted. "You haven't, they are mostly civilians and don't give a monkey's damn what your record is or what your rank is. I am going to draw my kit for the trip and I'll meet you at departure tomorrow morning at 6.30 a.m."

The squadron leader had not finished yet. "Report to me when you have drawn your kit, I want to discuss what I shall want you to do on this trip, I shall wait here."

"I intend to work the radio and navigate this Mosquito to Prestwick to the best of my ability and that's all there is to be said." I swung on my heel and carried on with my pre-flight chores.

When I joined the early bus the next morning, the squadron leader was sitting in splendid isolation on the rear seat. I ignored him and joined another Mosquito crew who were highly amused at my flying companion. "Dorval have been trying to unload him for over a week now," laughed the young RAF skipper. "He was sent to Washington on the Commission, lasted three days and was posted to Dorval for onward transmission to the UK. He is one of the most genuine bastards I know—makes a business of it."

"Can he fly a Mosquito?" I asked.

"No better than the rest of us," he replied.

The squadron leader waited for me at the check-in desk. "Which way do you want to go?" I asked.

His fishy eyes regarded me with a glassy stare, "You will be instructed on that when I have made up my mind," he replied.

"Make your bloody mind up in time for me to make out and file a flight plan, I'm off for a coffee," I answered.

A few minutes later he entered the coffee bar and leaned over my table.

"We'll go direct to Goose Bay today at 25,000 feet."

"Direct?" I asked. "But there's a perfectly good airway to Goose."

The squadron leader swung away from the table. "You have your orders, get to it."

I consulted with the Canadian squadron leader in operations about a direct flight across Labrador. "Make an airways flight plan to Goose," he said. "I will tell W—— why I have changed it when he signs in. I am not having Mozzys charging across that territory in this weather."

I did as he said and had just finished when W—— came back. He gazed at the flight plan and his eyes bulged. "I ordered you to make one for a direct flight . . ." but the ops man had seen the gathering storm and pushed into the party.

"You'll stick to the airway like any sane man and if you don't like it I'll get the head man out of bed to tell you so," he said. W—— stroked his whiskers first with his left hand and then his right and glared at the ops man but the latter stuck to his ground.

"What's it to be then?" he said quietly. W—— surrendered with poor grace "Unwarranted interference" and then signed the flight plan. I started to get my stuff together to load into the aeroplane and with the assistance of the ground crew, I soon had it stowed away in the cockpit and checked out with the radio. W—— climbed up the ladder and donned his oxygen mask, connected up his headset and settled back in his seat. For a moment silence reigned and then a single word was barked over the intercom, "Report". I replied, "Radio's checked and clear to start my side."

"I'll decide when to start the engines," he snarled.

"You just do that, Brother," I replied.

"Silence," he shouted.

What an atmosphere, I thought. I should have refused to come, murder will be done before we get to Prestwick.

Soon we were airborne, the Mosquito built up a bit of a swing on take-off, but he caught it and we were soon climbing along the airway to Quebec.

The flight was conducted in almost total silence. He flew the course I gave him and we stayed in thick cloud at 25,000 feet with considerable icing. I almost suggested that we dropped down to a temperature range when icing would not be expected, but one glance at the stiff, ridiculous figure opposite was enough to make me realise that the man in command would not appreciate such a suggestion. I wrote out the weather at Goose Bay and passed it across to him—"Vis. two miles in light snow, wind N 20 knots"—but it elicited no comment. Then the last of the airway beacons were behind us and I was talking to Goose.

"Clear to descend, you will break clear at 3,000 feet with half mile vis."

I made a last amendment to the course and then pointed down. W—— immediately throttled back and we started descending. Slowly the altimeter unwound in front of me and just as slowly the time crept towards our ETA—3,500, 3,000, 2,500 feet and then the murk seemed to lighten and we broke out over the desolate Labrador landscape with its miles of snow and fir trees. W—— continued the descent and then two minutes from ETA I caught the flash of the approach lights through the falling snow. I had been navigating steadily all day but I was still inexperienced enough to be elated when my sums gave the correct answer at the end of a flight.

I choked back a triumphant shout and instead, unemotionally, told the tower I had the field in sight. W——'s head jerked up at my statement, for a second I thought he was going to argue but I just pointed to starboard. We landed and taxied to the hangar and as I climbed down the ladder, I thought, "Now what. I don't fancy a dart up the fjord with this character."

Fancy it or not, at the ops room W—— stated with a few flourishes of his whiskers that he intended to leave the next morning for BW.1. He was advised to attend the film and turned to me. "You'll attend too"—it was an order.

"I've seen it and I've been up the fjord, and before you start any bloody silly arguments, I'm off to lunch."

At the transit mess I booked into a room with two other crew members and then went in with them to lunch. I saw W—— hanging around in the evening but avoided him by going to the camp cinema. Returning to the transit mess, I found that we were on departure the next morning and booked an appropriate call.

At breakfast I was in first and joined some friends at a small table. I met W—— again at the met. briefing; he was arguing about something with the American met. man so I picked up our folder and retired to make out the flight plan. He sat down beside me and when I had finished I pushed it along for him to check.

"I understand you have been to BW.1 before; you may be of some use to me today"—about as far as W—— was capable of extending an olive branch.

We left Goose Bay and headed out across the drifting icebergs of the Davis Strait at 10,000 feet. Slowly the ragged black cliffs of Greenland backed by the white bulk of the icecap towering above them came into view ahead. BW.1 reported its field, the fjord and BW.4 were all open, but I didn't like the way the white loom of the icecap seemed to hover over the cliffs. I remembered one of the old-timers telling me of a similar phenomenon he had noticed and I checked again with BW.1 that the fjord was in fact clear. W—— now decided that he would take a hand. "What's all this ditting and dotting about?" he asked.

"Don't like the look of the weather over the fjord and was just checking that it's still okay," I replied.

"You don't?" said W——. "I am still in command of this aircraft and it looks all right to me—don't use that bloody key again without my permission."

I decided to be conciliatory. "That damn alleyway in the mountain will be a real bastard if it starts to fill with mist after we get in it—no room to turn."

W—— was having none of it. "You civilians get on my nerves, there's a war on and this aircraft is needed in the UK. It amazes me that you have ever completed a delivery."

I dropped the discussion and gave him a course alteration to close the leg of the BW.4 range station. An hour later I thought I could distinguish BW.4 island against the now hazy backdrop of the fjord. I lined W—— up on BW.4 at last and said, "We've got twenty minutes to go for the island, but I don't like it."

W——'s reply was typical. "You're not paid to like it—only to deliver this aircraft."

84

"In one piece," I amended.

BW.4 island now started to appear out of the haze and it certainly was hazy. I had lost the coastline behind the island now altogether; I passed the course from BW.4 to the mouth of the BW.1 fjord to W——. "Fly that when I tell you but let's get down to the water first."

W—— started a fast descent while I concentrated on the BW.4.

"That island seems to be receding into the haze," shouted W——.

I looked again and then I realised what was happening. A bank of mist was drifting across our track between us and the island. "Climb, climb," I shouted over the intercom but no one was taking command of W——'s aircraft. He held his course. I glanced aside, the wing tips had vanished, we had lost our visibility and we were hell-bent for the coast of Greenland.

The roar of BW.1 beacon suddenly died away. "We're over the island—climb like hell on the new course," I shouted.

W—— for the first time did just as he was asked. He put the throttles through the gate and hauled back on the yoke. In that madhouse of howling engines and a shuddering aircraft, I remembered nothing until the sun flashed on the top of a mist bank which was backed by a wall of black rock streaked with snow. W—— saw it as I did and reversed the controls. We missed that rock face by inches and plunged back into the mist, climbing frantically. The next instant the cockpit was filled with a blinding white light—we had broken through the top. On my side stretched a glittering expanse of rolling mist covering the icecap, while directly below were the desolate black rocks of the coast of Greenland.

The Mosquito was still climbing and as I glanced at W—— the altimeter wound through 15,000 feet. Perspiration was running down his face and over his oxygen mask and he looked far from happy. I did a quick sum and gave him a course back to Goose Bay. He throttled back without a word and turned on to a new heading. I contacted BW.1 who told us to return at once to Goose Bay as the weather was treacherous in the fjord with drifting mist banks. I repeated this to W—— but now the hero of two tours began to reassert himself.

"Why should we return to Goose—why not Gander?" he said.

I did some sums. "Please your bloody self but it's at least eleven hundred miles away, you had better decide soon or the question of fuel will raise its ugly head."

W—— had had enough for one day, however, and we jogged back to Goose Bay in brilliant weather, sighting Cape Harrison at the mouth of Hamilton Inlet from at least seventy-five miles.

If W—— was expecting a hero's reception at Goose Bay, he was disappointed, the debriefing officer and the ops officer were openly bored with the story of how his quick reactions had saved the aeroplane. They also refused point blank to W——'s request that an enquiry should be held at once as to why he had not been informed of the weather changes. I sensed that he wanted to be told that a message had been sent and I had missed it.

The ops man got impatient. "The US Air Corps at BW.1 is responsible for the aircraft in the fjord, our radio people only monitored you until you contacted them and we heard them tell you that the weather was clear. For Christ's sake man, you got away with it, mist in the fjord can happen within minutes and without warning, your navigator did what he could, the matter is closed as far as we are concerned."

We retired for a late lunch but at dinner that night W—— started again.

"I am most displeased with your behaviour in the aircraft this morning. I shall report the whole thing at Prestwick and demand an enquiry."

"I only told you to climb, for God's sake what was wrong with that?" I replied. "There was a bloody great island in the way."

"It's the undisciplined behaviour in general that leads to this state of affairs," he answered, pompously sweeping away at his whiskers. "You can only make an observation to the officer in charge and he decides the action to be taken."

But I had stood enough, it had been a trying day without this. For five minutes I entertained him with all the bad language I had picked up in eight years at sea. He began to make feverish sweeps at his moustache and slowly turned a deep crimson. For a moment I thought he was going to have a fit and then a deep Southern drawl broke through my tirade. "I 'usta think that the British were a phlegmatic race, but just listen to that boy carrying on." I retired from the mess in some confusion.

In the lounge of the transit mess I was joined by the operations officer. "I heard that outburst and although I agree with your attitude we have still got to get that Mosquito to the UK. The CO is going to talk to W—— later and persuade him to go down to Gander and try again from there."

The CO got his way and we left the next morning in the usual frigid silence for a 400 mile jaunt down to Gander. The navigation was simple, it was a clear day and we flew a course to intersect a beam of the Gander range. At the met. briefing that evening a tail wind was forecast if a complex track was followed around two large depressions. W—— turned to me. "Do you think you can do that?"

I told him it should be possible and without more ado set about the flight plan. It came out at eleven hours to Prestwick and involved a considerable amount of course changing to make the best of the winds. My relations with W—— were now at an all time low; he accepted the plan without comment. There were three other Mosquito crews who decided to go that night; I took one of the most experienced navigators aside and asked his advice.

"Don't try to do too much. I am going to cut it down to three legs and my skipper agrees. Chasing around the edge of depressions is fine for a big aircraft and a navigator with nothing else to do but I cut the work load down to the minimum in Mozzys."

For a moment I thought of asking W—— to apply the same technique but then discarded the idea. He would at once have accused me of being incapable of following the complex tracks. Soon we were boring through the black night with the lights of Gander vanishing behind us and so started ten hours of concentrated work. There was none of the bantering conversation that Clyde and I carried on; I just lived alone in black night with my problems, never exchanging a word with the silent figure beside me. I took my first two-star fix which was within thirty miles of my DR position and presented myself with a problem—which was right? I later crossed a Polaris shot with a DF bearing from Bermuda which seemed to prove that perhaps they were both wrong. The next star shots fell into place and from then on the whole thing seemed to go right—and then it started getting light and there were no more stars. If my sums were right, we were one hour out of Prestwick. W—— grunted when I told him; I had almost forgotten he was still with me. Then, just where it was supposed to be, the Isle of Arran appeared and we were circling to land at Prestwick after eleven hours ten minutes. I left W—— in the debriefing room at Prestwick, he was demanding an enquiry into the fiasco in Greenland. I told a bored debriefing man that he knew where to find me and retired to bed absolutely exhausted mentally and physically.

This radio navigation job was much more like hard work than being a straight radioman. I never heard of W—— again but have often thought about him; he had been trained and had done all his flying under strictly controlled Service conditions—he was quite lost in Ferry Command.

CHAPTER TEN

On my return to Dorval, I lost little time in reporting to the briefing office; Clyde had returned from leave and I was told that we would be called for a Mosquito delivery within the next few days. Over a drink in the bar at the Mount Royal I told Clyde about my hair-raising ride with W——. He was deeply interested in the whole thing. "I heard in Dorval that you had been packed off with some guy whose face didn't fit," he laughed. "Must have scared the daylights out of you."

I considered that to be the understatement of the year.

A few days later we met again for another Mosquito delivery to Prestwick. It went without incident as did the succeeding four Mosquito deliveries. I was becoming reasonably competent at finding my way from Gander to Prestwick and then came what I have always called Black Friday. We were scheduled out for our usual early morning take-off and were asked to keep a lookout along the airways for a Mosquito that had been missing since the previous morning on a flight to Goose Bay. It was thought that it had crashed in the vicinity of Seven Islands. It was now late spring and a lot of the snow was gone. The flight proceeded normally in clear weather and we flew along the banks of the St. Lawrence in the hope that the Mosquito had forced landed on the shore or a sandbank. Twenty miles from Seven Islands we joined the range leg and dropped down to a few feet above the top of the fir-trees. Clyde rolled the aircraft from side to side so that we both had a view of the ground. I saw it first—a swathe in the fir-trees, the broken new wood seemed almost to shine in the sunlight and at the end of the swathe, a crumpled aeroplane with its tail lying on one side. We had found the missing Mosquito. Clyde did a couple of tight circuits while I fixed the position of the wreck as accurately as I could in relation to the airfield. We contacted Seven Islands tower who asked us to orbit until an air-sea rescue Norseman aircraft arrived. They had been searching the day before and had spent the night at Seven Islands. We made a very careful examination of the wreck but there were no signs of life. At last the Norseman arrived and swept low over the wreck and we climbed away along the airway for Gander. We landed at Gander and reported

88

our unhappy find in the ops room to be told that the crew of the lost Mosquito were old friends—the radio navigator had been an Englishman who had worked for me at Weston.

After a belated lunch we attended the met. briefing to find that there were six Mosquitos considering making the crossing that night. We were warned that there was a possibility of some ice and that the tops of a front at about 30 deg W could be as high as 35,000 feet but the winds were favourable. Clyde and I were both undecided about going. "Let's make out a flight plan and see what it looks like—no real reason why we shouldn't go but that prang we saw this morning has put me off my feed," said Clyde.

It worked out at eleven hours fifteen minutes. "Right Lad, go we must, we just haven't a logical reason not to, now that the other six are going."

The night was black with heavy overcast and within minutes of take-off we plunged into solid cloud. We were between layers at 20,000 feet and Clyde's voice came over the intercom, "Okay to stay here, Lad? You won't see any stars, have to use the radio for a bit."

We continued in cloud for about five hours and then broke out into the clear again. There was a moon up. Peering round for a couple of stars that I would recognise I found that there weren't any visible ahead, just a wall of cloud. "That's more than 30,000 feet high," I said. The moon sailed clear for a few seconds and the huge black towering mass suddenly became charged with menace.

"Don't like it, Lad, let's get some height, that looks more like a wall than a front," said Clyde.

He increased to climbing revs and eased back on the control column. The moon and stars had gone now and it was black dark. The aeroplane rolled slightly and bumped gently, I could see mist streaming past the wing-tip light, we were entering cloud again and then with a crash we suddenly seemed to stop flying; Clyde slammed open the throttles, my windscreen turned white, so did my side window.

"Ice." Clyde's unemotional voice was in my ears. "We're loaded down with the bloody stuff."

I flashed out a call to Gander, no luck, the aerial was grounded with ice. The aeroplane was beginning to wallow. "Push on the rudders and then the stick, with me," said Clyde. "Try and stop her really gumming up the works." He was now moving the throttles to and fro to try and stop the engine from surging.

"Ice in the intakes." Clyde still did not sound terribly impressed but I was. We seemed to be in real trouble. The airspeed indicator was frozen up, the engines were surging badly and the radio was out and the Mozzy was wallowing along like a lame duck. We struggled along like this for two hours. I could only sit and help with the controls on Clyde's quietly spoken instructions and gaze at the windscreen which glittered back in the panel lights. I remember thinking we are not only iced up we are also iced in. The aeroplane made queer whistling and sighing noises which only increased Clyde's frenzied struggling with the controls.

"We're getting into some warmer air, Lad, maybe we can shed some of this stuff and ungum some of our equipment." Clyde sounded hopeful. Through the corner of my eye I saw a flash and then through a jagged hole that had appeared in the ice on my side panel, I could see the glow of the exhausts and then the wing-tip light.

"We're in the clear," I called over the intercom.

Clyde nodded and I sat back again. Slowly the ice cracked and flew away from both windscreens, the engines smoothed out and the Mosquito began to fly like an aircraft again. The aerial ammeter was normal, we were coming back into business.

My call to Gander was answered by Prestwick. "You okay?"

I said we were and he asked, "Where have you been the last two hours?"

"We have been in heavy icing conditions," I replied.

Prestwick then roll-called the other six Mosquitoes, only two replied—both with the same story—badly iced up.

All the ground stations in the North Atlantic had been alerted and repeatedly called the missing four aircraft. None of them answered.

I reduced my navigation to an occasional Polaris star shot crossed with a DF bearing from Reykjavik and spent the hours scraping around the radio frequency in the hopes of hearing one of the missing ones. In all that ice it was logical to expect that they had lost their aerials but I had a feeling that they had gone. So the rest of the night passed and it seemed that our run of bad luck had ended. The weather at Prestwick was clear and we landed safely and taxied round to the dispersal area. The story, however, was not yet ended. We heard in the ops room at Prestwick that yet another Mosquito had crashed going in to land at Stornoway and both the crew were gone.

The losses of this night were caused by the abnormal icing conditions in that front that could not have been known when we left Gander. We were lucky in that we were climbing when it really hit us—perhaps the others entered the icing without the slightest warning. The onslaught could have been so sudden that within seconds the aircraft could have been so heavily coated with ice that all aerodynamic properties would have been lost. Later the Mosquito was to get a bad name in the North Atlantic and after a succession of losses that were never really accounted for, the delivery route was changed to the South Atlantic, away from the bad weather.

Clyde and I returned to Montreal and within a few days we met again in the briefing room for yet another Mosquito delivery to the United Kingdom. The forecast landing conditions for Gander during the next day were poor and we decided to schedule our flight "round the houses". That is via Goose Bay, BW.1, Reykjavik and Prestwick. We arrived in BW.1 to find the camp in the middle of a considerable dilemma. An RAF Boston on delivery to the United Kingdom had forced landed on the icecap. The crew had been found by a searching aircraft and the United States were faced with the problem of how to remove them from the cap in a reasonable time and without mounting a massive land expedition. The crew of three sitting on the icecap were pilot, navigator and radioman, the latter an old friend of mine. He told me the story later. They had taken off from BW.1 on a flight to Reykjavik and had climbed over BW.1 until they reached what they thought was a safe altitude before setting course. After some time, he said, he noticed that they had entered mist, it was obviously quite thin and as it was a brilliant sunny morning, the sun was shining through the mist and creating conditions of literally no visibility. The crew were completely blinded in this silver haze. Suddenly the aircraft bumped heavily, then again and next there was a heavy crunch followed by the oddest sensation that the aircraft was going sideways. That was in fact just what it was doing, blinded by the haze the pilot had inadvertently made a wheels-up landing on the icecap. It was quite a good landing and when the aircraft stopped sliding sideways a completely undamaged crew emerged from the almost undamaged Boston. They were in full flying kit and using their flying and "C" rations, settled down in the aircraft to wait until they were found. They were found next morning by a Norseman who immediately radioed BW.1 their plight. The next person to arrive was the famous Bernt Balchen with a rescue Catalina to see what he could do. After a long and detailed study of the ice area surrounding the crashed aeroplane, he made one last wide circuit and came in and made a perfect landing on the ice; he had both wing floats down—

the boat hull slithered across the ice in great fashion. The run ended about 100 yards from the stranded crew and the Catalina gracefully dropped its port float on to the ice and came to a full stop. The rear blister of the Catalina opened and the fixed metal ladder was put in place. Within minutes the rescued crew were in the Catalina, the hatch was closed and they were all set to go. For some minutes Balchen alternately gunned the two motor but the Catalina remained firmly glued to the ice. The heat generated by the friction of the boat's hull sliding across the snow during the landing had melted the snow and ice and after the boat had come to rest, this had immediately frozen again and welded the boat on to the ice. Balchen now unloaded everyone from the Catalina and they all congregated around the port float. As he now alternately gunned his engines, all hands heaved away to swing the float up into the air. At last it succeeded and as the port wing went up and the starboard went down, with a crack the ice broke away and the Catalina was free again. Balchen motored her slowly away from the group. Both crews were now stranded on the ice. As he slid slowly along, he set the throttles to keep the boat just moving, then the answer came—as he slowly slid past the group of waiting men, one of them broke away, chased alongside the rear blister and jumped on to the ladder and from there climbed into the blister. The problem was solved and continuing his slow taxiing he eventually had everyone aboard by this means. The take-off was extremely rough and Balchen eased the Catalina off the ice the moment he had flying speed. Within a few minutes he had landed on the fjord at BW.1 and the flying boat was beached immediately because the rough treatment had sprung a lot of rivets and it would soon have sunk.

The rest of our flight to England was without incident and Clyde and I returned to Montreal on the return ferry. Some days after we returned, Clyde was killed in a car accident. I lost a good friend and Ferry Command a good pilot.

When my next call came from the briefing office it was to say that I was scheduled to deliver a Boston to North Africa with an American civilian pilot. We met at the briefing and I found that I had been lucky again. Doug was in his forties, an ex-airline captain who was flying in Ferry Command more for interest than for gain. He told me once that he had been left a large sum of money and had abandoned the airline job with TACA in Central America and retired to the Southern States. After a year of boredom, he had applied to Ferry Command for a job. We discussed the flight, he had already made two Boston deliveries to North Africa, on both occasions to Maison Blanche where we were bound. Doug suggested that as I had not flown in a Boston we go over the aircraft together. This was a good idea. I found that the radio navigator was in a rear cockpit, isolated from the pilot, the navigator's cockpit in the nose was filled with equipment urgently needed in North Africa. One odd thing was that there were rudder pedals and a control column that could be brought into operation if the pilot was injured. Doug explained that as there was no auto-pilot, it would be a great help to him if I could hold the aircraft straight and level to give a few minutes' break. I said that I could just about do that. Doug hung a heavy nut on a piece of string and suspended it from the canopy, he then drew a crossed chalk circle on the metal cover over which the nut was suspended. As he explained to me "just keep the nut in the doughnut". When a flight was going according to plan, Doug didn't mind how long I played around at keeping the Boston right side up. His only complaints were that sometimes my manœuvres made him feel sick and sometimes they frightened him. He was a quiet sort of man on the ground but loved to chatter in the air over the inter-com; he would chat for hours about his flying experiences in the South and Central American States where his favourite aircraft seemed to have been a Ford Trimotor. He left the navigation entirely in my hands—"If it doesn't work out, let me know" was his only comment when I told him that I was far from being an ace navigator.

The next morning we met on the bus where he reaffirmed that Gander/Azores was the best way to go. The weather man promised good weather for Gander and then gave us an idea of Gander/Azores for the next day. It looked good, a zero wind component the whole way. Soon we were airborne and the aerial signboards of the airways system were going by—Quebec, Millinocket, Presque Isle and at last Gander itself. Doug flew the ranges by ear, he would tune each station down until it was inaudible to me and he actually flew along the edge of the beam in what is called "the twilight". His approach and landing at Gander were immaculate; Doug was a very experienced airline captain who believed in doing the job with the minimum effort. Over lunch Doug showed up another of his foibles—he didn't like flying at night very much. He claimed that night-time was strictly for owls with whom he had no affinity at all. I didn't mind, my experience with sun shots was minimal and we agreed to set off for Lagens the next morning.

At the met. briefing we were told that the wind would be about zero for the whole trip but there was a front lying across the track. It didn't look much to the met. man; he said we should be able to see our way round the tops of the clouds in daylight.

"See now why I fly by day," he laughed to me. "Some of these babies can grow up to be pretty hostile by late afternoon in South America; I like 'em best around high noon."

The flight plan came out at five hours thirty-five minutes and we scheduled our take-off at 10.0 a.m. local time after a large breakfast. At 10.20 we flew over the rugged coastline of Newfoundland and we set a course for the Azores some 1,700 nautical miles away. The cockpit was full of sunlight and the deep blue of the sea seemed to go on to the edge of the world. I commented on this to Doug. "It's better than scratching around in the dark, that scares me half to death."

The flight jogged along; after an hour a few high stratus clouds drifted across from the west. I watched the sea but it remained calm; there were no white horses on which I could take a drift sight and check if the wind was as forecast. I complained to Doug that he must be asleep while I did the worrying in the back. "Not on your life," he replied. "I am just an ignorant old airframe driver and my wife always packs an educational book in my bag on these trips in the hope that some of it will rub off."

"What you got up there this trip?" I asked.

"Guy called Lawrence, the book's called 'The Seven Pillars of Wisdom', know it?"

I confessed that I had not completely read it. Doug laughed, "Thought it would be above your head; my wife's an addicted woman, she used to be a school teacher."

My first fix was a sun line crossed with a DF bearing from Gander. I repeated this in thirty minutes and then again in another thirty minutes, but Gander was fading fast; he labelled the third bearing as second class. The sky was becoming obscured by now although the sun was still visible. I spent some time plotting out my three fixes and then Doug's voice came over the intercom. "That front's building up ahead, doesn't look anything much yet —just a collection of cu nimbs which we can fly around, we should be there in about twenty minutes."

I peered ahead at the front, the tops were nearer 40,000 feet than the estimate of 20,000 feet given us by the met. people.

"I'm going under this lot," said Doug. "I was going round 'em but they are higher than they should be."

We lost height rapidly and then Doug cried, "Check your seat belt," and the Boston plunged into what seemed to be a wall of rain. We twisted and turned around the darker patches under that cloud for almost an hour. I soon gave up trying to plot our DR position and just made a list of the headings and the time we were on them. Gradually the open patches became more frequent and the rain squalls intermittent. It had not been particularly rough and when we broke clear I was surprised to find that the sea was white with flying scud, a whole gale was blowing down there. Soon the front was behind us and the sun was shining over my right shoulder; it was time I did something about a position. Then came the first snag of Doug's fly-by-day philosophy. Neither Gander nor Lagens were audible on any of the frequencies. I called without reply and then asked Doug to climb up a bit and see if I could get some range from height; he was loath to use fuel for this purpose and suggested I waited until we were a bit nearer to Lagens. I busied myself with a sun line which plotted out almost parallel with my track but ninety miles to the west of it. I next plotted a DR position by averaging out our turnings and twistings in the front. Another sun shot made things look even worse—twelve miles west of track, about half-way between Gander and Lagens. The third sun shot put me 143 miles west of track and as I plotted it I felt the black fingers of panic creeping over my mind. Was my navigation at fault? Was the radio equipment out of commission?

The aircraft had no direction finder, we just had to get close enough to the islands to pick up the radio range. First I checked each of the frequency bands of the receiver; all the high frequency bands were deadly quiet. I tried the medium frequencies and strangely enough picked up distorted music. I asked Doug what sort of wind we had encountered under the front. "Not much, I don't think," was his reply. "It seemed to be blowing a bit on the edge though by the look of the sea."

"Drop down to the sea and let me take a drift sight," I asked.

Doug complied and I now found that I had a headwind with no drift to speak of. My instructor's advice came back: "If you think you're right, do something about it." I was rapidly getting in a complete mental muddle and I could feel hysteria hovering behind me. Over the intercom I gave Doug a big alteration of course to the east. He accepted it without comment and swung the aircraft round. I remember seeing the shadows in the cockpit swing round and thinking, "It's just got to be right."

Doug was quiet; he seemed to sense that I was panicky and made no comment but he seemed to sit up straighter in his seat. I gazed forward at the little piece of sky I could see between Doug's head and the edge of his windscreen, and just willed the Azores to appear. The sea below lost its white horses and I was just wondering if I had the moral courage to take another sun line and check that I was closing with my original track when very faintly I heard Lagens radio. I snapped out a request for a bearing to which he replied with a first-class bearing. With a dry mouth I plotted it, it went within twenty miles of my DR position. Lagens signals built up rapidly to very loud and I realised that I had been having HF propagation problems. I was soon able to prove that I was heading directly towards Lagens which was later confirmed by picking up the Lagens radio range station and later on Doug's comforting statement over the intercom, "Right on the nose—we shall be there in twenty minutes—makes us about thirty minutes behind the flight plan time."

A wave of relief swept over me, we had been displaced 120 miles in that front.

The rest of the trip to Maison Blanche passed without incident and during our two days in a rest camp waiting for a ride back to Rabat Sale I realised that I had been fighting a very comfortable war compared with some people.

Eventually an RAF Dakota flew us to Rabat Sale where we joined a South Atlantic Ferry Liberator operated by Ferry Command which carried us back to Montreal.

Back in Montreal I went to the navigational school and went over everything again with my old instructor. He could offer no solution except that perhaps Doug in his twistings had picked up a jet stream that had swept us sideways; an unlikely thing at that altitude but it was all good experience I suppose. His advice was to forget it, perhaps our compasses had both been affected and we had flown due west during our passage of the front.

Things were reasonably quiet in the two-man aircraft field and after a couple of weeks Doug was allocated a Dakota to deliver to Bari in Southern Italy and he asked if I could go along as his radio operator—this was agreed. The copilot and navigator were RAF sergeants in a posting to North Africa. We went via Gander, Azores, Rabat Sale, Tripoli without incident and then set out on the last leg to Bari. This turned out to be an enormous airfield and a hive of activity of both aircraft and ground vehicles, and over the whole hung a huge canopy of dust. There was some misunderstanding and after landing a follow-me jeep, instead of taking us to the RAF dispersal, led us into the British Army loading area. I went aft and as I set the ladder on the sill was almost bowled over by a red-faced Army major demanding, "What the bloody hell was all that junk doing in the aeroplane?"

I started to explain that they were engine spares from America for the RAF but it was like talking to a lunatic.

"I want this aircraft loaded with ammunition at once," he bawled. "Get this stuff out."

By now I had been joined by the two RAF sergeants and Doug but we just couldn't get anywhere.

"Get out of the bloody way, my lads will clear this lot," he shouted and clear it they did. A full cargo of much needed engine spares were flung into the dust and dirt of Bari. Still raving he ordered the Dakota to be loaded with boxes of ammunition. Appeals to his reason fell on completely deaf ears.

"Just take it to . . ."—a jumble of letters and figures, shouted the major as we were literally pushed back into the aircraft and the door slammed behind us. Doug sat in his seat and scratched his head.

"At least he didn't tell us there was a war on. I am getting out of Bari or I might find myself flying a fighter."

We started up the engines and Doug asked permission to taxi to the runway for a take-off. A very busy control tower operator at once granted permission. Doug turned to the two RAF sergeants: "Where did that clown actually want us to take this lot?"

The navigator shrugged his shoulders. "It sounded like some map co-ordinates but I haven't a clue about where they are."

Doug waved me up beween the two pilots. "I am going to take this aeroplane back to the RAF base at Rabat Sale," he said. "I am a civilian ferry pilot; let some other clever clot unravel this lot." I nodded agreement, it was no good trying to argue with the mad major who by now was standing gesticulating in front of the aeroplane; one could almost hear his raucous voice bellowing to get us airborne and on our way.

Doug gunned the motors and we trundled down to where a queue of aeroplanes were waiting to take off. At last it was our turn and we were on our way to Rabat Sale. We landed there and reported to the movements people that we had been sent there from Bari. No one seemed to care where we had come from.

The movements officer pointed out of his window. "There's a ferry Lib landing now on its way to Montreal, I'll put you aboard that." This he did and we were soon roaring across the North Atlantic again en route for Gander and Montreal. I met Doug about a month later, after our partnership had been dissolved, and he told me that when he was last through Rabat the Dakota was still standing where we had parked it.

After a few days' rest in Montreal I was scheduled out again with Doug on a Boston for the United Kingdom. This time we decided to go direct to Prestwick from Gander. All went well until we were at the met. briefing in Gander when we found we were the only Boston on delivery and that there was a possibility of widespread fog in the United Kingdom. It was considered probable that the northern half of the country would be clear and the winds for the crossing would be light. We decided to go. I listened intently all night to Prestwick weather and then it happened—as the dawn broke the whole of the United Kingdom closed in with fog, well beyond our point of no return, we just had to go on. As we neared Prestwick we could see the odd piece of high ground sticking out of the fog which covered Scotland and England like a blanket. The met. office at Prestwick said that we might find an RAF field over in Lincolnshire that would take us. By now the fog was at least 500 feet thick, while we flew in brilliant sunshine on top of it towards Lincoln. I had now gone on to the emergency frequency reserved for "Darkie" which was the distress call. My first call brought half a dozen replies. I explained that we were en route from Gander to Prestwick and had been caught out by the dawn fog. Each aerodrome told the same dismal tale. "Sorry we are shut in tight now, but we think we may clear when the sun gets to work on the fog. How long can you remain airborne?" Doug and I did our sums again. Doug leaned off the engines until the Boston was flying so slowly that it seemed she must fall out of the sky. Arriving over Lincolnshire I found all the big RAF bomber bases had been alerted and were listening for me on "Darkie". The story was depressingly the same—just no visibility at all.

We now computed that we could stay aloft for two more hours then it would be dry tanks. "We can't promise a clearance within two hours," Waddington told us. "We can hear your engines overhead, what do you intend to do?"

"We will hang around for a bit," I replied.

"We think that the Wash area may clear first," they said, "go down there."

This we did and soon Feltwell told us that they could hear our engines.

I knew now just where we were but a fine lot of good it did us. Doug's voice came over the intercom, "We can only hang around and wait, it's going to be a long hour and a half."

A new voice came up from Feltwell, it was their CO. "We have checked everywhere for you but see no prospect of you landing at any of the airfields around here for quite a while." He gave us a course and distance to fly, "that will take you over heathland; you can try and put her down there," and then came the fateful words, "It's that or bailing out."

Although I had unconsciously been aware of the alternatives, to have them spelled out to me came as a shock. I had been so busy with the navigation and radio that the inevitable conclusion had been pushed into the back of my mind.

"Doug, I know this part of the country, I went to school at Thetford, it's heath all right but it has been made over to forestry land and planted with fir-trees. There are also a lot of woods mixed up with it."

Doug was completely calm, "Okay, that settles it, we jump, give me a course to aim this old Boston out to sea and then we had best get on our way."

"Due north will do," I replied.

Doug's calm voice went on, "Okay, north it is and I am going up to 5,000 feet, now pull that parachute harness so bloody tight that you can't stand upright."

I looked around at the Boston fuselage, it looked strong enough to last forever, it was a brilliant sunny morning, even the blanket of fog below looked solid, surely I had not got to leave this world and trust myself to this square pack clipped to my chest. For a moment my mind ran away, were we over the land still? Had we made a complete mess of our fuel figures? Perhaps we had hours of endurance. Doug's voice, unemotional as ever, brought me back to reality.

"5,000—shove your canopy back and jump when you are ready. Don't forget to take off your glasses and disconnect your intercom plug and good luck old son—count ten before you pull the handle."

With the canopy back the roaring of the slipstream and the motors seemed to fill the cockpit with an unbearable noise. I pushed up on to my seat and swung one leg into the slipstream. It seemed that a giant hand jerked on my leg. I saw a blurr of black as the tail flashed by. I forgot to count ten, I remember thinking I must find the handle and then something flashed in front of my face followed shortly by a vicious jerk—I was floating down towards the fog, completely unharmed and feverishly clasping the parachute release handle. The first sensation was one of utter quiet, there seemed to be no sound and I floated downwards gently turning. Then I saw another parachute floating down a long way off—Doug was out. In the completely still sunny air, I seemed to be falling in a straight line and then suddenly the sun went in and an instant later I crunched feet first into a big gorse bush and the canopy flopped over me. My thick flying kit saved me from scratches and in a couple of minutes I was standing alone in dense fog in the middle of Brandon Heath. A feeling of relief washed over me like a wave, I had bailed out and got away with it without a scratch— thanks to Doug I had not even lost my glasses. I shrugged off my parachute harness and was just considering what to do next when I heard the measured clopping of a horse's hooves on a hard road. I shouted at the top of my lungs, the horse stopped, I walked towards where I thought it was and within a few steps I was able to see the loom of a milk float and a horse standing still in the middle of a road. At last I convinced that Norfolk farmhand that I was not the forerunner of a Nazi invasion and he agreed to take me to the nearest police station. This turned out to be Brandon in Suffolk, about three miles away. The sergeant at the station listened stolidly to my story but raised his eyes when I said we had come from Canada. There was a roaring outside the station—Doug had arrived sitting on the back of a farm tractor and also completely unharmed. The sergeant rang up Feltwell RAF station and soon Doug was talking to the CO. It was arranged that the police should give us rail tickets and put us on the next train to London. This was within an hour and Doug and I found ourselves parked in a first-class carriage with our flying kit tied up in two bundles on the luggage rack. At Liverpool Street the RTO took over and that evening saw Doug and me ensconced on the night sleeper to Kilmarnock. I was so completely exhausted both physically and mentally that I have no recollections until we were back in Prestwick.

As was the way of things during those hectic years of war, we never heard if the Boston was found but Doug and I were convinced that it was lost in the North Sea. Doug said that he had trimmed it to fly hands off and he rolled it over on its back so that he could fall out. He saw her roll back and the last he saw she was flying straight and level towards the sea. We reckoned we were about 20 minutes from dry tanks but it is a difficult thing to forecast just when the engines will stop—when all the gauges read zero.

CHAPTER ELEVEN

On our return to Montreal I found that the emphasis had gone off the delivery of Mosquitos and Bostons and I was posted to flying boats as a straight radio operator. The training base for Ferry Command to convert landplane crews to flying boats was at Bouchierville on the St. Lawrence. We were picked up in Montreal each morning and taken by bus to the flying boat base where we spent the days learning to adapt our flying knowledge to a very different type of flying machine. The radiomen flew as crew with the training captains and were taught the handling of the mooring ropes and the operation of the drogues. The first job was to single up the ropes holding the Catalina to the buoy until the aircraft was held only by one rope and a single turn round the bollard. When the pilot had both engines ticking over to his satisfaction, he would call out "turn her loose" and would then taxi off to the take-off position. On landing the aircraft would taxi up to the buoy and the man in the bow position would slip the rope through the ring in the top of the buoy, take a couple of turns round the bollard and gently ease the boat to a stop when she could be permanently secured to the buoy.

This was called "bow hooking". The crew assessed the pilot's capability by his ability to arrive at the buoy at just the right speed —too fast and the bow man wouldn't get the slip rope through the buoy ring, and even if he did he wouldn't have time to take enough turns round the bollard to hold the boat when there was always a chance of being jerked into the water. If the pilot couldn't get speed off the boat he would call for drogues which were conical sea anchors trailed in the water on either side to slow the boat down. Perhaps it was the effect of my eight years at sea but I took to boats and soon reckoned myself a top-class bow hooker and moorer-up.

The whole operation of a flying boat taught infinite patience, nothing was easy—a small engine fault meant rigging platforms from the wing; special tools had to be patiently fetched from the shore by the attendant dinghy which was always busy with another flying boat when you wanted it; anything dropped was lost for ever. To get aboard and ashore you were at the mercy of the dinghy coxswain.

In the air the boats were much slower than landplanes so that the added time of getting things started and the slow transit times made a flight a long operation. In the air the flying boat was roomy and quiet and I liked it after the noise and bustle of landplane deliveries. During my last week at Bouchierville I several times acted as "bow hook" for an American civilian who was converting from landplanes and one evening on the way back to Montreal he asked me if I would join his crew. He had been delivering Liberators before his conversion and had brought his navigator and flight engineer with him. Wayne was a tall, slim, white-haired Californian who I found out later was 62 years old. He was as tough as nails and had been flying airlines all over America for more years than he would ever admit to. Alex, his navigator, was a Canadian, a flight lieutenant from New Glasgow, and Wally, the flight engineer, was a civilian from Vancouver; he was the happiest man I have ever known. I joined this crew with pleasure and the flights in their company remain some of my happiest memories of Ferry Command.

Soon we were called out to the briefing room to find that we had been allocated a Catalina for delivery from Elizabeth City, North Carolina, to Largs Bay on the River Clyde, via Bermuda. We left Montreal by train the next evening for New York to change trains for Norfolk, Virginia, where we were to be met by bus and taken on to Elizabeth City. The Norfolk train left Grand Penn station in New York the following evening and then our problems started. The copilot was a handsome young American called Carl who had only recently joined Ferry Command and in the parlour coach he got into conversation with a very glamorous young woman who "just loved fliers". Carl took her to dinner and then apparently confided that he had some top grade liquor in his bag which he had brought on his last trip. He was in the berth below mine and later in the evening shoved his head through my curtains. "Got myself something going," he said. He was dressed in his pyjamas and dressing gown. "She's a couple of coaches up—I'll see you in Norfolk in the morning."

The next morning the rest of the crew met for breakfast in the dining car but there was no sign of Carl. I explained to Wayne that "he had something going in the front of the train".

Wayne looked at me for a second and then burst into a roar of laughter. "Did he say where in the front?" he asked.

"He said a couple of carriages," I replied.

Wayne's laughter increased. "The train was in one part when

we left New York but it divided during the night and the front half went on to Washington. I reckon lover boy is arriving in Washington about now in his pyjamas and dressing gown."

And so it was. We arrived at Norfolk, Carl was still missing and I put his B4 bag aboard the bus for Elizabeth City and off we set. Ferry Command had an office in the Virginia Dare Hotel and rooms had been reserved for us there. I booked Carl and myself in to a double room, Wayne reported Carl missing to the office and we settled down to await events. Carl turned up the next day just before lunch with quite a story. All went well, he said, for the first part of the night for after a judicious bribe to the porter he and his girl friend had settled down in her upper berth with a supply of paper cups and his bottle. His next recollection was of being roughly shaken into wakefulness by his girl friend. "For Christ's sake beat it, we are running into Washington." She was no longer crazy about fliers. "Get the hell out of it, I'm meeting my old man here."

Carl dropped into the passageway which was full of people getting dressed for their arrival at Washington. There was a new redcap on duty and he eyed Carl sourly as he pushed into the man's room. As the train began to slow, the room cleared rapidly and then the redcap poked his head round the door. Carl called him in and told his story and then for the first time heard of the train dividing. The redcap said he could only call the railway police and when the train had stopped he slipped out of the door and locked it. Soon Carl was being escorted across the crowded platform, still clad in his dressing gown and slippers, by two large policemen. He was taken before the senior detective in the station who roared with laughter when he heard the full story. Carl was without a ticket and means of identification but the detective got in touch with the British Purchasing Commission. Telephones buzzed between Washington and Montreal and late in the afternoon an RAF officer arrived; he had brought some secondhand clothes, some money and a rail ticket to Norfolk, Virginia. He insisted on buying Carl dinner and hearing the story firsthand before putting him on a train with a wealth of advice about talking to strange young women on railway stations.

In a couple of days we were called out to the US Air Force base and Wayne was assigned a brand new Catalina for delivery to England. It was standing on flotation gear on a slipway and it was decreed that we would do an acceptance test flight. The whole operation was most efficient. We were allowed to roll slowly down the slipway and as the Catalina became waterborne, frogmen released the undercarriage legs from the hull and they were towed away while we taxied up to a buoy. The test flight was successful and an hour later we were moored up again. The Catalina was fitted with radar and the next day Alex and I were given a one-day course on how to use it—my first introduction to radar.

The next morning we all arrived at the base again and set about going to Bermuda. The boat had been beached again, Alex produced a flight plan of eight hours while Wally and I checked the boat and stowed away our gear. The Catalina had a cockpit for two pilots, then a large compartment with the navigator's table on the port side and a radio desk and equipment on the starboard side. The next compartment had a huge auxiliary tank in it and access to the engineer's position in the vertical stub connecting the wings to the hull, it also contained the hotplate. Aft of this was another compartment with two blisters and aft of that again was a catwalk to the tail compartment which contained the flare shute for dropping smoke floats to measure the wind. Our Bouchierville training had made us reasonably competent at handling the boat and we were soon winging our way past Cape Hatteras for Bermuda. The Catalina was big and roomy, the radio equipment was extremely powerful—no problems about being able to raise anyone. After a couple of hours Wally climbed down from his eyrie under the wings. He switched on the hotplate and fumbled around in the grub box. I got out of my seat to help and we had salmon salad and tinned peaches for lunch with hot coffee—a big improvement on frozen cheese sandwiches and lukewarm coffee tasting of the thermos jug.

Slowly the hours passed with only the Bermuda weather to copy once an hour and the sending of a position report once an hour. I was hardly overworked. At last Alex turned. "By my calculations we are 100 miles from the island, would you try that magic box and see if you can confirm it?"

I fiddled with the radar and then I saw it—a tiny flash of light right at the top of the display tube. "Got something dead ahead seventy-five miles, Alex," I said.

"That's it," he said.

Gradually the tiny flash resolved itself into a blob of indeterminate shape and then I found two more blobs had appeared much closer in. Greatly daring I called over the intercom, "Two ships in line astern twenty miles on the port bow."

Wayne laughed. "Yes man, two Navy jobs. I'll keep well away from them."

Wayne took us for a joyride round Bermuda. It looked a lovely place from the air. Soon we were in touch with the control launch who gave us a direction to land by Darrells Island. Wayne greased the Catalina on to a gentle sea, I opened up the nose and the white control launch edged in and took us in tow for the buoy. We were accommodated in the Belmont Hotel and for a week Alex and I spent our time swimming, wandering around Bermuda and talking to the other crews waiting for the right weather conditions to make the crossing to Largs Bay—all 3,000 miles of it. Alex and Wayne visited the met. office each morning to return with the same dismal story—"Try again tomorrow", and then after a week, Wayne came back and said, "Crack of dawn in the morning lads, twenty-seven hours—a hell of a long trip but if we don't go now we may have to wait a long time for a second chance."

Wally went off to the boat to potter around, Alex vanished with his maps and I was left alone. We all met again for dinner and then went off to bed with a 5 a.m. call. I slept like a top. At 6 a.m. we were stowing our gear away on the launch that was to take us from the Belmont Steps jetty to the boat.

The Catalina was riding low in the water with a complete load of fuel; Wally had "loaded her up to the gills" he said. I took off my uniform and climbed into an overall and opened the front hatch. Assisted by the boatman in the launch I singled up the moorings to a short slip, I then checked out the radio and turned to Wayne. "I am ready to go when you are, skipper." The rest of the crew were also ready. I went to the front hatch and held on to the short slip, the two Pratt and Whitneys burst into life, Wayne was standing on his seat with his head out of the hatch. "Turn her loose and we'll be on our way." I pulled in the short slip and climbed back into the cockpit and took my seat in the radio compartment. The Catalina wallowed along into the Great Sound and then sluggishly turned into wind.

"She's heavy," said Wayne. "Not much bloody wind either, she'll run to hell and gone before she gets airborne."

With both engines at take-off revs we started to thunder along. After two minutes the thumps of the waves began to grow less. "On the step," yelled Wayne and about thirty seconds later the Catalina lumbered into the air, climbing slowly on course for Scotland. Wally informed Wayne that the motors had disliked that sort of treatment and had begun seriously to overheat.

"We'll nurse 'em now Wally, I thought she just wasn't going to unstick at all."

At 5,000 feet we levelled out and the engines were throttled back to long range cruise; we had started our long trip. Slowly the hours drifted by, lunch time came and then it began to get dark. About midnight a long message came through from Gander which when decoded gave us a new picture of the weather. Alex dived into his flight plan and came up with the news that the new situation gave us a flight plan time of thirty hours. Alex and Wayne hunched over the navigation table and then Wayne made his decision.

"We'll keep on, this forecast can be a bit pessimistic"—and keep on we did. Then it was getting light again; we had been twenty-four hours on the way. With the dawn the whole crew seemed to be overcome with fatigue and I nodded off at the radio table. I awoke with a start; I had slept for an hour and found that everyone had succumbed to sleep. I checked up, but with the autopilot engaged the Catalina was still getting on with the business of flying to Largs Bay. Wally and I now cooked up some bacon and eggs and coffee on the hotplate. It seemed to wake us all up and we settled down to the last part of our flight. Alex passed me a new ETA, the winds had not been quite as hostile as had been forecast —the flight was only going to be twenty-seven hours after all.

Some time later Alex asked me to try the radar. "See if you can interpret what you think you see into where I think I am." His faith in radar was not very great yet. I fiddled around until I got a picture on the screen and tried to interpret what I saw.

"Looks like a headland about 30 miles away on the starboard bow, and then a single island just slightly off the port fifty miles away"—dead silence from Alex for about ten seconds.

"Either you're a bloody good guesser or I'm a bloody good navigator. That headland is Bloody Foreland and the island is Eagle Island."

Wayne was as lacking in faith as Alex. "Let's see if that radar is telling the truth," he said, and put the Catalina into a gentle descent. We broke cloud at 3,000 feet.

"Damn right it is, there's Eagle Island smack on the nose."

Alex passed Wayne a new course and an ETA one and a half hours on. We settled down again for the longest hour of a long trip. Carl and Wayne were map reading and Alex fell fast asleep across the navigation table. At long last Wayne called me forward and I stood on the sill between the two pilots. Wayne pointed over the bow. "There's Largs Bay and the control launch is circling the landing area. Get 'em on the radio."

This I did and a voice with a thick Scots burr replied with landing instructions. Carl looked at me when I acknowledged. "What language is that? Didn't sound like English to me."

"Or me," said Wayne, "give me those instructions again."

Soon we were lined up for a landing and then came that indescribable tearing sound of a boat hull cutting the water. I opened the hatch and glanced at my watch—twenty-seven hours forty-three minutes from Bermuda to Clyde. The launch edged in and dropped a rope over the bollard that I had set up.

"Okay laddie," said the control officer. "We'll tow you to the buoy and moor you up, tell your skipper to cut the motors."

As the rumble of the idling motors died away, I climbed back into the hull and started packing up. I felt completely exhausted and drained of energy. We all slept on the bus taking us to Prestwick; I seemed to sleep for the next three days. We made a slow flight back to Montreal on the return ferry but it didn't worry me, I slept the whole way.

After about ten days, the briefing call came—another Catalina from Elizabeth City to the Clyde. We all met at the briefing office and found that we had been allocated a new copilot; Wayne had not been too impressed with Carl's capabilities. The new copilot was J. B. Cooke—Cookie as he became—a short, fat American civilian who claimed to be the only professional copilot in Ferry Command. He had been a copilot of every aeroplane that had two seats in the front.

The trip was as before—New York, Norfolk, where we managed to arrive this time complete with our copilot. Elizabeth City had a Catalina being readied for flight; it would be ready in a couple of days and I asked if I could go to the radar school until the aircraft was ready. The Americans were quite helpful and when I left I knew a little more than my previous trip. The trip to Bermuda was uneventful but we found the Belmont Manor Hotel full of crews waiting to get across to the United Kingdom.

The weather was unsuitable for about fourteen days during which we got to know some of the waiting crews quite well. There was Captain—later Sir—Patrick Gordon Taylor who had gained undying fame for his exploits as Kingsford-Smith's navigator on the *Southern Cross* and *Lady Southern Cross*. He was an unobtrusive, quietly spoken man who, according to his crew, would not discuss his previous flying experiences at all. Another captain was Hughie Greene, later to gain fame as a television commentator; a friend of mine was his radioman and he claimed that life in Hughie Greene's crew was an hilarious business. Day after day Wayne and Alex visited the met. and then at long last the flight was on—twenty-seven hours again, but we were all tired of waiting and the next morning found us taxiing into wind for another take-off. I don't know just how long we lumbered across the Great Sound, Wally later claimed that he had take-off power on for four minutes before we reluctantly took to the air. Slowly the hours passed, the light faded and then it was night, the huge great circle from Bermuda to Largs Bay took us comparatively close to Gander and then out into the Atlantic again. Alex was happy navigating away with plenty of stars until we drifted into fog over the Grand Banks but we were steadily falling back on the flight plan. Then it was light again and after helping with the breakfast I climbed into the co-pilot's seat. We were snoring along just below the cloud and glancing below I saw in the sea a lifeboat full of men. I called to Wayne that there was a boat filled with men on my side.

"Try and keep your eye on them while I make a gentle turn," cried Wayne.

Cookie shoved the binoculars into my lap but the boat was plainly visible to the naked eye.

"Got it." Wayne now had the boat in view and he dropped down to make a low pass. They were obviously in a bad way; some of the figures were lying down in the bottom of the boat and I could see that they were half covered with water. The lifeboat had a sail up; it looked like a dipping lug. One man was standing on a thwart with his arm round the mast and literally looked me right in the face as we flew over. Another man in a yellow sou'wester was crouching over the rudder bar. He waved feebly with one hand.

"By Christ, they look pretty far gone." It was Alex's voice from the rear blister. "Can't we do anything?"

There was quite a sea running and Wayne's voice was bitter. "If I try and put her down on that lot, we will all be smashed up."

I jumped out of my seat and called Gander. "We are circling a lifeboat half full of men and some are alive."

Alex pushed a position report into my hand which I immediately transmitted. Gander's reply was instant. "Can you land and help them?"

I replied that the sea was far too rough.

"Tell 'em we will try and drop them some water," Wayne's voice came over the intercom. I climbed again into the copilot's seat and as Wayne made another low pass at the boat, I studied the occupants carefully. This time the man in the yellow sou'wester

108

didn't lift his hand and the man by the mast seemed to have slipped into the bottom of the boat.

"Wayne, it's too late; they can't help themselves. If we can't land and help them they are goners."

I looked across the cockpit at Wayne. He seemed to have aged years in the last few minutes. "I can only circle and try to find a ship to guide to them," he muttered.

"And we can't do that for long," said Wally, "we're light on fuel already."

I called Gander who had a message waiting for us. "You are ordered to proceed, we will send surface craft to the lifeboat."

Wayne made one more low run and as we passed over the boat he raised his hand in salute. "Poor bastards, what a way to go."

Within minutes the boat was lost sight of astern. Just another war casualty in the North Atlantic. We never heard any more about it; in wartime these casualties were all too common.

We plodded away and still Alex reported that we were behind time, we had now been thirty hours on the way, the last six of it below cloud, and Alex was using HF/DF for his navigation when he turned to me and said, "Try the radar, you should see something soon."

I couldn't see a thing and then Prestwick came in with some disconcerting news. "Fog is forming at Largs Bay, the Glasgow balloons have gone up and the area is dangerous, recommend you land as soon as possible in the Solway Firth." Alex gave an alteration of course for the Solway Firth and I got busy on the radar and we found it without trouble.

The Firth was calm and fog was forming along the shorelines. Wayne landed straightaway and as we slowed I saw an RAF launch curve out from the shore towards us. The launch crew were most helpful, they literally took over the boat and towed it away to Silloth. Another launch came alongside the blister and we all disembarked—five very weary men; the flight had taken thirty-four hours twenty minutes. We were accommodated that night in the RAF mess at Silloth but I was so utterly exhausted that I remember nothing about it and the next day we were taken by bus to Prestwick.

I had become friendly with Bob Tuck, one of the radio operators who manned the radio station at Prestwick. We had originally met at sea years before and renewed our friendship over a few beers in the bar of the Orangefield Hotel at Prestwick. We knew each other well enough to recognise each other's "fist" when sending morse.

After our Bermuda to Silloth marathon, we met in the bar as usual, he admitted hearing me just after leaving Bermuda, having a day off and being amazed to hear me still pounding away when he came back on duty. He also told me a strange story about a lost Liberator that I have never heard satisfactorily explained. The previous week he said a Liberator had left for Gander to Prestwick; it carried the usual mixed crew—the skipper was an RAF wing commander, the radioman was a very experienced Canadian civilian while the rest of the crew were Service personnel on posting to the United Kingdom. For the first half of the crossing the situation appeared normal. The Liberator passed its position reports to Prestwick and occasionally asked for a DF bearing from Prestwick and Reykjavik. The operations officers plotted them and the Liberator seemed to be proceeding normally, then at about 30 deg. W it suddenly asked for a QDM from Prestwick. This means "give me a magnetic heading to steer for Prestwick in zero wind". The usual request for a bearing was QTE—"give me a true bearing from you". However, Prestwick supplied the QDM; the request was repeated every fifteen minutes for an hour. Gander, Reykjavik and Prestwick now took bearings and plotted the Liberator's position. It appeared to be flying almost due north. Messages to this effect elicited only a "wait" signal from the aircraft. At last Prestwick asked the Liberator to transmit for a bearing and Bermuda, Reykjavik, Prestwick and Gander each took a bearing and passed it to Prestwick. When plotted, they gave a small cocked hat position which was far north of the normal west/east track. Requests to the radioman in the Liberator from Prestwick elicited only the response that he had understood their messages and would they "wait".

After a long silence the Liberator opened up again, but it was only to ask for yet another QDM; plotted back at Prestwick this put the aircraft about 400 miles north of track. Again a message giving the aircraft's position and a suggested new heading to fly was receipted by the Liberator's radioman followed by the now infuriating signal of "wait please". Twice more in the next hour he asked for QDMs and that was the last that was ever heard or seen of that aircraft and crew.

I have often wondered what could possibly have gone on in that cockpit but have never been able to produce a solution that would even vaguely fit the circumstances. The only person we know who was operating normally was the radioman but had he communication with the rest of the crew?

A couple of nights later we were scheduled out on the return ferry and were most impressed to find that seats had now been fitted; the ghastly return flights back to Montreal, sweating or freezing under those eiderdowns, were a thing of the past. After the usual few days off, Wayne and I found ourselves on a new type of Catalina delivery. The Russians had been allocated some Catalinas on lease-lend by the United States and we were to assist a Russian crew to take over and complete the delivery to Russia. We had heard the odd rumours that this could be, at best, an odd experience and so it turned out to be. We made our now familiar train journey to Elizabeth City and settled down in the Virginia Dare Hotel to await the arrival of the Russians. I don't know how they came to the US base but one day the Ferry Command office told Wayne that they were there and arrangements had been made for us to do an acceptance test flight the next morning. I don't know if the language was the barrier or if we were just basically different but the next morning Wayne found that we had a real problem on our hands. There was a Russian crew of seven led by a full colonel. The US Air Force interpreter explained that the colonel would fly as captain, Wayne as copilot while I was to help the radio operator and the navigator. The meeting was far from friendly on their part and the interpreter explained that not one of them had a word of English or that they claimed not to have. The Catalina was waiting on the slipway and we climbed on board. Apart from the fact that some of the controls had Russian lettering on them, it seemed to be a normal type Catalina; the radar was conspicuous by its absence. I sat down at the radio table and switched on the equipment. It was promptly switched off again by a large crop-headed Russian who pushed a board under my nose which contained a list of Russian/English phrases. He pointed to "the equipment is working"; I searched for something like "so what" or "let me have a go" but the case didn't seem to be covered so I promptly switched on the equipment only to have it just as promptly switched off again. I swung round and leaned over the navigation table only to be elbowed aside. I somehow had the feeling that I wasn't wanted. I at last put on my headset and plugged in and turned on the intercom.

"What the hell's going on Wayne?" I asked, and then told him my problems.

He was having a similar sort of problem up front.

"They seem to be convinced that we are going to sabotage everything we touch, the stupid bastards."

The navigator's lips compressed. I thought that one knows English but the rest of the crew milling around gave no sign. The Russians took charge of the unmooring and starting of the engines, I used the R/T with Wayne waving his hands and pointing. At last we turned into wind, the colonel had the controls and slammed open the throttles. As the boat surged forward I was standing on the sill between the two pilots. I was yanked back into the cabin and my place taken by a large wooden-faced Russian. Wayne told me later that the colonel was a poor pilot and that he snatched the controls away from him halfway through the take-off. I did the test flight sitting on the catwalk between the cabin tanks. Wayne apparently landed the aircraft and then the boat was full of pushing, scrambling Russians mooring up. Wayne and I tackled the interpreter about just what we were supposed to do; he was sympathetic but could only suggest that Wayne did the flying while I just tried to help where I could. Meanwhile our crew had marched into the waiting transport with military precision, leaving one man to sleep on the boat. They obviously did not trust even the US Air Force to look after USSR property.

Wayne told the interpreter that we would leave for Botwood in the morning. Botwood was a flying-boat base on Gander Lake close to Gander airfield. The next morning our problems started again; the Russians grabbed the met. folder and after a long and noisy discussion produced a flight plan which the interpreter said gave a flight time of nineteen hours to Gander. As the distance was about 1,500 miles, this did not sound right at all. Wayne insisted that we do our own—this appeared to precipitate almost an international incident. At last the met. man gave us a copy of the met. forecast and Wayne and I set to and produced a flight plan of about seventeen hours and this was the one we filed.

The pattern of yesterday was again reproduced. Wayne made the take-off after I had operated the R/T and then I was immediately bundled into the blister at the rear where I plugged into the intercom. In the next couple of hours two attempts to go forward were physically blocked off. At last Wayne called me and asked if I had anything on the Botwood weather. I explained that I couldn't even get forward. "You'll just have to hack your way through and get on the radio, it wasn't too good when we left and we may have to divert." This time my passage was unobstructed, somebody who understood must have issued some orders. I plugged into the radio station, another large Russian was listening intently on the receiver to absolutely nothing. I leaned across and found it was 10 kilocycles off the guard frequency. As I returned Gander came blasting in with the Catalina's call sign saying she had a message for us. I watched his face—not a flicker of interest—that gentleman was either a brilliant actor or couldn't read morse. I switched on the transmitter, told Gander to go ahead and copied down a long message in code, without a glance from the radioman, if that's what he was. Decoded it gave some new wind velocities for the rest of the trip. I amended my copy of the forecast and offered it to the Russian navigator. His chart was absolutely blank—I found later that he covered his working chart when I was in the cockpit. I asked for and received the weather from Gander, it had improved on the forecast and I told Wayne.

"How's the flight going?" he asked.

"I don't know," I replied. "Nature Boy is either doing it all in his head or has hidden his chart."

"What a deal we've got," commented Wayne. "We seem to be doing all right, leave 'em be. You're not built to take on six large Russians, try and rustle up some grub."

As I turned away there was a roar of slipstream from the cockpit—a gale blew round the cockpit and maps and papers flew in every direction. Wayne and I there and then discovered a new type of instrument flight—when in cloud open the side window. Fortunately we only encountered the odd cloud because the colonel avoided all he could but when he did enter one, we had to endure the colonel's side window being open. When I went to the carton containing the food, it was bare. I just don't know—it was full when we loaded it but everything, including the cutlery, had vanished. Wayne was almost beside himself, he loved his food.

"What the hell have they done with it?" he asked.

I looked down my translation board but couldn't find "who's pinched the bloody grub"—another situation that the interpreters never thought would arise.

"Sorry Wayne, I expect it's going to feed the poor starving Cossacks," I told him over the intercom and I settled down again in the blister.

After a long time Wayne's voice over the Russian gabble said, "I'm going to alter course a bit, I think I can see Sable Island, I want you to plot me a new course from there to Botwood."

Again progress to the cockpit was unimpeded and again I found an absolutely clean chart. I plotted a course to Botwood, and worked out a time of arrival. "Tell me when we're overhead," I said to Wayne, "then I'll give you a new course and ETA for Gander."

After a time Wayne said, "Right over it now." I passed him the new information; we had about five hours to go. As I turned away from the navigation table, the Russian navigator started carefully to erase the pencil marks from the chart. Wayne map-read the rest of the way to Gander and then called me forward to work the R/T. It was now a routine procedure—Wayne landed the boat and the Russians moored it up, again leaving one man as a guard. In the bus taking us to the airport at Gander, the interpreter tried to smooth things over when Wayne and I complained.

"Every crew has the same problem," he said. "You've only one more leg to do and I can't really help except that I'll get you both lunch boxes for stowing in your baggage. I'm a second generation American, my old man's a Russian and I can speak the language but I can't understand them. They don't talk to me; any complaints I pass on to them from the Ferry Command crews they totally ignore. This business of pinching the rations has been going on ever since they started making deliveries."

The interpreter then went on to explain that they insisted on flying for maximum range even on short sectors; one irate Ferry Command captain claimed that the Russians were flying so slowly that over the South Coast of Newfoundland they were overhauled by a seagull which rested on the wing for an hour before taking off again and being lost sight of ahead. "This probably explains some of our time problems," said Wayne. "They pulled off power every time my back was turned—saving aviation fuel no doubt."

The next morning they produced a flight plan of twenty-four hours for a distance of about 1,800 miles but this time we let it go; all Wayne and I wanted to do was to get to Iceland. There would be a tail wind and we had completely full tanks. "The only thing I want you to watch, and create trouble if you must to get the information, is the temperature of the sea—it's too damn close to freezing for my liking; I don't want a load of ice when we hit the water," said Wayne.

We went through the familiar routine and soon we were winging away across the rocky coastline of Newfoundland on our long trudge to Iceland. I was relegated to my usual place in the blister soon to be joined by Wayne who had got out of his seat to stretch his legs after take-off and who then found his seat occupied by a Russian. Flying this Catalina was like playing a game of musical chairs.

Slowly the hours drifted by, Wayne and I opened up our baggage and took out the lunch boxes; Gander had done us proud but in the middle of our picnic we became aware that we were being watched by two Russians. They were, as usual, deadpan about it but we sensed that they considered it a waste of good food. At last Wayne and I forced our way into the cockpit, I pushed the radio operator out of his chair, collected a temperature report and some HF/DF bearings from Gander, Reykjavik, Prestwick and Bermuda, and Wayne plotted the bearings on a chart that was as usual completely unmarked. We both leant over the chart table and did a few sums under the unwavering stare of the navigator.

"Going a good bit faster than usual," said Wayne. "Must have a good old chuff wind." He poked his head into the cockpit. "Just about got her hanging on a sky hook; if he opens his window now, she'll stall for sure."

We moved aft again to our private office and settled down. About an hour before our estimated time of arrival, as distinct from the Russian one, we repeated our trip to the cockpit. As I plotted our position, I found we were making an excellent ground speed and should be over Reykjavik harbour in about thirty minutes. As I turned to go aft, I was rudely grabbed by a Russian who pointed to his translation board "The transmitter has broken down" and shook a large and smelly fist under my nose. I checked the transmitter, the valves were all right, it looked like a blown HT fuse. I crouched over the power unit and removed the cover when something hard was jammed into my back. It was a revolver held by one of the crew—I was sabotaging his equipment! Feeling most unwarlike I held the blackened HT fuse under his nose and then replaced it with the spare from the holder in the lid. As I stood up, the character with the revolver stood back, I checked the transmitter, it was working and I scrambled aft. That cockpit was no place for me! Later we went forward again and Wayne took control; I worked the R/T and after a trip of seventeen hours we swished down on to the harbour at Reykjavik. We climbed into the RAF launch complete with our baggage and chugged away from that Catalina with its Red Stars without a backward look.

I discussed our trip later with other crews who had assisted the Russians on Catalina deliveries and most of their experiences were different. Some Russians even spoke a few words of English, some appeared quite competent, others quite hopeless. Perhaps our crew were dominated by the colonel's high rank. The flight engineer, whom we called the Commissar, also appeared to be a person of considerable influence.

In the transit mess Wayne met a friend of his who was delivering a Dakota to Prestwick and he offered us a lift there. Next morning he circled the harbour for us and we found the mooring where we had left the Catalina was empty—they must have made an early start on their long trip to Russia.

When Wayne and I arrived in Prestwick we found that our record for the longest crossing from Bermuda to Largs Bay had been handsomely beaten by a Catalina that had taken no less than thirty-six hours forty minutes and after that prodigious effort, the boat had been lost. Arriving in fog, they had orbited over the Solway Firth area until nearly out of fuel and then, assisted by radar, the captain had positioned himself and let down at a constant rate of descent until he made a perfect landing in a glassily calm Irish Sea. Unfortunately, the Catalina was then taken in tow by a destroyer whose captain had only a fragmentary knowledge of flying boat towage. Full ahead on both engines resulted in the Catalina's nose being smashed in and the boat sinking. The crew were picked up and I gathered that all hands were entertained for fifteen minutes while an angry aircraft captain entertained an embarrassed destroyer captain on his own bridge in the language of the Deep South which concluded with the information that he was a cotton pickin' bastard.

CHAPTER TWELVE

Two types of flying boat that had been delivered to the RAF had proved to be unsuitable for their requirements. They were the Mariner, a deep hulled, twin-engined flying boat with a cranked wing, and the Coronado. It was decreed that the Mariners should be ferried back to the US. The Coronados were to be ferried to Boston where they would be fitted with seats to operate on the return ferry service. In the winter they were to fly between Bermuda and Lagos and ferry crews back from West African deliveries. In the summer they were to operate from Bouchierville to Largs Bay and assist on the North Atlantic ferry.

The boats had been collected at Wig Bay on Loch Ryan, the home of No. 51 MU of the RAF. As the MU were unfamiliar with the American radio equipment, I was sent to Wig Bay to assist in preparing the radio for the long trip back to the United States. When I arrived at Wig Bay I found it to be a dispersed site—the mess, the huts, flying control—they were scattered all over the Scottish countryside. When I first arrived a bus came early in the morning to transport us from the huts in which we slept to the mess for breakfast. After that, it made a circular tour of HQ, the hangars and stores. Runs were made later to collect people for lunch and for dinner at the end of the day. The Mariners and Coronados were scattered along the shore of Loch Ryan from Wig Bay to Stranraer, and in the first week I almost walked my way through two pairs of shoes. In the second week I was issued with an airman's bicycle, an incredibly heavy device but a vast improvement on walking everywhere. I wanted to get the job over with.

The first flying boat for delivery was a Mariner; the RAF ground crew had overhauled the engines and I was able to get all the radio serviceable in about a week. I rang Prestwick and they said they would send a crew down to do a test flight preparatory to its delivery to the States. Then came a bitter disappointment—I was not to be a member of the delivery crew, but was to turn my attention to a Coronado that was soon to be delivered to Boston. Wig Bay was not exactly an easy place to work at, the permanent staff were engaged on the repair and overhaul of Sunderlands for Coastal Command and I was definitely the odd man out. However, Prestwick assured me that I would be on the Coronado crew so I set about making its radio serviceable.

The story of the Coronado is that Consolidated Aircraft who built the Catalina were so pleased with its range that they decided to make their next flying boat twice as big in the hope that it would go twice as far. This resulted in the Coronado which was a huge aircraft and dwarfed every other flying boat except perhaps the Boeing 314. When I climbed over one beached at Wig Bay I was amazed at the size of the cockpit and the comfortable arrangement for the crew. In the bow compartment were two wide doors with platforms below them for "bow hooking". Then came another compartment with four comfortable berths, the main hull had two decks and on the top deck was a full cooking range and a 60 hp auxiliary power unit. The flight deck had really first-class radio equipment, two direction finders, radar and Loran. It was more like a ship's bridge than an aircraft cockpit.

For nearly a week I crawled around that Coronado finding my way around the complex equipments and making sure that everything worked. Then the chief technical officer tackled me. "We have got the mechanical side of that boat as near the top line as we can; if your radio is okay, ask for a crew to come and get it off my doorstep."

One of the resident test pilots overheard the conversation.

"I'll fly you up to Prestwick in the morning if you can fix me a ride on that Coronado when it test flies."

I agreed and so I met Wayne again. We left Wig Bay in an amphibious Walrus the next morning and we taxied up alongside a return Ferry Liberator at Prestwick that was loading crews for a return flight to Montreal. A stream of ribald comment swept over me as I poked my head out of that waddling amphibian when its clattering engine stopped. Wayne was amongst the Lib's passengers and in particular was most insulting. "Get your ass out of the box Boy and sling it aboard this Lib, I want you on my next Cat delivery."

The Wig Bay test pilot was asked pointedly if he flew it, rode it, walked it or paddled it. My friends were apparently not impressed with my conveyance.

I never saw Wayne again. He made several more Catalina trips and then retired to California—he was then well into his sixties.

Prestwick agreed to call a crew together for the Coronado and the Wig Bay test pilot and I flew back to Wig Bay and landed on Loch Ryan. During the ten days I waited for them to turn up I flew several times in Sunderlands and was again struck by the large difference in crew comfort between British and American aircraft. I appreciated that the austerity and paucity of equipment in the Sunderland was largely dictated by wartime conditions, but it did seem a shame that so little was done towards making the long arduous patrols on which they were engaged a little more comfortable. Bow hooking in a Sunderland was a hazardous game played in the front turret several feet from the water level. Compared with the wide door and platform of the Coronado a foot above the water, it was hard going indeed.

When the crew arrived I found that it was a pilot and copilot, two radio navigators of whom I was to be one and two flight engineers. The American captain went by the odd name of Henry Seagal and he was inevitably called Henry the Seagull. The test flight was satisfactorily carried out and the next morning we set out on the first sector of the trip—Wig Bay to Reykjavik. Henry the Seagull made a good take-off but ten minutes after there was a crack from the port inner; it was immediately feathered but the damage was done. Henry the Seagull had the lowest possible opinion of the dispersal site at Wig Bay and declined to return, instead he elected to fly to Iceland on three engines while I radioed ahead and asked for transportation for the crew from Iceland to America. It was an uneventful flight and the Seagull made a normal landing in the harbour where he secured to a buoy.

At the jetty we were met by an RAF officer who informed us that the US Air Force had booked us out that evening for Gander. We were taken by bus to the American base at Meeks Field where we were bundled aboard a DC–4 and soon were en route for Gander. The aircraft had passenger seats and we all slept away the flight. After a couple of days the Gander authorities found us seats on a Ventura on the Montreal/Gander milk run and we found ourselves back in Montreal.

On the strength of my overseas service in the United Kingdom I was able to wangle myself on a Loran course at Dorval. Loran was a long-range hyperbolic navigation system that had been brought to an operational state by the United States, although the basic idea was British, by the installation of ground stations giving coverage over most of the North Atlantic. It called for some practice in selecting the correct signals and then lining them up and I later became very proficient with it. Most full blown navigators preferred astro and the feeling of satisfaction that comes from a first-class three-star fix, but I found Loran quicker and when I became experienced, I could put a degree of confidence in a Loran fix that I was never able to do with my astro.

After the Loran course, I was called to do a trip as radioman on a Fortress to Cairo. The skipper was an ex-Air France captain whom I had met before; the flight engineer was an old friend and he introduced me to the rest of the crew who with the exception of myself were all RAF officers on a posting to Cairo.

I had not flown in a Fortress before and the flight engineer climbed all over the aircraft showing me around. It was a comfortable aeroplane, the navigator in the nose, the cockpit, a bomb bay and then a completely self-contained "office" for the radio operator. It had a table with a radio receiver on it, a transmitter under it and a large luxurious chair. A door in the rear bulkhead gave access to the rear of the aircraft containing the waist gunner's position and the rear and ball turret gunners. The guns were all stowed away, still in their oiled paper wrappings.

The next morning the skipper, a tall dark man with greying hair, who was a French Count in his own right, called us together. "I want you all to call me Dick," he said, "and I shall use your Christian names"; and so it was throughout the trip to Cairo. The first sector was the usual jog along the Canadian Airways to Gander; sitting back in the luxury of my office I took life easily.

The copilot did the airways flying and talked to the range stations. I just worked the HF and copied the weather; the Fortress was well soundproofed and the engines were such a long way away, they were only a murmur in my office. My thoughts went back to the hideous discomfort of that old Hampden—the war was improving.

We had a perfect flight to Gander but when Dick joined us for a late lunch, he had a face like a thundercloud. "We've got a passenger to Prestwick tonight—and a woman at that!"

"Why us?" asked the copilot. "Does she fancy me do you think?"

Dick was not amused. "She's a young Canadian woman who flies with Air Transport Auxiliary in England. She's been over here on holiday and is now hitching a ride back. She came from Montreal to Gander on one of the milk run aircraft and they have unloaded her on to us for onward transportation."

"We've got no spare seats. Where is she going to sit, Dick?" I asked.

He grunted. "She's a very determined young Canadian lady; maybe she will take my seat and I shall have to move into that box of yours in the back. She's told me ten times already that she has much flying experience and it seems the lowest position she will accept is maybe that of copilot."

The flight lieutenant copilot was not amused and broke in. "Keep her out of the cockpit for Christ's sake, Dick."

"I'll do what I can," said Dick, "but believe me, she's a famous pilot—I dunno, we'll see."

It was decided to leave that evening for Prestwick, and as we were eating our early supper we did indeed "see". Our passenger swept into the dining room and all the heads followed her progress to our table. Dick's reaction was simple—"Now we see I think."

She was smartly dressed in a dark blue uniform with golden wings and was a very pretty "young Canadian lady", as Dick had already pointed out—obviously a young lady who was used to getting her own way. As we all stood up to be introduced she dismissed the half wings of the navigator, engineer and myself and concentrated on Dick and the copilot. We all murmured a few polite banalities but Dick was soon under fire.

"Where do you want me to sit, captain?" she asked. "I would like to act as copilot if you don't mind," and bent a winning smile over our flight lieutenant. "You see I may have to deliver a Fortress in England one day so I would like to be checked out on them."

Dick was not committing himself—"My copilot I want, but later we see," and so the matter was left.

Later when we boarded the aircraft I set up shop in my "office" and our passenger vanished into the cockpit. After the usual run up at the end of the runway, Dick turned the Fort into wind and we rolled along the huge runway and gently took the air.

The Fort seemed to have some of the elegance of the old HP.42. After about half an hour the door from the bomb bay banged open and in flounced an extremely angry young Canadian lady. "That bloody old Frenchman has just told me that there are two places for a woman and the cockpit of a Flying Fortress on an Atlantic delivery is not one of them," she stormed. "He said go back and sleep with the radioman."

I bowed and tried to pour oil on troubled waters by explaining that Dick's English sometimes suffered in times of stress but actually radiomen never slept so she was not to worry. I unpacked my flying clothing and spread it out on the floor; the flight engineer poked his head round the door and contributed both his and the navigator's flying clothing and we made her quite a reasonable bed. At last she simmered down and fell asleep. She must have been pretty tired because she slept until I woke her up half an hour out of Prestwick.

During the night there was a change of radio operator at Prestwick and I recognised the "fist" of my friend Bob Tuck. I was tempted to add to the position report, "Twelve thousand feet over Mid Atlantic sleeping with young Canadian lady." I refrained because the German monitoring stations might have thought we were taking a secret weapon on the aircraft—perhaps we were.

Our passenger scrambled to her feet when I told her how near we were to landing. She looked tousled and very gummy about the eyes and immediately took my seat, balanced her pocket mirror on the receiver and set about effecting repairs. She marched away from that Fortress and its crew after landing at Prestwick without a backward glance.

We spent a couple of days in Prestwick. The RAF explained to Dick that we should have to make a night flight from Prestwick to ten degrees west longitude, fly down ten degrees west until we were abeam Gibraltar and then fly in through the Straits of Gibraltar and on to Cairo. The RAF navigator who had made the trip before, delivering Halifaxes to the Middle East, stayed with us.

We left Prestwick at dusk and flew due west to ten degrees west. We arrived there and turned south just as it became full dark. The sky was cloudless and with a full moon it was almost like flying in daylight. I heard the navigator telling Dick over the intercom that he would have preferred some cloud cover—the Fort was painted white and must have been pretty conspicuous in the moonlight. We had to preserve radio silence and as the hours slowly passed, it was difficult to keep awake; in the early hours of the morning I must have dozed off for I was suddenly awakened by a short and violent vibration of the Fortress. Dick's voice came over the intercom, "What in hell's that?"

For some seconds all was quiet and then the engineer said, "It wasn't the engines; it felt like the turbulence of another aircraft's slipstream." I peered through the small window alongside my table and then I saw it. Turning against the moonlight sky was an aircraft whose silhouette, with its blunt nose and two cylindrical engines, unmistakably identified it as a Junkers 88.

Speechless, I watched it complete what must have been a stall turn and then it was hurtling down at the Fortress. I found my voice—"An '88, diving on us from the port beam," I yelled. Then it was lost and I gazed up through the transparent panel over the radio table; there was a flash of moonlight on metal followed shortly by a shuddering of the Fortress from the buffeting of the '88's slipstream. I jumped to the starboard window, saw another flash in the moonlight and then nothing. Dick's urgent voice was in my phones.

"Watch out for him, all of you, the bastard's bound to come back."

For the next five minutes I peered intently through first one window and then another, a dozen times I imagined I saw that silhouette but nobody saw that '88 again. At last Dick said, "I do believe he's lost us or the sight of our radioman leering through his little window has scared him off."

The copilot broke in. "Patrols in the Bay are always warned about hunting '88s on the lookout for Sunderlands, but I didn't think they got this far west; you sure it wasn't a Condor?"

No one else had seen the aircraft but that plain view had been unmistakable.

"No," I replied, "a Condor's got four radials, saw 'em just before the war in Croydon. That was an '88 for sure."

That was the end of the matter but I have often wondered just what the '88 thought we were doing. Discussing it later in Cairo, we decided that he must have assumed we were a fully armed Coastal Command Fortress and decided that he didn't want to tangle with it. We were fully armed but the guns were still in their original cellophane wrappings and there was an acute shortage of gunners and ammunition.

Just before dawn we flew into dense cloud and the next thing we saw was the Nile Delta—a first-class piece of navigation; we landed at Cairo West on a blistering hot morning.

The American movements control could not offer us a ride back to the States at once but could supply a ride to Rabat Sale where we could pick up the South Atlantic Ferry Command Liberator for Montreal. Dick accepted this and we said goodbye to the RAF contingent of our crew before climbing into a Dakota loaded with boxes. We made an uneventful flight to Rabat Sale and found we had five days to wait for our onward passage. Dick, the flight engineer and myself were accommodated in a civilian hotel with several other crews. I can't remember the name but in the basement was a night club known as the Snake Pit—a place that was of necessity operated in almost total darkness. I am sure that no one would have gone into the place if the ladies who used it as a club for dates had been exposed to bright lights. The flight engineer and I spent a few hours there on our first night in Rabat Sale but our supply of Canadian dollars was soon exhausted. Rabat Sale had only recently been liberated and most commodities were in very short supply. The French were extremely short of clothes and a flourishing black market had grown up in secondhand clothes.

The next morning we met a flight engineer who was just rolling in wealth having just sold a prewar dinner jacket for an astronomical number of francs. The fact that there was absolutely nothing to buy in Rabat except bad booze and the charms of the ladies in the Snake Pit didn't worry him one bit. The flight engineer and myself went through our bags; he donated a pair of khaki drill pants that were patched in the seat while my contribution was two blue uniform shirts suffering from advanced old age. Our wealthy friend took over the job and vanished into an ornamental park where he had his black market contacts. He soon returned with a handful of francs which lasted us for one more evening in the Snake Pit. Fortunately the next morning we were called to the airport for our onward flight or I am sure that we should have made another raid on our joint wardrobes for the evening's entertainment and finished up by flying back to Montreal in bath towels.

There were several old acquaintances in the South Atlantic Ferry Liberator and the trip to Montreal via Lagens and Gander passed without incident. The radio office in Montreal said that I had been posted to No. 231 Communications Squadron which operated the "milk runs" and general communications services all over the world and was told to report to an RAF officer on 231.

Andrew was an ex-Coastal Command Sunderland pilot who had been given the job of organising the Coronado ferry service which was to be based in Bermuda throughout the winter and at Bouchierville in the summer. He had been in Boston supervising the equipment of the Coronados to a passenger carrying standard and he had now positioned them to start their service from Bermuda. He explained that the crew of a Coronado was to be a pilot, a copilot, two radio navigators and two flight engineers; this was later modified to include one full-time navigator. It was his intention that I join one of these crews in Bermuda but first we had a job to do.

The Coronado that I had deserted in Reykjavik had now been repaired and he wanted it flown to Wig Bay and loaded with spare parts, and then delivered to Bermuda. He had scraped together a scratch crew with himself as skipper and I was to be the radio operator. One of the return Ferry Liberators dropped us off in Reykjavik on its way back to the United Kingdom and that evening in the transit mess, the base engineering officer explained that he had fitted a new engine but that he was generally unhappy at the state of the boat. It had been sitting around on slipways in the UK and in Iceland without any attention for too long and it needed a thorough overhaul before tackling the long flight back to Bermuda. "She'll let you down somewhere," he concluded.

We had two RAF flying officer flight engineers and their faces dropped; this didn't sound like an easy trip for them. Andrew explained that the boat was being taken to Bermuda to act as a reserve only; his main concern was the problem of the boat icing up on take-off from freezing spray. We visited the boat the next morning and I must admit that she did look bedraggled as she swung forlornly round a buoy. She had originally been painted in a light blue camouflage and it looked as though she had been acting as a roost for all the gulls in Reykjavik harbour. I found that some wag in the operations department had allocated her the radio call sign of Bright Blue William and Bright Blue William became her name until she was deliberately sunk in deep water off Bermuda after the war. Inside the same air of neglect was evident; she smelt of stale water and oil while the wash of the tide against her hull and the drumming rain on the wings played a dismal dirge for the whole operation. We all worked round her for a couple of days, did engine runs and checked out the equipment and at least made the old lady smell a bit sweeter. Andrew watched the water temperature carefully and then decided we would go. One of the great advantages of a Coronado was that there was reverse pitch on the inboard engines and water handling was much improved. Andrew, I found, was particularly adept at this and when we unmoored for a taxi run around the harbour, he returned to the mooring buoy by placing it gently alongside the front door, I had only to reach down and put the slip rope through the buoy ring. Gone were the days when you dashed past the buoy at the rate of knots leaning far out to try and slip the short slip through the ring and the string of abuse from the skipper when having got it through the ring you couldn't get enough turns on the bollard to hold the boat.

The next morning we left for Wig Bay, the take-off was uneventful and although the spray probably did freeze, it did not affect the flying. The flight to Wig Bay was uneventful, the controller at Wig Bay recognised my voice on the R/T, as did the pilot of a Sunderland on a test flight. There were some terse comments about Canadian rejects and undesirables—it was like coming home. Andrew had several friends among the local test pilots and really showed off. He put Bright Blue William down on Loch Ryan for the landing of her life. We received a hearty welcome from the resident staff and a remarkable amount of beer was consumed in the mess that evening to the accompaniment of some pretty tall stories. Andrew later claimed that the last straw was when he heard me claiming that we had actually chased that Ju '88 in the Bay of Biscay with the Fortress and forced it into a stall into the water.

The next day there was a decided chop on the loch which set Bright Blue William rocking and I for one was very glad when we at last swung into wind for the take-off for our short flight down to Mountbatten.

A very smart Australian squadron operating Sunderlands was in residence at Mountbatten and Bright Blue William must have cut a sorry figure as we taxied between the trots of immaculate white Sunderlands. At least there was no excitement of buoy grabbing, once again Andrew laid the mooring buoy right at my feet and Bright Blue William was soon tied up. We spent several days in the mess at Mountbatten while arrangements were made with the RAF for our long flight to Bathurst in West Africa. The navigator was issued with the necessary maps, I carried a world wide route book and didn't play much of a part in the pre-flight preparations. Then Andrew informed me that a signals officer was on his way from Pembroke Dock to brief me on what I was to do with the radio between Mountbatten and Bathurst; this had to be done in his presence.

A very important little flying officer arrived the next day; he was a signals officer from Coastal Command and he was amazed and disgusted to find that he was to brief a civilian in an odd uniform for this highly irregular flight. He started the briefing by suggesting that perhaps Andrew had best send me back to Prestwick and he would find a "proper signalling expert" from Coastal Command for the trip. The soul of tact, he said this in front of me. Andrew explained that I had had some experience with this particular radio equipment and I might be hard to replace at short notice. All that dreary afternoon he told me silly things about radio communications that the lowest AC.2 was familiar with; my repeated sarcasms he put down to lack of training. At last we got down to the Coronado's two direction finders which I had carefully calibrated in Wig Bay before her original flight to Reykjavik; the long range one had a large error curve—about ten degrees in the worst case, I believe. This was far too big, much more than he could possibly accept.

"I think it better that we bring in a signals officer to do this calibration work again."

Andrew was growing bored and tired. "Just what is wrong?" he asked.

"The error on the second DF is too big," stated our friend firmly, "much bigger than that in a Sunderland."

"But a Coronado is a much bigger boat than a Sunderland, therefore the error must be bigger," said Andrew reasonably.

The briefing officer at once cheered up. "Of course, Sir, I never thought of that," and at once cleared the flight.

Andrew led me firmly into the bar which had just opened and placed a pint of beer in my hand. "Takes all sorts to make this man's air force," he laughed. "Your friend will return to Pembroke Dock convinced in spite of what I have said that you have no 'entitlement' to be on the crew of Bright Blue William."

The following evening we loaded up and just after dusk set off on our haul of almost 3,000 miles. The route was out to ten degrees west, then south down the ten degrees line until we were abeam Gibraltar and then direct to Bathurst. Slowly the night passed, then it was dawn; Prestwick radio station faded out but there was Gibraltar. It was a clear morning which turned hazy with sand as we started to follow the bulge of Africa round to Dakar. Port Etienne came in on the radio and then we were flying over it; it looked a godforsaken hole if ever I have seen one—just a sandy spit enclosing a bay from which some Coastal Command Sunderlands on detachment from Bathurst operated as a self-contained unit. I could see one building which someone told me later was the old Air France radio station; there must have been an airstrip down there but it was hidden in the dust haze. Gradually the desert changed into jungle and we were circling the RAF boat base at Bathurst. It was called Half Die! When I enquired about how it came to get that odd name, it was said that years before the area had been devastated by plague and half the people had died—an easy answer.

I had been having some trouble with the main communications transmitter during the flight, its power seemed much down. As Andrew edged up to the buoy, an RAF launch took up station alongside and the first man through my door was a man wearing a Ferry Command cap. "I'm a radio engineer cum Russian/Canadian interpreter," he introduced himself. "I'm stationed here to help the Russian crews through. I heard you tell the radio station that your power was down and I have come along to help."

I was only too grateful to hand it over to him and get ashore for some sleep. We had dinner and a good night's rest before our 1,800 mile trip to Natal in Brazil. We were away from our buoy at first light and with the radio fully serviceable again—but then we found a problem.

The tropical morning was utterly still, the water was glassy calm and our first attempt at a take-off had to be aborted; the engines were overheating before the boat got up on the step. Andrew taxied back making a wide "S" turn to try and ruffle the water as much as possible. The trick worked; on the second run we crashed through our own wake twice and then Bright Blue William took to the air. The cylinder-head temperatures were well above the red line; there was obviously a time of the day on which to take off from Bathurst and this wasn't it.

The day passed slowly until lunch time, when one of the engineers and myself set to and produced a two-course lunch in the galley—soup, salmon salad, biscuits and cheese with coffee. I found then a useful device in the Coronado—in the galley was a trunk which ran through the hull to the step under the boat; it was there to break the airlock under the hull during take-off. It was like a vacuum cleaner—all one had to do in flight to clean dirty plates was to hold them over this trunk, everything went down that trunk —tins, paper, refuse, it was easy to keep the galley clean.

The intertropical front which usually lies across the track from Dakar seemed to be having a day off this trip, just a few isolated clouds with heavy rain on the sea beneath, which we avoided without trouble and the sky was cloudless again. Then we were looking down on the Rocas. From our height it just looked like a completely barren circle of sand with the white cream of breakers round it; we knew then that we had about 300 miles to go. We landed in Natal river alongside a US Navy launch. There was a line floating in the water supported by red and white cork floats, one of the launch's crew picked up the floating line, dropped a loop in it over our bollard and then, "That's it, Captain," said the coloured Petty Officer in charge of the launch, "leave the rest to the US Navy." The floating rope tightened and the Coronado was nudged neatly into a U-shaped dock. After some of the wild work that I had indulged in in trying to moor up with a tide and a stiff wind, this was luxury indeed.

We spent the night in the Navy mess and the next day set off to Belem in Brazil, a short flight of about 1,000 miles. Belem lies on one of the mouths of the Amazon and we found conditions on the water very different from those at Natal. Andrew landed quite well and then started to taxi towards the buoy. There was a strong current in the mud-coloured flood and the buoy was a big, flat round iron buoy with a ring in the middle. Andrew angled up but the surging current had tipped the buoy up and I couldn't reach the mooring ring and then I made a big mistake; I jumped down on to the buoy which immediately tipped more and I found myself hanging on like a limpet with my legs up to my knees in the river Amazon. One of the engineers had been on the mooring platform with me and at once tried to hook the boat hook into my belt but Bright Blue William had had enough, the starboard inner engine cut dead. She was immediately swirled away by the current and within moments she had vanished round a bend in the river. Things looked decidedly unpleasant; the launch that had attended our landing dashed off in pursuit of the flying boat, the American crew of the launch later claimed that the boat was in more danger than I was. "We have had men marooned on those big flat buoys for hours," they laughed. Perhaps they were right for when I scrambled up to the mooring ring to get my feet out of the water, the buoy did level off so that I could sit with my arm through the ring. As I sat in the middle of the Amazon, I began to wonder if in spite of my marine background, boat flying really was the best method of flying for a living.

After about twenty minutes Bright Blue William came surging back round the point, all four engines roaring and hotly pursued by the launch. Andrew edged up to the buoy, the engineer leant out and handed me down the short slip, I passed it through the ring, he then snapped on enough turns to hold her against the current. The launch put his foredeck on the buoy and I jumped aboard and from there transferred to the Coronado. Everyone thought it was most amusing but Andrew said I was taking seamanship a bit too seriously when I jumped on to the buoy; he claimed that it reminded him of the navigator who bailed out to find out where he was when he was thoroughly lost.

Ashore in the Navy mess I was soon fitted up with a new set of American KD—much smarter than my own, and a pair of Navy shoes with the compliments of the US.

The next day we flew on to Trinidad and landed at the boat base there at Chaguaramas, that had been laid down by Pan American. Mooring was the same as at Natal—an orderly business with the boat moored in a float. We spent the night in the RAF mess at Piarco Field and the next flew the last 1,600 miles of the trip to Bermuda. We landed at Bermuda in perfect weather and moored Bright Blue William up at Darrells Island. She did not fly again; she was later hauled ashore and cannibalised to keep the rest of the fleet going. After the war the hull was towed out beyond the reefs and scuttled in deep water.

CHAPTER THIRTEEN

WE settled down for a few days in the Belmont Manor Hotel and became acquainted with the rest of the crews who were operating the West African Ferry. There were three RAF captains, who had done a lot of boat flying in Coastal Command; there was a Canadian civilian who had gained most of his experience on float-planes in the Canadian Arctic and lastly there was an American civilian pilot called Dick, whose crew I joined.

Dick was a most versatile pilot; he had been a chief petty officer pilot in the American Navy before the war and had gained considerable experience of all types of flying boats. He had then flown airlines for some years and joined Ferry Command on the day it was founded. He was a copilot of one of the seven Hudsons that made the first Atlantic flight from Hatties Camp to Aldergrove. Dick's crew consisted of Neil, the American civilian copilot, Nick, the English RAF navigator, and one other radio navigator besides myself—a Canadian called Stevie and two Irish RAF flying officer flight engineers. I took the place of a French Canadian who had returned to Montreal.

Dick was the most competent pilot I have ever flown with—a natural on both aeroplanes and flying boats. He was one of those rare pilots who maintained command without effort and without changing from his extremely happy disposition. Our first trip was scheduled out in a couple of days—Trinidad, Belem, Natal, Bathurst and on to Lagos, the end of the line. The trip was without incident except for an unfortunate mistake by our two flight engineers in the BOAC resthouse at Ikeja. The resthouse was in fact a series of semi-detached bungalows which were extremely light and airy; a pleasant place for a night stop. The bar was a pleasant place too and our two Irish friends spent an hilarious evening in it. Their return to the bungalow was a noisy business and accompanied by a few renderings of "The Wearing of the Green". The resident of the next bungalow to theirs took exception to the noise and had the temerity to tell them so. Within seconds, what had been a legitimate complaint had become an Irish–English battle which ended with the Irishmen evicting their neighbour and the furniture from his bungalow and piling it on the lawn. The next day at breakfast Dick told us that both the engineers were "inside"—they had been arrested during the night. It transpired that their neighbour had been a high ranking Provost Marshal for West African forces and that he was not amused at his treatment. It took Dick and the local RAF C/O most of the day to "spring" them so that they could start the trip back to Bermuda the next day. Back in Bermuda, Andrew as CO had to take a hand and he could only pass the matter on to Headquarters in Montreal. Meanwhile the two engineers remained in the crew. Years later I met one of them on the Berlin Airlift and asked him how the matter finally ended. He was still in the Air Force and still a flying officer but admitted that the episode had given him a black mark that had taken some living down. His compatriot had left the RAF at the first opportunity and the last time he heard from him he was running a garage in Cork.

Back in Bermuda I found that Andrew had rented a cottage just opposite to the flying boat base at Darrells Island. He offered me one of the bedrooms which I accepted; it was to be a pleasant change from the Belmont Manor. The rest of the official "residents" were one of the RAF skippers, a Canadian radioman and the Canadian skipper, but with the crews going in and out it always seemed to be full. It was an old coral cottage built into the side of a low hill overlooking the boat base. The top storey was a large room with a passage running back into the hillside off which the three bedrooms opened and which terminated in the bathroom. From this large room a wide stairway went down to another room which we rigged up as the bar. The dining room and kitchen opened off this. The cottage was surrounded by cedar trees which grew out of the hillside. A coloured woman "did" for us all; she arrived each morning before breakfast on an old-fashioned lady's bicycle and went home after dinner. How she managed to feed us all, do the washing and keep the place tidy, I don't know, but she did and remained eternally cheerful about it. It was in this cottage that I was to receive a fright which made all the odd scares I had had in my flying career look like nothing.

Andrew had brought across from Darrells Island one of the Alsatians that had adopted the flying boat base. He was a friendly soul who pottered around with me all day long and slept on the floor of my bedroom. Bermuda was a lovely spot, the weather superb and the days were filled with golf, swimming and deep sea fishing—we all had a wonderful time. One day several of the crew members living in the Belmont Manor and myself hired a boat and spent the day fishing on the edge of the reef. We had a good day's sport and when the boat dropped me off at the jetty by the cottage, I took several of the best fish with me. The housekeeper was pleased with this addition to the larder and promised me a dinner of fish and chips. She also told me I should be alone, as everyone was away. The dinner was excellent and after she had done, I was left alone reading in the top lounge. The dog snoozed away in front of the empty grate; the day at sea in the sun and the wind had made me very drowsy. I retired early to bed and the dog moved his bed from the hearth rug to the mat alongside my bed. I was asleep within seconds and then, what seemed like hours later, I came wide awake with a start, aware that something was wrong. The first realisation was of an absolute stillness—with the sea breeze forever in the cedars and the croaking of the tree frogs, it was never quiet at night in the cottage. The window was wide open and a full moon was shining across the bedroom floor towards the black oblong of the open door to the passage. Standing on the floor was the dog, absolutely rigid. I reached out and touched his back, it was stiff and he never moved. Then I heard it—the tread of leather shoes on the stairs up to the lounge. One, two steps and then on the third step, the squeak of the tread that had always been there. Still the incredible silence persisted outside, then the steps reached the top of the stairs. I was paralysed with fright, afraid to move my hand from the dog's back and gazed, mesmerised, at the black oblong of the door. Slowly the steps moved across the lounge to the entrance of the passage and then into it. The steps were heavy and deliberate, they passed the door and then moved towards the bathroom at the end of the passage where they faded out. There was a strong smell that I can only describe as compounded of books growing mouldy in the dark. Suddenly the night breeze sighed through the cedars, the frogs started croaking—it was a normal Bermudan night again.

I jumped out of bed and switched on the light in the passage, then the lounge lights, but there was no one there. Back in my bedroom I found the dog trembling. I got him a drink and he settled down again but I didn't get over it so easily, I was still wide awake when the dawn came. There was only the door to the bathroom and no window—it was cut directly out of the hill. For days I kept my experience to myself but one day I had some hours to spare in Hamilton and visited the agent who had rented us the cottage. She said that it was one of the oldest cottages on the island and had been owned by a Bermudan family who had never used it as a home. It was always rented to visitors and it was said to have been built on the ruins of a slave baracoon, the slaves being landed from boats at the cottage jetty. I was never alone again in that house at night.

We made several trips to West Africa and back without incident. Nick, the navigator, was first class at his job and looked sideways at the efforts of Stevie and myself. He was strictly an astro navigator and considered that the Loran system of navigation was only suitable for use by the "half educated ones" as he called Stevie and me. He always carried a reserve chart on which we were allowed to operate. I remember once getting a Loran fix every minute for thirty minutes and plotting each one; it looked most impressive to me but still Nick was not sold.

Then the spring came to Canada and arrangements were made to shift the operation up north to Bouchierville. The farewell party was something to remember for those that were capable of remembering. Some of the guests lost their pants which were used in an abortive attempt to burn down the stairs. We took back to Montreal a full passenger load of Canadian civilian ground engineers and their wives. Although the Great Sound was choppy in a stiff wind, Dick had the greatest difficulty in getting the Coronado airborne; we were almost in the open sea by the time it had climbed to fifty feet. Dick's voice over the intercom sounded really worried.

"What the hell went wrong?" he asked the engineer.

"Nothing back here, Dick, all the engines were giving full power."

"Why in God's name didn't she take off then? What's the weight like, Nick?"

Nick was non-committal. "Fair amount of passenger baggage, Dick, but still well below our safe take-off weight, I just can't understand it."

The trip proceeded to Montreal and then, as we circled Bouchierville preparatory to landing, we received the first warning that all was not well.

"Proceed to the buoy but no one is to disembark until the ship has been cleared by customs," said the control launch.

"Customs, now what?" said Dick. "Never heard of those chaps bothering Ferry Command."

We all agreed. As we motored up to the buoy and I swung open the door, a smart marine customs launch was following the mooring launch. As Dick put the mooring buoy alongside the bollard, I was joined by half a dozen customs men. They were completely impervious to any ribald comments from the mooring launch crew.

The crew were told to unload their personal baggage first and then we were taken ashore while the waterguard boys took charge of the passengers. We had to wait ashore for five hours while they searched that flying boat from nose to tail. She was found to be loaded down with cases of whisky—they even found cases stowed away in the wings. Every nook and cranny must have held its individual bottle. Dick ruefully surveyed the huge pile on the jetty. "No wonder she couldn't take off, we must have been hundreds of pounds overweight."

The crew were then dismissed from the affair. I forget the real culprits but the customs in Montreal had apparently been warned that cases and cases of liquor had been bought in Bermuda in the week prior to our departure. Scotch and rum were rationed in Canada, so someone had set up a real killing. During the next week, the rest of the Coronados arrived in Montreal but not to the royal welcome we had received.

We made our first scheduled North Atlantic crossing about a week later—Bouchierville/Botwood one day and the next afternoon we set out for Largs Bay. The evening and night passed without incident but the next morning with nearly a thousand miles to go we had trouble; the starboard outer propeller came off, smashed into the starboard inner and within seconds we had two engines out on one side. The nearest flying boat base was a place called Castle Archdale on Lough Erne in Northern Ireland and we limped in there early in the afternoon. In conjunction with Killadease, Castle Archdale was an operational-cum-training base for flying boats and the launch crew were well used to coping with lame ducks. The landing Dick made was incredible under the circumstances; he held the wing with two dead engines until just the right time and then dropped the wing-tip float on to the water at exactly the right moment. Two crash launches were alongside as soon as the weight was off the float and they took charge of the whole operation. We were soon loaded bag and baggage into a launch and put ashore.

We were allocated a Nissen hut between us until it was decided what should be done. At breakfast in the mess the next morning the CO came across and sat down. "Well chaps, your disposal instructions have just arrived—a Catalina will take you across to Helensborough this morning and a bus will be waiting there to take you to Prestwick."

Those simple words ended my flying boat career.

It was as he said and within a couple of days I was back in my digs in Montreal. A few days later another Coronado was lost through running ashore—it was manœuvring in a high wind at Invergordon where it had been diverted when flying from Largs Bay to Reykjavik. Flying boats were not too lucky on the North Atlantic and the service was closed down.

Back in Montreal I was assigned the odd communications flight but already there was evidence that now the war was over Ferry Command were slowly disbanding. Deliveries were down to a trickle and civilian crews were going home; all the English radio-men went home by sea in a Blue Funnel ship and I knew that my turn would be soon. In the middle of November 210 Squadron said that I was free to go. The radio office of Ferry Command was almost deserted, the girl clerk though, was pleased to see me. "I have to find a radioman for a Dakota delivery to Prestwick in the morning," she said. "I have asked the few R/Os we have left on the books but they are so busy trying to find civilian jobs that I have been unable to pin one of them down."

I made a decision; I had hoped to spend a week or two in Montreal while my transportation was arranged but a quick break was perhaps the best—I too had to get myself a job. "I'll take it," I told her.

I found that the Dak was one that had been used for training and had been damaged but was now repaired. The captain was an Army captain—just what he was doing in Dorval in November 1945 I never found out but, like me, he wanted to get home. The two other crew members were RAF sergeants from the training school at Three Rivers—also keen to get home. We flew over the old familiar route for the last time—Gander, Iceland, Prestwick and then the war was over for me too.

CHAPTER FOURTEEN

I STAYED home for a few days and then started to shop around for a job. The state of civil aviation could only be described as chaotic; everyone wanted to get into the act. BOAC were obviously going to be one of the giants but already some of the prewar aeroplane companies whose names had been lost since the first day of the war were talking about the routes they wanted to run. My prewar licence stood me in good stead; I was offered jobs by a dozen companies whose problems were twofold—no licensed crews and no aeroplanes —the job was to decide which company was most likely to make good. I didn't apply to BOAC, they still had a considerable number of prewar people around from whom they would form their radio department. I was sure that I would do better in one of the new companies and so it was to be. I was called for an interview with British Latin American Airlines at an office in Dover Street, London. The interview was conducted by Mac, a radio engineer I had met during the war; a man of considerable ability and experience in the erection of radio stations in Ferry Command, and who was to become the radio superintendent, and a prewar BOAC captain who was to be operations manager of the new airline.

Having by now amassed a considerable number of flying hours and holding the necessary licence, I was taken on immediately. By the end of the year the policy of the Government was established. There were to be three main airline corporations—British Overseas Airways Corporation to operate roughly in the northern half of the Atlantic, to Africa and to Australia and the Far East; British South American Airways, who were confined to the southern half of the Atlantic, and British European Airways, who were to operate the internal and continental routes.

While these momentous decisions were being made, British Latin American, or BSAA as it subsequently came to be called, went ahead with the problems of opening an air service to South America. Short of licensed aircrews, ground engineers and aircraft, the one thing they were not short of was enthusiasm. Led by Air Vice-Marshal Bennett of Pathfinder fame, everybody was desperately keen on making it a success; perhaps this keenness was overdone for it doubtless led to some serious situations and the eventual taking over of the corporation by BOAC, but this was in the future. In 1945 everyone was keen to establish himself in civvy street.

I found the Dover Street offices positively buzzing, ex-RAF pilots swotting desperately for the coveted "B" licence, the qualification then necessary before you could fly for "hire or reward". Office accommodation was so desperately short that I have even seen them sitting working on the stairs. The first problem was passenger aircraft and suitable equipment to operate them. The corporation's policy was to carry no navigators or flight engineers; those jobs were to be covered by pilots. They were forced by the facilities available over the projected routes and the type of equipment availabl to carry radiomen, but any chance of cashing in on my now venerable Second "N" was firmly squashed at my first interview. I became the senior radio officer. The only aircraft available were ex-bombers; six Lancastrians were on order—Lancaster bombers with a metal nose and tail with thirteen passenger seats running down to a lavatory in the tail. The radioman sat on a small seat with his back against the main spar. Behind this was a small space used by the stewardess as a galley. Beside the radio operator's seat was an adjustable step on which the navigator stood to get his head into the astro dome—this usually entailed sitting on the radio operator's shoulder. Ahead of this was a long table for the navigator and then the two pilots' seats. With four Merlins roaring away in the wings, it was a cramped and noisy aeroplane to operate but it was all we could get. The radio equipment had been designed just before the war and mass-produced to fill the RAF requirement. It was unsuitable for airline operations, but again it was all we had and we made the best of it.

The next problem was to get radio operators; there were plenty of ex-Service people available and they were doubtless quite competent, but they did not fulfil the legal requirement of holding the necessary licence. These were stirring times; the excitements of war had not yet faded into memories and the inevitable reaction when told they would have to get an Air Ministry Licence was: "I was good enough to fly in the RAF during the war, how can a bloody civilian say whether or not I can fly now?"

The next gimmick was a letter from the CO which usually proved that the applicant was a radio genius—a second Marconi himself. By the middle of December we had managed to lure in a couple of men with marine experience who had obtained their air licences just prior to the outbreak of war. Then came a great thrill—we were to go and collect our first aeroplane; it was at the A. V. Roe factory at Woodford, and with a crew of captain, ground engineer and a stray navigator on leave from the RAF we set off by train.

We were met at Manchester station and driven out to the airfield at Woodford where we were royally entertained by Major G. A. Thorn, the chief test pilot; he was later to be drowned in a tragic accident to a Tudor. We spent a couple of days at the guest house during which we carefully checked over our pride and joy—"Starlight", Lancastrian G–AGWG. The next day the AVM himself arrived and within an hour we were on our way to Heathrow, an airfield in Hounslow which was to grow into the London Airport of today. It was only a short flight and we were soon in the circuit. The airport consisted of one runway running roughly east–west with a taxiway and a small parking area. The AVM parked the aircraft in this area and the back door was opened by a young man in a raincoat and trilby hat—BSAA's first traffic officer.

The aerodrome was not officially open; the story is that the only previous aircraft to land there had been an American Thunderbolt which had landed short of fuel. There was one hut with about four offices at the top of the parking strip for BSAA at London Airport. All servicing was carried out in the open, but we now had an aeroplane and were due to start a scheduled airline to South America. Unfortunately, it could not be claimed that this was the first airline between Europe and South America. The great French Aeropostale Company had begun operating a through mail service on March 1st, 1928, with obsolete destroyers carrying the mail between Africa and Brazil. The trip took eight days. They were followed by the Germans who made the first crossing with the airship "Graf Zeppelin" carrying passengers in 1931. From April, 1932, regular airship services ran fortnightly during the summer season between Friedrichshafen and Rio de Janeiro. The service was closed down after the disaster to the "Hindenburg" at New York in May, 1937. The trip took between 80 and 120 hours. I remember when I was at sea in a tramp steamer on a voyage from Barry to Santa Fé being overtaken one night by an airship flying along quite low with its searchlight shining down on the sea. I immediately called on the radio CQ—all ships—can anyone hear me? I was answered by a powerful transmitter which gave the call sign of the "Graf Zeppelin" and asked for my position.

There was a later development by the German Lufthansa when the ocean crossing from Africa to Brazil was made by Dornier Wal flying boats. A special ship, the *Westphalia*, was stationed midway between Africa and Brazil. The aircraft landed in the sea and were then taxied on to a mat towed by the ship. They were then lifted on board, refuelled and catapulted on their way. Later on in Natal we were to find one of the old French transatlantic planes that had been abandoned there at the outbreak of war. It looked a fragile job for such a task compared with today's aircraft.

There was one first, we could claim—we were to be the first airline to operate from England to the Argentine. The crew for the first flight almost picked itself—the AVM as captain; the chief pilot, Captain Cracknell, as first officer; the deputy chief pilot, Captain Alabaster; Mac, the radio superintendent, and myself as first and second radio officers with our one and only stewardess, Mary Guthrie, and two ground engineers to look after the aircraft. Our passengers were a mixture of fare-paying passengers and ex-RAF officers who had been employed to become station managers at the airports throughout which BSAA were going to operate.

At last came the great day—January 1st, 1946, and a few minutes after twelve we were climbing away from Heathrow on the first leg to Lisbon. With Mac manning the radio and every passenger seat occupied, I was obliged to crouch in the galley until Mary started to serve lunch. An ex-ATA pilot, she did her best but the knack of serving a four-course lunch in a tiny space and then climbing to and fro over the main spar to wait on the passengers was not picked up in a few minutes. To her eternal credit she managed some sort of a meal and I tried to help her clean up the mess afterwards but the galley was a shambles. Looking back, it was altogether too ambitious an operation and we landed at Portela Airport in Lisbon literally knee deep in dirty dishes. While the flight plan to Bathurst was being prepared, the mess was cleared up and as we had off-loaded one passenger, Mr Hall, our Lisbon stationmaster designate, Mac decreed that I should work the radio from Lisbon to Bathurst while he occupied the vacant seat. It was dark soon after take-off and I had a real introduction to operating in a Lancastrian.

The navigation did not appear to be going too well, for the three pilots spent half their time hopping up and down to the astro dome; once there, they would spend a long time half sitting on my shoulder. I contacted Bathurst early in the trip and then lost him for hours. The old Air-France medium frequency direction finding stations had been reactivated immediately after the war but offers of QTEs to the navigators were not appreciated. At last I was able to hear the Bathurst radio beacon but found that the pilots insisted on using the direction finder themselves. After several mistakes I offered to take over but was fairly curtly shut up. We landed at Bathurst early in the morning. I for one was tired and irritable; I had obviously to reorientate myself when operating with ex-RAF crews. The atmosphere in the cockpit caused by the navigational problems and my inability to get in touch with Bathurst was not pleasant and I was all for handing back to Mac for the next sector.

The reason for not raising Bathurst was solved on arrival. The fine tuning of the transmitter had been moved fully one way during the scrambling around of the navigators and Bathurst could not possibly have heard us. It was inexcusable not to have found out what had happened, but like the rest of the crew I was trying too hard to do my best and working under difficult physical conditions had not helped. The break at Bathurst eased the whole situation, we set off on the next leg to Natal in better heart. I was able to maintain continuous contact with both Bathurst and Natal and was now allowed to make intelligent use of the direction finder. The rest of the night passed away peacefully and soon after dawn, the big US Army base at Natal came into sight. I was able to contribute a little to the accuracy of our landfall by using the direction finder aurally as I had always done at sea. Relationships were improving as the appreciation of each other's capabilities increased. The flight from Natal to Rio was made in daylight using the Pan American radio facilities and early in the afternoon the wonderful harbour of Rio came into view. The big international airport at Governor's Island had not been completed and we were forced to use Santos Dumont which was decidedly short for a Lancastrian; it was literally right in the city. The aircraft pilot-operated voice radio was too weak and reception had to be by the main receiver and then fed into the intercom for them to hear the reply. The result was chaos again; in desperation I used the main transmitter and tried to do the radio telephone landing procedure from the radio position. This was okay until, using established American procedure, I receipted a clearance to landing by saying "Roger". The AVM had had enough, he sarcastically enquired if I was carrying on a conversation with my Uncle Roger and went straight into Santos Dumont and made a spectacular landing in front of an audience that seemed to consist of half the city. British Latin American Airlines had originally been formed by a combination of five shipping lines—Royal Mail, Booth Lines, the Vestey interests, Blue Star and Pacific Steam. They had all pulled out when it was nationalised but for several months until we became organised, they acted as our agents in South America. The Royal Mail manager took over all the arrangements and the crew were soon bustled off to the most elegant hotel where accommodation had been reserved. After a long and leisurely bath, punctuated by two large scotches, I stretched out on the bed and reviewed the flight. One thing was obvious—civil flying was going to call for some considerable readjustments in my outlook; the leisurely flying of the prewar era and the sense of comradeship engendered by wartime flying were obviously out of date in the postwar aviation field. Still, it was a living and a way of doing things to which I should have to adjust myself.

My musings were interrupted by the Royal Mail man collecting the crew for the reception and dinner to follow. We were treated like heroes and the conflicting emotions that had been bred of tiredness and tensions in "Starlight's" cockpit were washed away with alcohol and good food. The dinner that followed was wonderful; I was introduced to heart of palm with the most wonderful steak I had ever eaten, its only fault was that there was too much of it and two-thirds of the way through I had to give in. I must have collapsed into bed and remember nothing until the morning.

The next few days went in a whirl! I was adopted by the local manager of the Marconi Company and his great friend who ran the Rio side of Cable and Wireless. They fed us, wined us and introduced us to dozens of people. One visit on my first flight to Rio remains a vivid memory—a ride in the cable car up to El Cristo and being told half-way up that the cable had never been replaced since it had been built.

The flight down to Montevideo was a peaceful ride compared with our first efforts to Rio, and at Carrasco Airport we received another wonderful welcome. A round of parties started and one morning about three days later I woke up in the elegant room at the Beach Hotel where Royal Mail had put us up and decided that I must have a walk and shake down some of the food I had consumed. I saw the Shell man in the lobby to whom I explained my plan. He said he would run me to town and I could walk back— nothing simpler. Walking back was simple, I just aimed at the sea but it was a glorious day and I just kept on walking. I looked at my watch—I had been walking for three hours and no sign of the sea. I was in a very smart suburb of Montevideo with the houses lying well back from the road and not a soul in sight. I walked on but the pleasure was gone—my feet and legs were beginning to ache, the sun was getting higher and hotter, and the few thin hairs scraped across my dome were not adequate protection against the midday sun in Uruguay. I trudged on, the houses were getting wider and wider spaced and at last I came to a white police box. A policeman in a white suit was inside and looked far from friendly but the situation was getting desperate so I presented myself at the door of the box and used my one word that might sound like Spanish "Inglesi". The policeman replied with a flow of Spanish but I could only repeat "Inglesi, Inglesi, Inglesi". He now looked as worried as I felt, then suddenly he smiled, grabbed his telephone and after a short wait he handed it to me. The cultured English voice came over, "I am the court interpreter, can I help you?"

I unloaded my problem, the interpreter laughed. "Good heavens, you must have walked about twelve miles. You will be on the borders of Paraguay unless we get you turned round. Give me back to the policeman."

In a few minutes the policeman burst out laughing, pushed me into his chair and handed me the phone.

"It's all under control," said that silvery voice, "the police are going to pick you up on their motorcycle patrol and take you back to your hotel. Have a good flight home and give England my love."

Soon the policeman and I were carrying on a fluent conversation in sign language. I removed my handkerchief and pointed to my red scalp but he had an answer to that; he rummaged in a locker under the table and produced an off-white baseball hat. I clamped it on my head and I wore that hat until it fell apart. Soon a huge American motorcycle drew up and I was firmly parked in the side-car by my new friend; we shook hands all round and then roared off. The arrival at the hotel coincided with the return of the rest of the crew from a shopping expedition. My driver, complete with revolver, crash helmet and high leather boots, escorted me to the door of the hotel and shook me warmly by the hand before climbing back on to his motorcycle. The truth of this spectacular return has never been accepted, the only story that was accepted without question was that I had been slung out of a waterfront dive.

The next day we flew across the River Plate to Moron, the old airport for Buenos Aires, passing over the sunken *Graf Spee* on the way. All that could be seen was some rusty iron sticking out of the muddy river, *sic transit gloria mundi*.

We had another great reception in Buenos Aires and were accommodated in the City Hotel. The warmth of our reception throughout South America was I think largely due to the fact that there had been no interchange of peoples during the war years between Europe and South America and perhaps in us they saw the first concrete evidence that the world was returning to normal. Buenos Aires was the end of our flight and after a couple of days we retraced our journey back to London Airport.

We all learned something from that trip and Mac and I arrived back with stacks of information on radio facilities and operational procedures that had to be turned into a route manual. We found that the uniform was totally unsuitable for tropical flying. A blue serge tunic with blue shirt and black tie and a heavy peaked cap had obviously been modelled on merchant navy uniform and used the same principle as the French Foreign Legion dress for keeping cool—that of keeping the heat out!

Mac decided rightly that each radioman must do at least one trip to South America under supervision. This meant that I was heavily committed to a training programme. Most of the radiomen were perfectly competent after one trip, some needed two, but then we found a young man who failed at the end of two trips and needed a third. He was an ex-merchant navy radioman who had made two long trips in lifeboats after his ships had been sunk. I found him incompetent and deeply resentful of being told what to do. Mac and I were grateful when he left to join another company. Then another young man made two trips under supervision and again I was called to make a trip to decide what we should do. Sitting beside him on the trip from London to Lisbon, I formed the impression that he hadn't any idea what was going on. Eventually Lisbon started calling him and I watched his face; the signals were loud and the telegraphy immaculate but there was not a flicker of interest; to any competent telegraphist, this was roughly the equivalent of shouting his name in his ear. I leaned across, received the message into his log book and gave a receipt. He smiled pleasantly. "Have you a clue about what's going on?" I shouted and above the snarling of four Merlins he explained that he had picked up a brief-case in Paddington Station containing a licence and passport and presented himself to us for a job. He had had two months' pay and two trips to South America out of it. This seems terribly inefficient now but the pressure under which we were working must be taken into account. He had a new licence, so must have recently been at school; he had been in an RAF highspeed launch that carried a standard RAF equipment, the same as our Lancastrians, so he was well versed in handling the equipment. We assumed that we could teach him the procedures. By the time we got to Lisbon I was determined that he must go north on the next aircraft. This decision was taken out of my hands—the last I saw of him he was ducking through the usual crowd at Portela Airport. There were a lot of aircraft staging through in those days—charters and war surplus deliveries to all parts of the world, he doubtless got a ride to somewhere. We at least did not see him again.

Slowly BSAA was expanding into an airline, we now had six Lancastrians and crew training was going ahead, then came our first serious setback. At two o'clock one morning there was a thunderous knocking on the front door where I found a policeman. "There's been an accident and your firm want you to be waiting at the end of this road in half an hour's time."

He knew nothing more, he was just delivering a message so I packed my bag and was waiting well within the half hour. Then a hire car drew up and I found a glum looking AVM and the chief pilot sitting in it. They had no intention of discussing what had happened and it wasn't until we arrived at the BSAA office at London Airport that the chief pilot called me aside and explained that there had been an accident at Bathurst. No one was injured but we were to fly out a relief aircraft to pick up the passengers and carry them on to South America. The aircraft was ready for us and we were bundled aboard and with the AVM at the controls, we were soon climbing away into the night sky. I found the radio serviceable and then asked diffidently where we were going.

"Bathurst," the answer snapped back.

"Yes, but are we stopping for fuel?" I asked.

"You worry about your radio and I'll worry about the fuel," was the uncompromising reply. The chief pilot, who was navigating, slid a piece of paper on to my desk.

"London–Bathurst direct, longish way, but don't worry."

I signalled the radio station at Uxbridge with my departure message, "Departed London for Bathurst direct." One could sense the operator at Uxbridge lifting his eyebrows. "Direct?"

"Yes," I replied.

There was a silence for a few minutes and then, "That's nearly 3,000 miles," came the reply.

I was feeling brave now. "I know, don't worry." I shifted over to the night frequency and there, working with Natal, was Bathurst itself. I called him and much to my amazement he replied. He accepted my departure message but his reaction was the same as Uxbridge—aircraft were not supposed to fly direct from London to Bathurst.

Long flights on very noisy aircraft have always had the effect of making me lose my sense of relative time; the hours drift by without the conscious knowledge that the passing of each one was bringing us closer to the end of the trip, and so it was now. Over North Africa I was able to offer considerable assistance to the chief pilot in his navigation by using the prewar Air-France medium frequency direction finding stations. I wound out the 200 feet of aerial to improve the range—Agadir, Sidi Ifini, Cape Jurby, Villa Cisneros, Port Etienne and Dakar—the radio operators all seemed to be as bored that hot morning in the Sahara as I was and a request for a bearing was answered by every station that could hear us. Cape Jurby offered to switch his beacon on if we would wait twenty minutes. I didn't know he had one, but as we were still some miles north of him I asked him to turn it on. He did and we took several bearings. Some time later he said he was going to close down for twenty minutes while he turned the beacon off. One could imagine the operator mounting his camel and trotting away into the desert to do this chore. I heard later that it was actually a marine beacon and miles from the Air-France station, so this could well have been true. In the middle of the afternoon we plunged into a build-up of rain clouds that gave a rough ride for a few minutes and then we broke out over the lush green of Gambia. As we circled for the landing we could see a forlorn Lancastrian sitting on the end of the runway with a collapsed undercarriage. The AVM really took charge on the ground; he held an enquiry on the spot, exonerated the captain from blame and decreed that he should carry on with his passengers in the aircraft we had brought.

The Lancastrian was more badly damaged than was at first apparent and months later, after everything of value had been removed, it was abandoned by the insurance and the hull was sold to an African scrap dealer.

Meanwhile we were accommodated at Bathurst in the BOAC resthouse—a collection of bungalows with a central mess and bar by the sea. Waiting here for a couple of days before we could hitch a ride back to England, I got to know our chief pilot much better. Captain Cracknell, who later became a senior captain in BOAC, was known as "Crackers". I found that his problems of selecting and training suitable pilots was a much magnified edition of our own; I also found that he too had flown on the Air Dispatch paper run to Paris before the war.

While at Bathurst there was an accident of a sort that was only too common immediately after the war, when crews with experience were at a premium. A Bristol Wayfarer landed at Bathurst on a delivery flight to Brazil. I found the first officer-cum-navigator-cum-radio operator was an old acquaintance from Weston Airways; we were in each other's company quite a lot during the days they laid over at Bathurst. The north-bound planes were all carrying two radiomen and a full passenger load, so I was stuck in the resthouse for over a week. During this time the Wayfarer started off one evening on the next leg of its trip to Brazil. Throughout the night and the next day, the flight Bathurst–Recife appeared to be going according to plan, but then the ETA Recife came and went and although the aircraft was still flying and communicating with Natal, it had not arrived there and admitted that there was no sign of the Brazilian coast. At last the Wayfarer realised the situation was serious—it was completely lost and fuel was getting low. Unless they could find out where they were, they would have to ditch it in the sea. The Wayfarer then said that they were flying in a heavy rain storm and the met. office at Natal did a brilliant piece of investigation. They checked through the Pan American network all along the Brazilian coast and found that a heavy squall had passed over Aracaju and gone out to sea earlier on. Taking the chance that the Wayfarer was now passing through the same storm, they gave them a course to fly for the coast. This they followed and although they did not actually sight the coast it brought them into the shipping lanes for the Wayfarer now signalled that she had a steamer in sight and that they were going to ditch alongside it as the fuel situation was desperate. They made a good ditching close to the United States cargo ship *Tulane Victory* which was bound south for Rio. Scrambling on to the wing my friend became the only casualty of the whole operation when someone put their foot in his face. They were picked up by a waiting lifeboat and conveyed aboard the steamer. Reconstructing the whole episode later, it became evident that a compass error had led them south of track for the whole flight and instead of sighting the coast, they had finished up flying parallel to it about 200 miles off. We heard later that the Wayfarer continued to float with its hull full of empty fuel tanks and as it was deemed to have become a danger to navigation it was sunk by a destroyer.

Most of the big international aircraft operators were having trouble training ex-wartime aircrews to operate in the civil environment. Air-France suffered from a shortage of pilots with a good enough knowledge of English to operate into places like New York where all instructions are passed to the pilot by radio telephone. The story goes that one afternoon when the visibility was poor enough to use GCA, a considerable number of aircraft waiting their turn to land were orbiting at different heights over the entry beacons for the New York area when a voice broke in: "New York, this is Air-France Fox Able Charley, am I clear to land?"

For one horrified second there was dead silence and then the dazed voice of the controller replied, "Air-France Fox Able Charley, where the hell have you come from?"

"I just come through harbour entrance," replied Able Charley.

"Climb on heading of 360 degrees magnetic, report passing through 1,000 feet, 2,000 feet, then alter course to 20 degrees magnetic and continue climbing and report passing through 3,000 feet, is this Roger?"

Silence for a few seconds then Fox Able Charley again. "No, this not Roger, this Maurice. Roger still in Paris—I can see runway, okay to land?"

Roger is the radio telephony term for "understood"!

Back in Dover Street, I found the radio department had been much strengthened by two more radio operators. Bob Tuck, my erstwhile friend from the Prestwick radio station, and Andy Ruthven, both ex-marine radiomen with some prewar flying experience. Another prewar flying operator had also appeared, Tommy Clark—we were slowly building up strength.

My next job was to go to Yeadon to form part of the crew to accept the first of our new aeroplanes, an Avro York. The York was a military transport conversion and although far from ideal, was a considerable improvement on the Lancastrian. It was a high wing aircraft with four Merlin engines and carried twenty passengers with two lavatories amidships and a galley aft.

The cockpit crew accommodation was a marked improvement— two pilots, a radio station complete with a chair behind and below the captain, with the navigator on a platform behind the first officer and under the astro dome. The nomenclature of "Star" was carried on; I think the first York was "Star Haze". "Crackers" was captain on the acceptance flight and we flew it back to Heathrow. He was now faced with the problem of converting all his crews to the new aeroplane; it fortunately carried the same radio as the Lancastrian so we had no conversion problem. From the point of view of a passenger, the main problem of the York was noise, the front row of seats was in line with the Merlins and the noise became painful if they were occupied for long periods. I remember on one trip noticing an old lady sitting quite happily there from London to Lisbon. I found her walking beside me as we disembarked and moved towards the terminal. Wishing to apologise for the hellish din she must have endured for the last five hours I said, "Sorry about the noise but I am sure the Stargirl (as our stewardesses were now called) will find you a better seat for the next flight."

She smiled sweetly and produced a pad and pencil. "Do you mind writing it down, I have been stone deaf since birth." She must have been the only satisfied passenger who rode in the front row of a York.

There was another incident in a York that indicates well the growing pains to which a budding airline can be subject. An hour out of London, a Stargirl was accosted by one of the passengers. "Eh lass, you don't half give us a good ride for ten bob." The impossible had happened! Queueing for a ten shilling flight over London in a Rapide, he had somehow got mixed up with the queue for the passengers in the York. A message was sent back to London Airport and his wife was contacted and the position explained to her. The passenger was as pleased as could be; he had a good lunch and when he arrived at Lisbon was taken out to a hotel in Estoril where he spent two days waiting for a north-bound aircraft. He was taken back by a York on which I was flying and he was one passenger without a single complaint about BSAA.

Another "growing" incident occurred in Rio. As Santos Dumont airfield was too short for Lancastrians, it was agreed that we could land on the new unfinished field on Governor's Island. When an aircraft was due, Royal Mail sent a tug with the customs and immigration authorities to handle the ingoing and outgoing passengers. I was flying with a new captain who was imbued with the press-on spirit. At each stop he cut the allowed time on the ground and by the time we arrived in Rio we were over an hour ahead of schedule. The tug with the authorities had not arrived but the captain would not delay, he dumped the passengers and their baggage in the shade of the partly built hangar and within minutes we were airborne again on the way to Monte. The authorities, I heard later, were extremely put out and it called for delicate negotiations at almost President level by our local manager before that little episode was forgiven.

Most of the York flights from Natal to Bathurst, and later to Dakar, were made during the hours of daylight and the navigation in the middle of this sector had to rely on dead reckoning and sun shots; this was usually quite satisfactory but sometimes the inter-tropical front would manifest itself as a high layer of cloud which made sun shots impractical. Recourse was then made to the following method of obtaining a position. The radioman would revert to the international distress frequency of 500 metres which is guarded by all shipping and transmit a call to all ships, followed by "QRK" —"Does anyone hear me?" There are a lot of cargo boats on the route between Europe and South America and mostly someone would reply; we would then ask him to transmit on another frequency and take a bearing of the ship on the direction finder. The ship would then supply his position from which the aircraft could plot the bearing. If several ships obliged, the aircraft finished up with a position to which no great degree of confidence could be attached but which was far better than dead reckoning. I often used this system and having a merchant navy background, prided myself on being able to pick out ships from the regular lines whose positions were bound to be accurate. One afternoon my call was answered by a ship with a Greek call sign; he said he was the *Evangeline Strathotis* bound from Rotterdam to Rosario. He was most helpful—when asked for a position he replied, "Captain asleep, will call you in two hours' time." On another occasion a British tanker, when asked to transmit for a bearing replied, "No need to, old man, ten minutes ago you flew directly overhead," and gave me his position at that time.

A BSAA radioman and first officer did a smart piece of work one morning flying from the Azores to London. A message was picked up from an aircraft saying it was lost; the aircraft subsequently turned out to be a Catalina which was being ferried from the States to Port Lyautey in North Africa. We never heard who the crew were but they had thoroughly lost themselves and complained that both their fluxgate and magnetic compasses appeared to be faulty. The BSAA radio officer gave the Catalina the frequencies of the Consol stations at Lugo and Seville, told him to listen to each station and count the number of dots and dashes that he heard. He made the Catalina also take bearings of the two stations and give him the readings of his magnetic compass. From this information the BSAA aircraft plotted a position for the Catalina. The Catalina was then given a course to fly for the coast recommending that he used the magnetic compass as this was least liable to error. This procedure was repeated at half-hourly intervals and it was established after an hour and a half that the magnetic compass was reasonably accurate at any rate on that heading. Eventually the BSAA Lancastrian, which had been steadily flying to London, received a jubilant message from the Catalina that they had Port Lyautey in sight.

I once heard our early flights described as "bombing our way through South America"; for years the route from Buenos Aires to Santiago had been made by aircraft flying through the "pass" in the Andes. It was a flight which demanded clear weather and the flight could be delayed, sometimes for days, during periods of bad weather over the mountains when the pass would be filled with cloud. BSAA now decided to extend their service from London to Buenos Aires to Santiago in Chile by using Lancastrians which could cross the Andes at 25,000 feet if needs be, rather than wait for fair weather in the passes. I was sent to Buenos Aires to take part in the proving flights. The Lancastrians were unpressurised but had an oxygen supply which gave each person a rubber tube to suck with masks for the crew. The first flights were made in clear weather and it was the most impressive scenery; the actual Andes range is quite narrow but is perpetually snow-covered and it is dominated by Aconcagua, a monster peak of 29,000 feet. Once across the Andes, a very steep descent was called for into Los Cerrillos, the airport for Santiago. It was decided to open the service with the proviso that under no circumstances were the aircraft to enter cloud which can pile up over the Andes in the most alarming manner. If the aircraft couldn't top the cloud it was to return to Mendoza. For a while all went well and then a captain on his first trip in command went missing over the Andes. It was never established if he did enter cloud and an enquiry could only establish that from signals received, the aircraft, it appeared, had already crossed the Andes. Years later, a contrabandista, as the smugglers are called who operated in the high Andes across the Chilean–Argentina border, was arrested and found to be wearing a watch belonging to one of the crew of the lost Lancastrian. He stated that he had found the wreck of an aircraft in one of the high valleys and from the way it was scattered it was obvious that the crew and passengers had been killed instantly. The Chilean authorities had made a comprehensive search for the lost aircraft but they now mounted an expedition to the site of the wreck. It was found to be in a deep, narrow valley where it would not be visible from an aircraft unless the sun was overhead; nothing was found that indicated the cause of the disaster.

Because of the difficult terrain and weather conditions it was decided that a special captain should be posted in Buenos Aires to fly the trans-Andes sector of the route. Captain Cliff was the first captain to hold this post. I had several trips over the Andes with him and only had to turn back on one occasion when we landed at Mendoza. On this occasion the cloud was towering high over the mountains and as we climbed closer the tops appeared to be moving as though they were boiling. On another occasion on a check flight, the first officer was navigating and I was sitting in the copilot's seat. It was a brilliant day and we were crossing at 20,000 feet with Aconcagua just to the north of us showing a trail of cloud streaming away from the summit. Suddenly the pilot pointed through my windscreen; crossing our path at about a hundred feet above was a huge bird, an Andean condor. It is the highest I have ever heard of a bird flying.

On another trip we had a very rough passage, we ran into some clear air turbulence which was shaking the Lancastrian in an extraordinary manner. I felt a hand shaking my shoulder and looked round to find the Stargirl leaning over the spar; she looked utterly exhausted and was pointing dumbly back into the fuselage. I hopped out of my seat and into the passenger cabin where I found chaos. The Elsan had carried away and dumped its unsavoury contents which were advancing down the narrow aisle between the seats. I unhooked the carpet and rolled it up towards the approaching tide. Eventually I pushed the unsavoury bundle into the lavatory and jammed the door closed. I then tried to help the Stargirl with her charges and was amazed to find that two tiny babies which she collected from their prostrate mothers were the only two of our passengers who had not been violently sick. In fact, one of them was quite happy sucking condensed milk from the handle of a spoon when I looked after them in the galley.

Home again, I found that we had had another disaster; a fully loaded York leaving Bathurst for Natal had crashed into a man-grove swamp on a night take-off with the total loss of passengers and crew.

BSAA decided to move their operations to Dakar where the French had now opened up the old United States base at Mallard Field as an international airport. It was a much better airfield but the accommodation for crews in Dakar was far below the standard of the BOAC resthouse at Bathurst. The war had left Dakar short of everything—water, electricity, hotels—everything had been allowed to run down and was now trying to start again. The only accommodation available was in the Metropole Hotel which was crowded out. The captain and the Stargirl had separate rooms but the rest of us, sometimes four or five, had to crowd into one large room, the floor of which was covered with beds. With water available only for a few hours a day and the discomfort of the heat and overcrowding, the Dakar stop was not looked forward to. Back in

Dover Street, another route was decided upon—London, Santa Maria in the Azores, Bermuda, Jamaica and Caracas. I went on the first proving flight preparatory to opening the service. Santa Maria was a US military field that had been handed over to the Portuguese civil authorities. The flight was uneventful; we picked up Santa Maria Island at about fifty miles but the radio telephone conversation with the control tower was most peculiar. It later transpired that the tower operator was sick and his place had been taken by an operator whose English was fragmentary. He used a list of standard replies from a board left by the Americans which he gave us regardless of what we said. The end of this exchange of information came when he ran out of replies. I reported, "Island in sight."

He replied, "Clear to taxi," and that ended the matter as far as telephony was concerned.

We found Santa Maria to be a huge American base with plenty of hangar space, vehicles and acres of tarmac but no staff. The authorities were converting a series of huts into a transient hotel which was called the "Terra Nova" but like so many countries in the immediate postwar years, the Portuguese were desperately short of materials and tools and the hotel took a long time to complete. We spent twenty-four hours here and the next afternoon set off on the next sector—Azores, Bermuda—a distance of some 2,300 miles. We did the flight in just over twelve hours against the prevailing westerly winds; some of the later flights took much longer—one was actually in the air 16½ hours. The wartime long-range direction finding stations had been partly abandoned so the whole flight had to be made using astro navigation. Sometimes the winds forced us to fly low and when the stars were not visible navigation was by dead reckoning.

Later we were able to equip the aircraft with Loran and this was of great assistance to the navigator, for the whole of the sector was covered by Loran at night, but until this was done and the pilots became proficient in its use I always disliked this long sector; with cloud cover and a failed radio system, finding Bermuda if it was closed in by bad weather would have been a well-nigh impossible task. The American Air Force base at Kindley Field had been turned into a civil-cum-military field. It had a high-powered beacon which could be used in conjunction with the aircraft direction finder and two radio range stations.

Accommodation had been reserved for us in the White Horse Inn at St. Georges; it was a big rambling old place that became the home of the slip crews when they were in Bermuda. It was always called "Arthur's and Rosy's" after the owner and his wife who did everything possible to remove the normal stilted atmosphere of an hotel.

The next day we went on to Jamaica, landing at Palisadoes Airport where we all received the typical Jamaican welcome—a large glass of planter's punch. We stayed the night in the Myrtle Bank hotel, it was usually called the Turtle Tank, and sampled a few more of the planter's punches. The next day we made the short flight from Jamaica to Marquetta, the airport for Caracas. The ride from the airport to the city, which is up in the mountains, was the type of journey that you remember for always. The road seemed to be hacked out of the side of the mountains while at each corner were small memorial stones and shrines to people who had driven over the edge. I had the feeling that the taxi driver put on a special show of squealing tyres and near misses with cars coming down from the mountains especially for us. If the object was to scare us, in my case it was most successful. The only thing I remember about the hotel in Caracas was that one of the other crew members and myself went into the bar and ordered two whiskys; the bill came to nearly a pound—not quite our line of country.

The next day we started the long journey of retracing our steps back to England. It was decided to base a York in Jamaica to cover the West Indian services. This was later moved to Nassau and the fleet increased to cover the Panama Canal zone and on to Lima and Santiago, thus BSAA completely encircled South America. The routes were now divided into two, the east coast from the UK to Santiago via Lisbon, Dakar, Brazil and the Argentine; and the west coast via the Azores and later Newfoundland through the West Indies to Peru and Santiago. On the two routes a total of approximately fifty crews were employed, with the majority of the senior captains on the west coast.

By now the initial training and familiarisation of the radio staff was complete and I settled down to ordinary route flying. The standards of flying of the captains varied enormously and I used Rio harbour as the yardstick by which I judged a pilot's ability. In aircraft equipped only with a hand-operated direction finder and unsuitable radio communication equipment, an approach into Rio in bad weather could be quite an experience. The harbour is ringed with hills, one particularly nasty-looking lot we called "The Fingers", and the accepted method of approaching was to establish oneself overhead and then orbit round the radio beacons until one broke cloud. Communication was by transmitting on one frequency and listening for the reply on the beacon. The voice radiation was slightly offset from the beacon frequency and unless it was carefully tuned, English spoken with a Portuguese accent could become very garbled. With a flight from Dakar to Natal behind you and arriving at Rio mid-afternoon with an impatient captain who didn't understand the radio instructions, the atmosphere in the cockpit could get tense. The situation was later improved by equipping the aircraft with automatic direction finders as they became available in the civil market and with Rebecca equipment which gave the pilot his distance from the beacon he was orbiting on.

I remember one unpleasant experience of breaking cloud in a York and seeing through the big round window beside me a huge statue of Christ, which is perched on one of the hills, pass by the wing-tip with what appeared to be inches to spare. Another captain lost heart orbiting in dense cloud and decided on a new approach; he climbed out of the hole, flew over the sea and then let down to sea level and made a run for the harbour mouth in spite of the protestations from the ground control that the cloud was down to the sea in the harbour mouth. We roared along at literally nought feet and plunged into cloud. The York suddenly rolled wildly and then plunged into clear air beneath the cloud in the middle of the harbour. I heard on the intercom, "Christ, man, we missed that mast by inches," and so it proved to be. A ship had been right in the harbour entrance as we went through. We heard no more of that one but assumed that our local manager must have gone through his smoothing down routine with the local authorities.

On another trip to Jamaica, we found that Santa Maria was out with weather and the captain elected to go to Prestwick, Gander, Bermuda and Jamaica. All went well until we were approaching Gander where the weather was just in limits to allow us to land. In those days there was a ground controlled approach radar at Gander jointly operated by BOAC and Pan American. This was a system of giving the pilot guidance instructions for flying via voice radio down to the runway threshold. Any aircraft could use the system if they so desired but for each approach a charge was made against the aircraft's operating company. The only other method was a range type let down. The radio telephone conversation went something like this:

"Gander, this is Lancastrian Uncle George, estimating your field in five minutes."

"Roger, Uncle George, vis. one quarter of a mile in snow, what let down do you elect, GCA or range?"

The captain was aghast at the thought of the company being charged for a GCA and, in spite of the fact that he was by no means an expert at range flying, he replied, "Elect to do a range let down."

"Roger," replied Gander. "Clear inbound at 5,000 feet, report high cone."

Our first attempt was a dreadful hash. I listened in to the whole thing on my receiver at the radio station. There was obviously a strong beam wind which repeatedly blew us off the range leg and instead of trying to assess the drift and edging back, we made steep turns in an attempt to rejoin the range leg, we would then fly right through it. Then the range characteristic changed. "Report high cone," said Gander. Over the intercom I told the pilot he had missed it.

"You keep out of this," he snarled but nevertheless turned 180 degrees and made another attempt to find the approach leg.

"Report your position," said Gander.

"Just joining approach leg," replied the pilot.

"Report high cone," said Gander.

Again wild course changes for ten minutes and again the cone of silence eluded us.

"Report your position," said Gander.

This time we had no idea; "Standby" was the only thing we could say.

Then a rich, deep assured voice broke in. "Gander this is Pan American flight seven, give that son of a bitch a GCA on Pan American, we'll save money that way."

During our gyrations along the range legs, no less than three aircraft had arrived and were orbiting while awaiting their turn to approach. GCA at once took over and gave us height and courses to fly to position us for an approach. When we had settled on this, GCA said, "Captain's name please?"

He started to reply, "Uncle, Sugar, Willy, Willy, Uncle, Roger er, er . . . what's the phonetic for Tee?" he asked me over the intercom. Before I could reply GCA broke in, "Never mind, just sing it or say it, sonny."

I felt that somehow people were getting a little tired of us in Gander. It was a slightly shamefaced crew that climbed out of "Uncle Willy" into the whirling snow at Gander airport a few minutes later.

Then came a great day in the life of BSAA, we were to fly in a BOAC Tudor I at London Airport and assess its possibilities for use in BSAA. We found a big, roomy cockpit and a chair and table to operate from and what, to us, was wonderful radio equipment. It had duplicate equipment of the type which was fitted to the first Hudson I had flown to England in Ferry Command. The Ministry had ordered a number of Tudor Is for a North Atlantic operation by BOAC. The story was that this order was placed without consultation with BOAC and now they were refusing to accept them. They were twelve-seaters which even if they were full every trip they made, would have been an odd operation in that they needed a crew of two pilots, a navigator, a flight engineer, a radio operator and stewardess—half as many crew as passengers. The aircraft was deemed suitable with some modifications to the cockpit and the passenger seating arrangements and when this was completed we returned to Woodford to take delivery of the first BSAA Tudor. Alas the American radio equipment and the automatic direction finder had vanished, we were back to the old wartime equipment of the Lancasters and Yorks, but this time it was duplicated.

The first trip of the Tudor "Star Lion" was to Jamaica for tropical trials. We had retained the "Star" title but it was now followed by mostly animal names. We were scheduled to go to Santa Maria and then a gigantic hop of no less than 2,750 miles to Beane Field in Antigua. From there to Trinidad and on to Jamaica, Nassau, Bermuda, Gander and home again. The AVM and "Crackers" were in charge of the flight. The first setback was that Santa Maria was closed with bad weather and the flight had to be re-scheduled via Prestwick, Gander, Bermuda to Trinidad. That was an extremely lucky piece of bad weather, for when flying from Prestwick to Gander we had fuel transfer problems and arrived at Gander with a large amount of reserve fuel which was not accessible; this could have created quite a situation on the Azores–Antigua sector. The Air Registration Board were satisfied with the performance of the Tudor under tropical conditions and arrangements were made to put them into operation on all our routes.

CHAPTER FIFTEEN

I NEXT made several training and familiarisation flights with "Crackers" before returning home to find that I had been scheduled out on a charter to New Zealand. Twenty-one Greek seamen wanted transportation from Athens to New Zealand to crew a ship that the Greeks had recently purchased there. A York had been scheduled for the job and the AVM was in command, with one of our Australian captains, Macphee, as first officer. The AVM's wife and secretary were the hostesses and myself and another radio operator looked after the communications.

The AVM was a man who never showed fatigue and on this marathon he was at his best. London Airport to Athens, where we landed at Hassani, the old airport for Athens, Cairo West, Karachi, where, owing to a hitch in our passengers' yellow fever inoculations, we caught a four hours sleep; Karachi to Dum Dum, Calcutta and then on to Singapore, Darwin and Sydney. The last stop was the main New Zealand Air Force base in South Island. The AVM was still going strong but I was completely bushed; I remember being given a pint of beer in a silver tankard by the signals officer and nothing more until the next day when we flew to Brisbane's Archer Field. Brisbane was the AVM's home town. We were met by a large number of people and in the evening we all attended a reception which was slightly marred when someone tried to introduce me to the AVM—an honour which he firmly declined. The next day we started our long trip back to London. By sleeping alternate sectors, we eventually made it home without night stopping again. Looking back, I sometimes think that my main contribution to this trip was acting as the go-between between the Greek seamen and our catering staff. The official interpreter was the Greek radio operator whose English was of the Tiger Bay variety and my eight years at sea gave me the knowledge to turn this into English suitable for a lady's ears.

Not being assigned to any particular route, I found that I was a natural for all the emergency flights that came up. A passenger York force landed in Casablanca with an engine out and one morning I found myself flying from London to Casablanca in a freighter York with Captain Rodley, complete with a spare engine and some engineers to fit it into the grounded plane. We found accommodation in Casablanca completely unobtainable; they could serve us food in the airport restaurant but we would have to sleep in our aircraft. The crew of the passenger York supplied us with blankets and we found that their two Stargirls were also sleeping in their aircraft. A night foray by Captain Rodley and myself was thwarted by the captain of the passenger York locking his crew inside the aeroplane. After two days we ran out of cigarettes but we had become friendly with a customs officer who had fallen in love with one of the Stargirls. Captain Rodley and I gave this affair all the encouragement we could because, as he said, it pays to have friends in high places. When we explained our cigarette shortage problem, the customs officer waved his hands: "No problem, I show." A crowd of passengers on an Air Atlas aircraft were just lining up in front of the customs desk. In a fervour of zeal M. le Douanier attacked their baggage; he found carton after carton of American cigarettes which were contraband and then he castigated them with a flood of French; he let them off their fines but confiscated the cartons and later presented them to us. Then the passenger York, complete with a new engine, departed northwards while we stayed another day to load the removed engine into our freighter.

Then another salvage operation turned up. A York had landed with an engine out at Atkinson Field, just outside Georgetown, in what was then British Guiana. Once again we set off with our spare engine and engineers and flew to Lisbon, Dakar, Natal and Atkinson. Working conditions at Atkinson were difficult as the field had been largely abandoned and we were stuck in a hotel in Georgetown for about a week. The captain had just bought a new house in London and was an enthusiastic carpenter. We spent hours searching the riverside timberyards for some very special wood for the top of his homemade bar. At last he settled for a slab of crabwood; it looked perfect—grain, thickness and guaranteed by all the timber merchant's ancestors, never to warp. At last the engine change was finished and we received a cable to proceed via Bermuda, Azores back to London. The crabwood was carefully loaded in the hold in a special wooden framework. It was a hot, still morning when we took off for Bermuda. I was standing between the two pilots and I was conscious that we were accelerating very slowly; the captain at last eased back the stick but it stuck; he pushed it forward slightly and pulled back with all his might, but it stuck again. We now had flying speed but with a jammed stick, a crash seemed inevitable—then I saw it . . . where the copilot's control column went through the floor was a leather skirt, this was old and had sagged down, and lying in the sag was an empty coke bottle, it must have rolled from under the co-pilot's seat during the taxi run. I snatched it out, the captain heaved back on the controls and the York took off from the last ten yards of concrete. Inquests were pointless. Literally anyone could have pushed the coke bottle under the seat.

The rest of the trip was without incident but an hour before reaching London the captain called me back; he had been aft to admire his crabwood bar top. I don't know if it was the heating system or that the coloured timber merchant's ancestors had slipped up but the captain's famous crabwood bar top had split clean across.

My next job in BSAA was on the flight refuelling programme. Flight Refuelling Limited had four Lancaster bombers—two of them were modified into tanker aircraft and two were receivers. The programme was that the two tankers would be positioned in Santa Maria with Flight Refuelling crews and that BSAA would operate the receivers direct from London to Bermuda and would refuel in mid-Atlantic from the tankers which would fly out to meet them. In addition, each tanker and receiver was fitted with a Rebecca/Eureka equipment which allowed each of them to measure the exact distance between the two aircraft. The minimum dis-tances to which these equipments would measure was about one mile and as all interceptions were planned to take place in daylight and clear of cloud, they were quite adequate.

The first London to Bermuda flight was commanded by the AVM; the first officer was Wheatley; there were two radiomen and myself and a Flight Refuelling engineer to handle the hoses from the tanker. Sir Alan Cobham came along as an observer—he was the chairman of Flight Refuelling. The interception was planned to take place some 300 miles north of the Azores. We were airborne from London about 9 a.m. and set course for Bermuda. I don't know if the rest of the crew were tensed up but I remember sitting glued to the Santa Maria radio frequency waiting for the tanker to signal he had left. Right on time, I heard him tell Santa Maria that he was climbing on course for the rendezvous. He replied to my first call and confirmed the position and time of the rendezvous. I now transferred my attention to the Rebecca cathode ray tube; I watched the maximum distance area at the top of the tube with deep concentration and then a tiny, steady pulse appeared.

"I've got it, 185 miles away," I said, but the radioman on duty pushed his logbook under my elbow.

"Got you at 190 miles," it said; the tanker was as good at that game as we were. After a while the AVM was talking to the tanker on VHF, then came the visual sighting. Soon the tanker was roaring along overhead; Chalky White, the Flight Refuelling operator, picked up the hose and 2,000 gallons of petrol were transferred from the tanker to a special belly tank in our receiver. When the operation was complete, the tanker reeled in her hose and wheeled away south on her trip back to the Azores. The captain of the tanker was David Prowse, a famous pilot of British Airways before the war. We were left alone to trudge out the many weary sea miles to Bermuda. The cabin of the Lancastrian was fitted up with four bunks and I was asleep on one of them when one of the radiomen shook my shoulder—I was wanted up front. It was now dark, the AVM had been transferring fuel from the belly tank to the wing tanks and found that things were not going well. I found that we had burnt out both generators. Everything electrical was switched off to save the aircraft accumulators to drive the transfer pump to empty the belly tank into the wing tanks. This was done and we finished with a dead flat battery. The AVM set himself to navigate by astro but we soon ran under a cover of high cloud and were reduced to dead reckoning. Slowly the long flight wore on; there was nothing to do but wait and hope we would hit Bermuda on the nose; our fuel reserves would not stand a long search for the island. At long and weary last, the ETA Bermuda came up but there was no island—just night and a black sea. An hour went by and in the midst of explaining to the AVM that if we put all the ship's batteries in series we might have enough juice to work the little range receiver, the first officer called, "I see a light"—it was the Cooks Point lighthouse, Bermuda. A few minutes later we were rolling down the long runway at Kindley Field, nineteen and a half worried hours out from London. With a fully serviceable aircraft, our return trip to London was an anticlimax—it went off perfectly. I made five of these return flights to Bermuda that summer, every one was highly successful and the only criticism I could find with refuelling in flight was the psychological effect on the passengers of the tanker flying over their heads during the interception.

While the flight refuelling programme was being carried out, Tudors were steadily being delivered to BSAA and taking their place in the general route structure. They were popular with both passengers and crews and in spite of considerable competition from new airlines that seemed to be appearing almost daily on the South American routes, the company was expanding. Then disaster struck —we had moved from the rabbit warren in Dover Street to a large new building in King Street in which I had been allocated an office. I was early for work that particular morning and as I climbed the stairs a white-faced secretary stopped me and pointed to the phone in her office. I picked it up and a voice said, "This is United Press. Can you give me the names of the crew of your aircraft that was lost early this morning in the North Atlantic?"

It was only too true. "Star Tiger", on her way from the Azores to Bermuda, had failed to arrive and must now be considered as lost. There was little to tell. She had left Santa Maria with a full load of passengers on a fairly long flight plan to Bermuda, they had decided to fly at 2,000 feet to avoid the stronger head winds at the greater altitudes. All night long, Bob Tuck, the radio operator, who had been my friend at Prestwick during Ferry Command days, had sent his position report every hour; the only discrepancy was that he reported his altitude as 20,000 feet instead of 2,000 feet—a mistake of putting a zero instead of an x in the height group. With some four hours to go, he sent his normal position message and that was the last that was ever heard or seen of "Star Tiger". The United States Air Force mounted a massive search operation, combing the area with radar-equipped aircraft operating in conjunction with surface vessels, but not a trace was found of "Star Tiger". For weeks the papers reported the usual crop of rumours that follow a disaster of this magnitude; there were the usual distress messages picked up by all sorts of odd people on all sorts of radio frequencies and when these died down we were regaled by people's ideas of what might have happened. The more preposterous, the bigger the coverage they seemed to rate in the press. One solution in particular was handed to me to investigate and which I have never been able to sort out in my mind. A letter from the matron of an old folk's home in the North of England enclosed a further letter from one of the inmates. The matron said that the lady whose letter was enclosed was very old and not very literate but she had insisted on writing down her "dream" and sending it to us. She said she had been flying in the cockpit of a large aircraft; there was one man sitting down facing forwards (the navigator?) and another man sitting facing sideways (the radio operator?), then she smelt a strong smell of gas and both men fell forwards over their tables. The aeroplane flew on and on for hours until the roar of the engines stopped and she stepped outside and found herself on a tropical island. She gave the name of the island and after searching through several atlases without success I eventually found it marked on a large-scale Admiralty chart—it was an uninhabited speck of land in the Philippines. She might have pieced the first part of the letter together from guesswork but how did she figure out the name of the island?—it was in Spanish.

There was now a great outcry that the Tudors should be grounded. Uninformed articles appeared in the press questioning the aircraft's safety and the ability of our crews. They pretty well questioned everything that we had ever done. The inevitable result was a public enquiry which was held in Church House, Westminster. It was my first experience of anything of this nature and, perhaps because of my emotional involvement in the whole thing, it was unwise to have attended. But attend I did and found that although the basis of the enquiry was to ascertain what had caused the loss of "Star Tiger", what was actually happening was that the legal gentlemen representing all the interested parties were trying to find out who could be blamed for the disaster; it seemed to be working backwards. I heard a ground engineer grilled for stating that the captain had told him to "fill her up to the gills", a term that has meant full tanks ever since Wilbur Wright invented an aeroplane; I heard the manager of BSAA, Bermuda, cross-questioned about his initiation of "aircraft missing" action as though he was personally responsible for its loss. I left that enquiry convinced that nothing but bad feeling would come out of it and so it proved.

A firm recommendation came out of the enquiry that the training of pilots must be put on a much more orderly basis. Captain Rodley was made training captain and Don Brown was imported from BOAC as training manager to set up an organisation to carry out the recommendation. While this was being set up the AVM left BSAA to form his own charter company. He was replaced by Air Commodore Brackley from BOAC.

CHAPTER SIXTEEN

After months of hindrance to both road and rail access to Berlin, the Russians closed all entry except along an air corridor. The allies determined to keep this open at all costs and to maintain Berlin by means of an airlift. We became involved in this airlift when the Ministry offered BSAA a number of Tudor V aircraft at a low cost as long as they were specifically used for this operation. If we decided later to use them as airliners, a much higher charge was to be made. The Tudor Vs were modified for the carriage of fuel oil by the installation of tanks in the passenger compartment. Our freighter Yorks were pressed into service for carrying coal and flour. The RAF put all their York freighters in, Aquila Airways flew supplies into Wannsee Lake with their Solent flying boats, the AVM turned up with a Lancaster and later with a Tudor in which he performed the amazing feat of taking off with his control locks on and landing safely again using the trim and moving his crew around.

I was sent to the RAF headquarters at Wunsdorf to look after the radio side of things for BSAA, where we were accommodated in an attic in the old German Air Force mess. The operation of the airlift was a triumph of organisation by the RAF. Twice a day at least, the mixture of aircraft were loaded and assembled in a line on the taxiways at Wunsdorf; this was called a wave. Two air routes were used, one into Gatow in Berlin and one back from Gatow to Wunsdorf. These corridors were defined by beacons, both medium frequency and radar. The aircraft were all fitted with voice radio and each one started up its engines and taxied round to the take-off position on instructions from the control tower. When the aircraft had been run up and the mags checked, they were instructed to take off at two-minute intervals, thus the whole wave became airborne in the corridor at two-minute intervals. By maintaining a constant airspeed they all arrived at Gatow in the same order. If any aircraft was unable to maintain this sequence on the ground, it stayed on the ground until the next wave.

The crew's duties fell into natural roles; the captain flew the aircraft and worked the voice radio, the navigator watched for the checkpoints while the radio operator watched the weather reports from Wunsdorf and Gatow. The BSAA captains on the airlift were mostly first and second officers who had been upgraded to the position. To a man they did an excellent job and have since all become senior captains with different airlines—it was certainly a forcing house for captains.

The aircraft were landed at Gatow in the same order as they had left Wunsdorf, the approach to the runway was over devastated Berlin, the last checkpoint being called the Christmas Tree. As the British wave landed, there was usually a wave of American Air Force DC-4s waiting to take off after the last of our aircraft had landed. If an aircraft failed to land on its first attempt it returned to Wunsdorf.

Some of the dialogue on the voice radio between the two fleets of aircraft is worth repeating. I don't know what the qualifications for the RAF controllers at Wunsdorf and Gatow were but they were the quickest thinkers and fastest talkers I have ever heard on the air. Coming into Wunsdorf I heard an American say "Them Limeys have sure been scraping the bottom of the barrel for kites on this airlift, Al."

"Sure have," replied Al.

"What's that one in the slot now, Al?"

"This is a Wayfarer," said a bored English voice.

"Roger, Wayfarer—I thought it was the Mayflower, Al."

"I say again 'Wayfarer'," said the English voice.

"Okay Bud. Think he made it himself, Al?"

On another occasion we were coming in with a Tudor V—a long aircraft that was difficult to land without bouncing.

"What's that boy in the slot now, Al?"

"That's a two door, Bud."

"Al, I got a dollar what says that boy's going to bounce that old two door," said Bud.

"That dollar's covered, Bud," said Al.

Our young skipper who was struggling to keep his heavy aircraft straight in turbulence grabbed his mike. "For Christ's sake, shut up," he snapped.

But it wasn't his day, he touched just too hard and the Tudor ballooned up and it needed a burst of throttle to get her down.

"Lookit that boy bouncing your dollar," said Bud.

"Yes," said Al. "Looks as though he's got kangaroo piss in his oleos."

I heard of an American flying behind a York who claimed that he was following a Limey boxcar by the Christmas Tree. The Berlin airlift almost produced a new language in three months.

After a few weeks, we moved into a T-Force hotel in a nearby town, where accommodation and food were much improved. Flying in tankers, we never spent more than ten minutes in Gatow—just time for a cup of tea in the Malcolm Club and then back to Wunsdorf.

We had a scare one afternoon when we were flying in the wave in dense cloud; the captain called to the control "Over Volkenrode." As he took his thumb from the mike button, the York ahead said "Over Volkenrode"; the reactions of our captain and the York captain were exactly the same—both dived and we broke cloud seconds before the York broke cloud 100 yards ahead of us.

BSAA now seemed to be dogged with bad luck, our new chief executive was drowned on holiday on Copacabana beach in Rio; this was a grievous loss for he was just starting to rebuild the corporation morale after the reverses suffered from the loss of "Star Tiger". We then suffered the final blow which meant the end of British South American Airways. Another Tudor, "Star Ariel", left Bermuda on a flight to Jamaica and about 200 miles out of Bermuda went missing. The radio operator had reported, quite normally, 150 miles from the island, flying in clear weather at 18,000 feet, and that was the last that was seen or heard of "Star Ariel". The Americans mounted another massive air and sea search but no trace was ever found. The Tudors were now grounded which was perhaps a reasonable decision in the knowledge that two of them had been lost without any indication as to what had happened, but it meant the end of the Tudor as an aircraft and the end of British South American Airways Corporation.

The only common factors were that both aircraft were Tudors and they had both been lost without warning and without subsequent trace. The differences were considerable; they were lost in different locations, flying at different altitudes and in different weather conditions. My feelings are that "Star Tiger" flew into the sea. Operating for a long period at low level with one pilot doing the navigation with the other monitoring the autopilot, his attention may have been diverted while the trim of the aircraft was changed by a movement of passengers from the after part of the cabin, where the toilets were, to forward seats. This supposition will hardly fit the case of "Star Ariel".

Some years later, an enterprising private company took some of the grounded Tudors and converted them into unpressurised freight aircraft and called them Super Traders. Even then they were still dogged by bad luck for one of them and its crew was lost in the mountains of Turkey.

For a while BSAA carried on operations with the Lancastrian and York fleets but it became obvious that there was only one solution to the problem of shortage of aircraft and that was a merger with BOAC.

Some time earlier BSAA had taken over British West Indian Airways and we were in the process of replacing their fleet of Venturas with ex-BEA Vikings that were being modified at the maintenance base at Langley to British West Indian Airways requirements. One morning I received a visit from an old friend of mine, Captain Des Vertiule. He had originally been a second officer in BSAA and was now a captain with British West Indian. He was back in England to ferry out the last of their Vikings to Trinidad and wondered if I would go along with him. Considering the atmosphere of gloom that was pervading the King Street offices, I jumped at the chance.

The Viking had been modified for operation by two pilots and was fitted with American radio equipment controlled from the co-pilot's seat. Des did the flying and navigated mostly by HF bearings plotted on his lap. It was a leisurely flight; we flew only by day and it made a pleasant ending to my hectic flying career in BSAA.

We made a daylight flight to Lisbon and spent the night at a small hotel in Estoril. The next day we flew in perfect weather along the African coast to Dakar. Here we found that the local manager had been unable to find hotel accommodation and apologised profusely for putting us in the Air-France resthouse. Perhaps the rooms were not the best in Dakar but the dinner that night most certainly was. Not too early the next morning we set off for Natal, again in perfect weather. The intertropical front was having a day off, just a few cu-nims towering into the sky which Des had no trouble flying round. With our high-powered American radio, we were able to hang on to Dakar and Port Etienne and they supplied us with bearings until we were able to pick up the radio beacon at the Fernando Noronha island, the Brazilian penal settlement 250 miles out in the Atlantic. We had a look at St. Paul's Rocks on the way, a desolate-looking spot, and then we were circling the field at Natal. After a night at the Hotel Grandi where the dinner compared poorly with Air-France's effort twenty-four hours earlier, we set out on the last leg of the flight to Trinidad. On the way we had a good look at Devil's Island which appears to be a nice place to live from the air, and then we arrived at Piarco Field, Trinidad. This was Des's home and I spent a pleasant two days living in the Queens Park Hotel and visiting the beaches.

Then the expected news came. BOAC had taken over the remains of BSAA and I was to return to London as a passenger. BWIA flew me round the islands to Jamaica where I joined a BOAC Constellation which brought me home to London Airport. The next day I visited King Street. The only person left was Max, the doorman, who had transferred to Crittals, the new owners of the building. I went home. So ended my connection with an airline that started life with high hopes and good prospects. It was born during the time when BOAC were losing £9,000,000 a year and in our efforts at least to break even there is no doubt that some of our practices were open to criticism. The philosophy of carrying more than adequate fuel reserves was not encouraged.

In the early days training was not followed too closely; there is a story that one captain scheduled out on a York complained bitterly to his first officer at the end of the runway at Heathrow that he had never flown a York before. Our ground services, especially abroad, were rather sketchy and we seemed a natural mark for stowaways. One young Portuguese hid in the main wheel wall of a York in Lisbon and rode there all the way to London. He must have been paralysed with cold but he hung on until they arrived. He then waited until the aircraft had been towed away to the hangar and when it was dark he dropped to the ground, right into the arms of an airport policeman who happened to be passing. Another stowed himself away in the tail cone of a Lancastrian and gave Captain Dickie Alcock a worrying flight while he tried to figure out what made the aircraft so tail heavy. A loader in Jamaica hid himself under a panel in the passage way of a Tudor. He scared the Stargirl out of her wits by climbing out of the panel under the carpet after the aircraft had been airborne only a few minutes.

When two corporations merge, inevitably something gets lost in the shuffle—this time it was me. For days I met the postman at the door expecting my marching orders. At the end of the month I visited the bank, yes, my salary had been paid, so I just gave up and waited. Ten months went by, the West Indians were playing in England and it was a beautiful summer. Occasionally I thought that perhaps I ought to do something about BOAC but they continued to pay my salary and I assumed that they would get around to finding me something to do some time.

One evening after a pleasant day watching England being

hammered all over Lords, I found myself sitting in the tube next to the ex-operations manager of BSAA who had by then reverted to his old job of a senior pilot in BOAC. He asked me which line I had been attached to and was most concerned to find that I was still unattached, although on full pay, and promised to see what he could do. Action followed fast. Two days later I received a letter from Mr. Whitney Straight, the managing director and chief executive of BOAC, summoning me to his office at 2.30 p.m. the next day. I spent the next few hours in harassed speculation of what could possibly be the purpose of this summons. The only thing I could visualise was dismissal, yet why from someone so high? I had flown with Mr. Straight before the war in a Q6 of Weston Airways when it was part of the Straight Corporation.

I set off from Ruislip Manor underground in plenty of time and then at Eastcote a door jammed and the train had to be removed from service. I just had to get to Green Park Station in time for the interview. I dashed out of the station—no taxis, nothing. I asked a porter if he knew anyone that I could hire; he didn't but he said he would run me up himself on the back of his motorbike. He dropped me at Green Park Underground station ten minutes before the meeting. I pushed two pounds into his hand and started to run for it. That Eastcote porter was a real hero. Red-faced and completely winded I blundered into the office of Mr. Straight's secretary to be greeted with the news, "Don't panic. Mr. Straight has been delayed twenty minutes; just sit down and relax and then after you have recovered you can tell me why you cut it so fine."

All my guessing had been wrong as I found out as soon as Mr. Straight arrived. My name had been given to him as an employee of BSAA not yet assimilated into BOAC and when he called for my papers he recognised that I was an old employee. He said it was his intention to post me to the Comet fleet that would be forming in about a year's time and in the meantime he wanted me to get more experience of the UK–Australia route. I was to be posted immediately to the Australian Constellation fleet.

The repercussions from this interview were not long in coming. Two days later I received a curt letter to report to BOAC head office at Brentford. It was generally known as the "Nuthouse" and I was soon to find out why. I was shown into the office of a character who had not the courtesy even to look up and I was left standing in the middle of the floor while I was supposed to go to pieces. His system worked. I became furiously angry and within minutes we had a first-class row going. He ranted about making me pay back the ten months' salary and I replied with criticisms about his organisation that allowed such a thing to happen. Threats of the sack were mixed with complaints about lack of respect for his position and in the middle of all this unpleasantness the secretary came in with a memo in her hand which she slid firmly under his nose.

"Perhaps if you read this . . ." she said quietly.

He read the memo and then turned and gazed down at the traffic on the Great West Road. After a while, he turned back and fixed me with a look of black hatred.

"I am posting you to Bristol for training on the Australian Connies," he grunted.

I refrained from comment, it wasn't the moment to display any flippancy.

I found training in BOAC was a well conducted affair. I was booked into an hotel in Bristol and went through a comprehensive course on the American radio systems as fitted to the 049 Constellation. I passed easily and during the course found that the Australian Connie fleet was very much a closed shop—an exclusive club, in fact, of which I was very lucky to have become a member. Regardless of experience, it was decreed that everyone must make one trip under supervision. In those days BOAC owned a dormy house at Sunningdale golf course and every member of the crew had to spend the night before departure there. It was a good scheme because it meant that the crew were all together and could be taken out to London Airport in a bus the next morning. I found that the term "an exclusive club" was an accurate assessment. Not a soul spoke to me that evening, not even the radioman with whom I was to fly the next day. It was the same the next morning and not until we were actually getting into the aircraft did anyone deign to notice my presence; the navigator then introduced himself and in turn introduced me to the supervising radio operator, Bryan Jenkins. He and I later flew together several times and became firm friends; his gesture that morning was never forgotten. He suggested I sat in a spare seat behind the navigation table. I claim that the Constellation was the best-looking aircraft that has so far been built; it even looked as though it was flying when it was standing on the ground.

The captain was one of those veterans whose methodical and accurate flying had been instrumental in building up BOAC's great safety record. He was completely unapproachable and dealt with the crew through the first officer. I was to leave the crew later on in Singapore and by that time I had never heard him address a remark to anyone except the first officer. It was to be very different from life in BSAA.

Soon the big Wright Duplex engines coughed into life and we taxied round to the take-off position. The Connie was smooth and quiet on take-off—at least I was going to like BOAC aircraft. The flight to Rome was uneventful. I sat alone drinking coffee in the restaurant with the rest of the crew chattering at the next table when Bryan Jenkins came in from making out the flight plan for Cairo and joined me. "Odd lot, old boy," he said, commenting on my isolation, "but they treated me the same way when I came here from boats a year ago. They'll get over it. Your problem is that you have been pushed into this line and you are not even from BOAC and this line is considered the cream."

I laughed. "It doesn't worry me, I just find it odd."

Half-way to Cairo the supervisory radioman came back to the navigation compartment. "It'll be okay for you to take over now," he said. "I will just listen and see how you get along."

So at last I was allowed into the holy of holies, the cockpit of an 049. It was a bit crowded with the engineer and the radioman sitting back to back but it was quite comfortable compared with a Lancastrian. I was left alone until we landed in Cairo. I must have passed my "test".

We spent the night in the Heliopolis Palace Hotel and the next day flew on to Karachi, an hour there and then on through the night to Dum Dum airport where we arrived in the morning. Here we handed the Constellation—it was called "Bangor", I believe—on to a new crew who would fly it on to Sydney while we went to the Great Eastern Hotel. Again I had to hand it to BOAC for organisation. In the Great Eastern a room for each member of the Australian Constellation had been set aside and air conditioned. These rooms were never occupied by anyone else; they were always waiting for us and were greatly appreciated in the heat of a Calcutta summer. Another thing I liked was that we were handed a sum of money to cover the purchase of food during the waiting period. My previous memories of Calcutta were of loading coal in Kidderpore docks in the height of summer in a British tramp steamer that shut down the dynamo at dusk to avoid paying overtime to the donkey-man. I thought of this the next morning sitting beside the swimming pool in the Calcutta Swimming Club of which all BOAC air-crews were made members. Perhaps I had bettered my lot.

For three days we waited for the next aeroplane from England.

We spent most of the time by the pool and the rest of the crew unbent enough to exchange a few words. We met the incoming aeroplane at Dum Dum early on the fourth morning; again I was just stared at by the arriving crew as a stranger in the camp. I shared watchkeeping on the trip with the other radioman and early in the trip contacted Singapore. He had a message for us—"Radio officer of northbound service in hospital, understand you have two radio officers on board, require one to operate the northbound service."

I handed it to the silent captain, he wrote "You" on the bottom and handed it back. The matter had been settled.

I saw another Constellation waiting on the ramp at Kalang airport, Singapore—my ride home without doubt. As I walked into the restaurant, a large, fair man jumped to his feet. "You the spare radioman?" he asked. I agreed I was. He introduced himself as Captain Green and shook me warmly by the hand. "Sorry to upset your first trip old son, what's your name?" He introduced me to the rest of the crew—what an incredible change from the last lot. Captain Green sat beside me. "It's going to be a hell of a graunch, but we are a lot behind schedule and I want to fly Singapore, Calcutta, Karachi, Cairo; there are two of everyone except you—think you can cope?"

I agreed that I would try.

"Don't worry," he laughed, "if you fall asleep, we'll wake you up for the position report."

We flew just as he planned and we arrived in Cairo back on schedule. In the Heliopolis Palace, Captain Green and the reserve captain joined the crew on the verandah. Again he thanked me for turning round at such short notice. I was to find that BOAC crews were much more mixed than I had been used to.

Cairo, Rome and then London, quite a trip, but I had still not made the stipulated trip to Sydney under supervision. With obvious assistance from Captain Green, it was now considered that I was competent to fly to Sydney and back as the radio officer of a BOAC 049 Constellation.

I spent about eighteen months on the London–Australia service; it was a pleasant run which allowed plenty of home life. It took me some time to settle down to the different conditions in BOAC but at least I began to realise that this was obviously the only way to operate such a vast organisation successfully. The trips were in the main quite uneventful, perhaps the best part of the trip was the slip in Sydney where we were accommodated in the Ben Buckler Hotel. It had a golf club behind it and a beach in front.

On one trip we flew through the heaviest turbulence I have ever experienced, between Karachi and Cairo. It appeared as a red curtain hanging from the sky right across the horizon. We had to fly through it or turn back so the captain dropped the wheels and flaps in an attempt to help the aircraft to ride through the turbulence. It was actually a gigantic sandstorm and once inside it, the cockpit was filled with an eerie red light. After twenty wild minutes, we rode out into brilliant sunshine and the wild heavings and plungings smoothed out. The sand in suspension had been so thick that the first officer later claimed that, in the heart of the storm, he had seen a camel walk past.

One evening on a flight from Rome to London, I looked up to see a very worried stewardess talking to the captain. He turned to me: "You handle this lot, I don't know anything about it," and climbed back into his seat.

"One of the passengers is going to have a baby before we get to London," said the stewardess, "can you give me any advice."

I certainly couldn't give her any myself but called the radio station at Birdlip and told him of our problem. In a short time he had an expert in these affairs on the phone—a specialist from a hospital in Cheltenham. The stewardess had meanwhile written out a resumé of the case which I passed to Birdlip who phoned it to the waiting doctor. In no time I was in the midst of a stream of two-way messages. The stewardess was a real heroine, she read the messages over my shoulder as I wrote them down, scribbled the reply and dashed back to her patient, while I transmitted them on. For two hours I worked harder than I had done for years but the rest of the bold aviators in the cockpit wanted no part of it. The captain in particular read a few of the messages flashing in and out of his aeroplane, shuddered and climbed back into his seat. The Birdlip operator asked if the stewardess was a midwife. I replied that she wasn't but she and I would be qualified by the time we got to London. But the baby actually won—it was born in an ambulance at the bottom of the steps ten minutes after we came to rest on the tarmac. I forget exactly how this happened but I remember that the mother, a stateless person, had bought a ticket to London, disguised her condition in an all-enveloping cloak and climbed aboard the aircraft like a normal passenger.

I had heard rumours for months that a Comet fleet was being formed and then in January 1951 I received the magic summons. I was to report to the Comet Flight at London Airport on the next Monday morning. I found them in a small hut set between two hangars at London Airport. The flight actually consisted of two captains—Captain Majendie, an ex-flying boat captain, and Captain Rodley, an old friend from BSAA; the manager, Captain Alderson, also an ex-flying boat pilot; two first officers, a navigator, a flight engineer and myself. We made a humble beginning for what has now grown into BOAC jet operations.

I found that de Havillands had two Comets actually flying, the very first Comet G-ALVG and a second prototype G-ALZK which was soon to be handed over to the Comet Flight for development of an operating technique for jet aircraft. At this time it must be remembered that commercial jet operations were unknown, jet flying had been confined to short flights of fighters and all passenger carrying aircraft had piston engines. The great day was May 22nd when we piled into Captain Majendie's car, which was to become the Comet fleet transport, and drove over to Hatfield. There we were met by Roy Sisson, the BOAC representative at de Havillands. The rest of the crew had been there before but it was my first sight of a Comet and I was most impressed. It hadn't the grace of a Constellation but somehow gave an impression of great strength— an impression which was later unfortunately proved to be incorrect. The cockpit was crowded—two pilots, a navigator, a flight engineer and a radio operator—but we were all so keen on our new toy that no one complained. It was arranged that de Havilland's test pilot would fly us all in G-ALZK and give me, at least, my baptism of jet flying. At three o'clock we were all in our seats and the engines were started up; the whine with which we were all to become so familiar was in strong contrast to the coughing of a Wright Duplex. At twelve minutes past three John Cunningham eased ZK off the Hatfield runway and two hours later to the minute he eased it back again—two hours in which we had flown nearly 1,000 miles; the highest and fastest I had ever flown.

The first and most noticeable thing about this type of flying was the smoothness and absence of noise. The fatigue which almost became exhaustion on a long flight in a piston-engined aircraft was entirely due, in my case, to the incessant hammering of the engines. For the rest of my flying career I was to be free from it. On this flight I met de Havilland's chief flight engineer, Braxton Brown, and he and I were to remain close friends until his tragic death in 1966.

We now took part in a considerable amount of local flying from Hatfield in Zebra King, as G-ALZK came to be called, and on April 4th, with both captains qualified to fly the aircraft, we flew back to London Airport.

For the next six weeks the aircraft was flown intensively on tests to prove that the theories developed by the two captains were suitable for Comet operations. On May 24th we set off on our first overseas proving flights—London to Rome, two hours fifty-one minutes; Rome to Cairo, three hours fifteen minutes, and then the next day Cairo to Nicosia, one hour thirty-one minutes and then back to Cairo in one hour seventeen minutes; Cairo/Beirut, Beirut to Cairo and back to London via Rome. The whole flight was extraordinarily successful and each sector a record. The problem of integrating this fast and high flying aircraft into the conventional pattern of lower and slower aircraft had raised no insuperable problems.

The established techniques of navigation worked well enough when one became used to covering eight miles in a minute. Communications from 40,000 feet were much the same as lower down except that ranges were somewhat greater. We thought we had an absolute winner. I was now made flight radio officer of the Comet fleet and was joined by two more very senior radio officers. New pilots were joining us and we were suffering from growing pains in our small hut. The next job was a move into more spacious accommodation. In July we made our first proving flight on what was to be the Comet's first passenger service route. We left London on March 17th, 1951, for Cairo, Entebbe and Johannesburg. Wherever we went we always seemed to be breaking a record of very long standing. Five hours and a quarter from Cairo to Entebbe, Entebbe to Johannesburg four and a half hours. We had a great reception especially at Johannesburg, a city that was new to me. One day we flew to Pietermaritzberg which had been designated an alternate airport in the event of Jo'burg being closed by bad weather. Here the local people turned up at the airport in their hundreds, the crew were promptly adopted by different parties and driven off to a local hotel where we were regaled by a wonderful lunch while we in return regaled them with tales of the fantastic speeds at which our new aeroplane could fly. I found that the man in charge of the radio station at Pietermaritzberg had been at school with me; we had never heard of each other since leaving school and have never heard of each other since. Back at Entebbe via Lusaka and Livingstone, we were unwise enough to challenge the local side to a cricket match from which they emerged victorious in spite of some pretty underhand work by members of the Comet party.

Khartoum airport was not yet ready for traffic and we landed at Wadi Seidna, an old military field that left much to be desired in almost every direction. The radio beacon was an old wartime aircraft radio transmitter set up in a mud hut and watched over by a man and a bicycle. If it stopped working, he cycled off for help. Hardly a reliable approach aid for a valuable aircraft.

At the end of September we set off again with Captain Majendie to survey the route to India as far as Calcutta. Cairo, Karachi and then Ahmedabad, where we received a fantastic reception. I had stayed behind to rectify a small radio fault when Braxton, who was in the cabin, shot into the cockpit. People were just pouring into the aircraft from both front and rear entrances; within seconds we were jammed into the front of the cockpit by hordes of struggling Indians. The heat and noise were fantastic and it took the police an hour to extricate the struggling mob by which time Braxton and I were more than slightly wilted. What they expected to see, I don't know, but the whole mob had been suddenly overcome by a mad desire to get inside the Comet. Ahmedabad, Delhi, Allahabad, Calcutta and then home again via Basra.

Zebra King was the second prototype and had a single wheel undercarriage each side. This raised a problem in Basra. It was incredibly hot and after Zebra King had parked for a while, it was found that she was slowly sinking through the runway; this problem was solved by the engineers who produced two large sheets of boiler plate and then taxied the aircraft on to them.

In October, with Captain Majendie, we set off for a proving flight into the Far East, this time extending beyond Calcutta to Singapore and Bangkok. After this was completed I was loaned to de Havillands for the de-icing trials and I was able to combine radio and navigation again. The crew of Zebra King was Peter Boise, a de Havilland test pilot; Braxton and myself and the aircraft was based at Prestwick. Searching for ice is always a chancy business; when you deliberately set out to find it, it eludes you and then when you are unprepared for it, you suddenly find far more than you want. For nearly a month we made long flights into areas where the met. office promised that ice should be present. It was usually up towards the Arctic Circle, sometimes north of it, and I found that the Consol navigation system was invaluable. We would fly to the area recommended by the met. office at Prestwick and then search around at different heights to try and pick up ice. It was impracticable to try and plot just where the aircraft went; I just plotted its position every fifteen minutes and connected the points by a straight line—hardly ethical, but it never failed in practice. When our fuel was getting down, we headed back for Prestwick and made a landfall with the weather radar. At last the Air Registration Board observers were satisfied that the de-icing services on the Comet were satisfactory and we returned to Hatfield.

I thoroughly enjoyed this interlude; I was able to navigate to my heart's content. Peter Boise was happy for me to keep track of where we were and have a course ready for him when it was time to go home. Back at London Airport I found that the Comet Unit had now received several of the operational Comets with the 4-wheeled bogey undercarriage.

I made two more round trips to Johannesburg and then came the great day—the first scheduled passenger flight of a jet aircraft. One crew flew the aircraft to Beirut, a waiting crew took her on to Khartoum and the last crew completed the flight to Johannesburg. The procedure was then reversed with the first crew flying the aircraft back to London; I was a member of the first crew. Captain Majendie first officer and navigator, Jimmy Woodill, Wally Bennett, the engineer and myself. We were airborne from London at three minutes past two in G-ALYP—or "Yoke Peter" as she was called—May 2nd, 1952. I personally felt very proud; this was a notable "first".

Two hours forty-eight minutes to Rome, where there was a little light relief when a passenger sidled up to me as we walked across to the terminal and said, "What's all the panic about? I've flown this route often, never seen anything like this before."

I couldn't resist it. "Didn't you notice the aircraft hasn't any propellers?"

He looked over his shoulder. "Damned odd, never noticed that."

Were the public already getting used to jet travel? We arrived at Beirut at 8.55 p.m. to find the next crew under Captain Brentnall ready to go on to Khartoum. We returned to London early in the morning of May 6th, the first return passenger service by jet to South Africa had been a great success.

I was now loaned to de Havillands again, this time to take part in a flight of which I have always been proud to have been a member of the crew. It was to take the Queen Mother and Princess Margaret for a trip round Europe in a Comet. With John Cunningham and Peter Bugge at the controls and Braxton and myself looking after the rest of the business we set off from Hatfield at 11.17 a.m. on what was hoped to be a four-hour flight. Everything went right for us, the day was perfect, there was no haze or cloud and visibility was literally unlimited. We set off across Europe for Genoa; half-way through the climb we could see Genoa. When overhead, we set course for Bordeaux and could see it clearly and then we turned for Hatfield—the Channel and Thames Estuary were all laid out in front of us like a gigantic map. We landed at Hatfield after a flight of four hours three minutes. It was one of the clearest days I have ever experienced over England.

I was being loaned to de Havillands for odd jobs during the next few months and at last they asked me if I would go and work for them. They wanted someone to assist them with new radio installations that were being asked for by their Comet customers and John Cunningham wanted a radio operator cum navigator to assist on overseas flights which he was being repeatedly asked to carry out. The job appeared to be made for me; the salary was right and I accepted.

When I joined de Havillands, Captain Peter Cane was the flight superintendent of the Comet Fleet and he was to give me what turned out to be a prophetic warning. "I know DH is booming, they are full of Comet orders, but you are putting all your eggs into one basket. If anything happens to the Comet, then what will you do?" We parted the best of friends but his words were never forgotten.

I had one more flight with BOAC before I joined de Havillands —a proving flight to Japan. Captain Majendie was in command again, the flight was Rome, Beirut, Bahrein, Karachi, Delhi, Calcutta, Bangkok, Manilla, Okinawa, Nagoya and Tokyo. On the return flight we took in Saigon, Singapore, Rangoon, Colombo, Bombay and Karachi. Once again the whole operation was a completely successful prelude to opening up a passenger service to the Far East.

Braxton was still on loan to BOAC from de Havillands and he and I had a most interesting experience in Saigon. We were sitting on the verandah of the bar on the airport which was crowded with people who had come in from the city to see the Comet, when we were accosted by a little man who looked a typical Frenchman from the Midi. He was dressed in blue denims, wore a greasy black beret and needed a shave. He smelt strongly of sour wine and strong tobacco but he spoke English; it was obviously his mother tongue although his use of it was somehow rusty. There was a tiny hesitation before some words—as though he was searching for the right expression—but his accent was pure Cockney. We asked him to sit with us and he unfolded a strange story. He had been a mechanic in a motor pool in the RAF based at Singapore before the war. As we had guessed from his accent, he came from East Ham. When the Japanese captured Singapore he was taken prisoner and for a time he was in Changi jail with hundreds of others. He was then picked out with several others to be sent to Japan; he had no idea why, but perhaps it was because he was a motor mechanic. They were herded aboard a Japanese cargo boat and locked into pens in the 'tweendecks and they then sailed for Japan. The Japanese guards were not apparently the type that have made themselves such an appalling name in the war histories, for they allowed their prisoners to sit on the hatches in the sun during the afternoon. On one such afternoon, when there wasn't a cloud in the sky, just a trusty old cargo boat plugging along on her way to Japan, there was a colossal explosion. Our friend said he had not the slightest idea what had happened and his memories of the next few months were hazy, but he was apparently picked up floating on a hatch board by some Indo-Chinese fishermen. He was exhausted and badly sunburnt and they took him back to their tiny fishing village; he didn't know how long he was convalescent—one day was so much like another in this village which was utterly isolated from the war. He learned the language, married and was the father of two children. He became a fisherman and his memories of the RAF and East Ham faded; the village was never bothered by the Japanese and the natives just stuck to their fishing. Gradually he became aware that there was no longer such a dearth of shipping passing off-shore as there had been. Then a rumour came through that all the Japs had gone and he decided to go down to Saigon and find out what was going on. They made the journey in his father-in-law's fishing boat and in Saigon he found that the war was ended. He made enquiries and eventually found what he called some British "authorities" to whom he told his tale. They promptly arrested him as a deserter. He was incarcerated in a stockade with dozens of other Indo-Chinese who were under suspicion and he just as promptly escaped and got back to the harbour where his father-in-law's fishing boat was waiting.

They hugged the coast back to their village where he became a fisherman again. When the turmoil of war had died down he wrote a letter to a local parson whose name he remembered, to enquire about his folks. The reply stated that their street had been wiped out by a bomb and his family must all be presumed dead. Some of the fishermen were turning over to engines, and as motor transport began to reappear, he earned his living again as a mechanic. He said that he had read that the Comet was visiting Saigon and he had made the trip from his village to Saigon on a Chinaman's lorry to see if there were any English people for him to talk to. As he finished telling his story, we had to rejoin the Comet for the short hop to Singapore; it was a pity because Braxton and I were just bursting with questions.

Back in London I now severed my connection with BOAC and on September 1st, 1952, I joined de Havillands. I did some local flying and then came my first overseas flight for them as navigator and radio operator. It was on the original Comet G-ALVG and, with John Cunningham in command, we set off to Khartoum on tropical trials on a water injection system to improve the thrust of the Ghost engines. Hatfield, Rome, Cairo, Wadi Seidna—I was almost wearing a rut along this route. Both the navigation and radio behaved themselves and we returned to Hatfield at the end of October.

Now started a really busy period. Air-France and Canadian Pacific Comets were coming off the production line. With the local flying there was a lot of liaison work with new customers—Pan American, Venezuela—everybody seemed to be buying Comets.

Mostly I found myself flying with Peter Bugge and Peter Boise, the two de Havilland test pilots, with John Cunningham and Braxton. A pleasant, co-operative atmosphere was present in the cockpit at all times. One day we demonstrated a Canadian Air Force Comet in Lisbon and stocked up with the famous Lisbon baskets—the aircraft interior looked like a market on the return flight.

Then came more tropical trials in Khartoum with a weekend in Entebbe to make a break from the almost intolerable heat. A month later there was another set of trials in Khartoum. Then in January 1954 we set off again to Khartoum, this time in G-AMXA, the first of the improved Comet IIs. It was decided that we would try for the London–Khartoum record. I had been working to improve my astro navigation during the intensive local flying, using the periscope sextant and, surveying our route, I found that we were going to be a long time crossing the Sahara where we should be without any aids from the radio. I made a direct steal from Sir Francis Chichester's book on his flight from New Zealand to Norfolk Island in a Tiger Moth, and drew three graphs of the sun's altitude in relation to our proposed track. Knowing Braxton's and John Cunningham's habit of sticking to times, the graphs were drawn round our published time of departure. We were airborne at Hatfield at 7.33 a.m. and we landed at Khartoum six hours twenty-two minutes later, having made a ground speed of 481 mph, beating the previous record held by a Lincoln by over eight hours. Sir Francis Chichester's navigation worked like a charm; I was beginning to feel that this navigation business wasn't quite the black art that I once thought it was. With the tropical trials completed in Khartoum, we flew on to Johannesburg for high altitude tests and then home again via Entebbe and Cairo.

Looking back through my flying logbook about this period, I find that I was flying in all types of aircraft. I remember a long flight in a Hastings for the Guided Missile Department of de Havillands. I remember this because the aircraft was fitted with Gee, a military navigation system from which it was possible to get an accurate fix in about half a minute, and after an hour's flying I found that we had flown precisely fifty miles into a 100 mph head wind.

Another series of flights in a Venom fighter which was fitted with an automatic direction finder, then proving flying in G-ANLO—the first and only Comet III. Then, early in 1954, disaster struck. We had already lost a Canadian Pacific Airways Comet at Karachi; it was being delivered by a CPA crew to Sydney and crashed on take-off with a heavy loss of life—now we lost another BOAC Comet, G-ALYV. Climbing through heavy weather after leaving Calcutta for Delhi, it apparently disintegrated in mid-air. Then G-ALYP climbing away from Rome crashed into the sea off Elba and, later, the final blow, G-ALYY operating the South African service was lost in the sea just off Naples. BOAC had no option but to withdraw the Comet from service. The Government enquiry into these crashes was the biggest and most thorough accident investigation so far attempted and successfully completed and the world's aircraft industry were to benefit from the findings. It was found that repeated pressurisations of the hull had caused metal fatigue.

While Comets were being placed in tanks and repeatedly pressurised to discover their weakness, the faith of de Havillands in the Comet remained unimpaired. Comet operators grounded their fleets and cancelled their services; public confidence fell to zero.

When the fault was located, a large programme of strengthening of the fuselage had to be undertaken. During this period, my work fell to literally nothing; some of the time I was employed by the Guided Missile department as a relief navigator. This was a new departure; the aircraft was a Meteor NF11 fitted with an air interceptor radar and a Gee for navigation, both the equipments were fitted in the rear cockpit and they were operated from a seat that could be raised or lowered to bring you on a level with each piece of equipment in use. The Meteor operated in consort with two Venoms, one carrying the missile and the other the camera equipment. It was a fascinating exercise.

The pilot of the NF11 was Jimmy Phillips, later to gain fame in the automatic landing field with the Trident airliner. Accompanied by the two Venoms we would fly from Hatfield to Valley in Anglesey. The missile range was in Cardigan Bay where Fairey Fireflies were flown as targets. It was quite uncanny to see a Firefly, operated from another Firefly several miles away called the Shepherd, flying jauntily along with both cockpits empty. The drill was for our trio to formate on the target and theoretically shoot it down with our dummy missile. After airline work, I found it a hair-raising form of flying. When we broke for home, I never got used to the two Venoms formating in by our wings with the pilot peering down over my shoulder to see how good my navigation was.

As a demonstration of de Havilland's faith in the Comet design, it was decided that the prototype Comet III G-ANLO should make a flight round the world.

Over the years a change had been taking place in the crew composition of the civil airliners. High-powered radio equipment had been designed which was completely automatic in operation and long-range communication was now carried out by radio-telephone. The free world had a network of radio-telephone stations covering all the long ocean and land crossings which supplied the aircraft with terminal and alternate weather conditions and en route wind changes. The operation of this voice radio was taken over by the pilots and the carriage of a specialist radio officer became uneconomic and unnecessary. Considerable advances had also been made in the field of automatic navigation. Direction finders had become completely automatic and electric sextants had simplified astronomical navigation. Doppler navigation equipment had been produced and this had really removed the "black magic" from the navigation of aircraft. The pilot had now only to dial into the system the track he desired and the distance along that track he wished to fly. Guidance information was now generated in the Doppler system and fed into the automatic pilot. As a back-up the pilot had my old friend the Loran sytem to guard against gross errors. Doppler was later followed by an inertial navigation system which did all that Doppler could do and did it more accurately. This progress created the condition where a specialist navigator became unnecessary and the navigator's qualification became a part of the commercial pilot's licence.

Routes between population centres were defined by radio ground stations which literally marked out airways in the sky and navigation was a simple routine following these stations. G-ANLO was therefore equipped to meet these requirements, as it was decided to carry senior captains from airlines who would possibly operate Comets over sectors of their routes. Unfortunately, the strengthening modification had not yet been carried out on G-ANLO and without pressurisation, it was necessary for both crew and passengers to use oxygen from 15,000 feet upwards.

The crew consisted of John Cunningham, Peter Bugge and Braxton with a full team of ground staff to maintain the aircraft. We also had Captain Peter Cane as an observer from BOAC and he undertook the majority of the navigation and communications. The programme was to fly to Sydney via Cairo, Bombay, Singapore and Darwin, then Melbourne, Perth, Sydney, Auckland, Nandi, Honolulu, Vancouver, Montreal and London. I think we were all glad when it was over—long periods on oxygen are extremely tiring. Unfortunately, an engine defect as we were climbing out of Montreal on the last leg to London caused us to miss Christmas at home—we actually arrived back on December 28th, 1955.

During the heyday of the Comet, we had sold two Comet Is to the Royal Canadian Air Force and they had been laid up in the de Havilland factory at Downsview since the initial grounding. It was now decided that one of them should be flown back to Hatfield, unpressurised, to be modified up to the full passenger carrying standard. John Cunningham and Peter Bugge set off for Canada in the Empress of Britain while Braxton and I went in a BOAC Stratocruiser to Montreal and Toronto to get the aircraft ready for the return flight.

A couple of days after Peter and John arrived, we did a five and a quarter hour test flight to assure ourselves that VC5302 was a going concern after her long lay up in the back of the hangar. It was confirmed that all was well and the next day two hours thirty-five minutes along the Canadian airways system brought us to my old stopping place—Goose Bay, Labrador.

The met. officer promised us a fifty knot tail wind to Hatfield which gave us a flight plan of five hours five minutes and we set our departure from Goose Bay for 0400 GMT. A last check before departure showed all was well with the Hatfield weather and we decided to fly a composite great circle to take fullest advantage of the tail winds. We actually set course at 0436 GMT and I set myself the job of a position fix every thirty minutes and to operate the telegraphy radio every thirty minutes. We used Loran until 40 degrees west longitude when it faded out. We next used Weather Ship Charlie for a running fix on the direction finder and at 30 degrees west the Consol navigation system was being received and this was used until we picked up the Irish coast on the weather radar at thirty miles distance at 0956 GMT. We were overhead Hatfield at 1000 and landed at 1002 GMT—five hours twenty minutes after leaving Goose Bay.

My flying career which was now ended had started when the value of the aircraft was measured in hundreds of pounds and the number of passengers could be counted on two hands. Today's aircraft is valued in millions of pounds and the passengers can number well over a hundred. The responsibility of the aircraft captain has increased enormously and it is my firm opinion that the day is fast approaching when this responsibility will become an intolerable burden for a human to shoulder. I have flown behind hundreds of pilots, among them natural pilots are rare enough but supermen are non-existent. They are just ordinary men, trained to a pitch of efficiency which varies from brilliant to poor; they unfortunately suffer the same ills as ordinary men and the only safe and sure method of operating tomorrow's monsters of the air is by automatic means in which the possibility of failure has literally been designed out.